Trusting God to the Promised Land

About Monday Blues to Sunday Pews

Monday Blues to Sunday Pews Ministry is a grassroots series of Christian books that will lead us on a journey through each book of the Bible, one step at a time. They will cover critical verses and topics within each chapter that were life-changing then—and are still life-changing today. They will inspire and encourage the "intentional" believer to move from that rut of complacency to a life that brings value to the Lord by how they live. Through this journey, we will broaden and deepen our knowledge of God's expectations for us. We will learn the importance of obtaining the message from God's word and sustaining it daily—real-life application!

Most importantly, Monday Blues to Sunday Pews will donate half of its profit proceeds to support the mission field, help the needy, and assist organizations in distributing God's word globally. Remember this passage in Matthew 16:24: *We're called to be intentional followers of Jesus Christ—daily!*

Monday—Meditate on one scripture in an area where you need help to refresh your mindset.
Tuesday—Tell someone about your daily journey as you begin. Someone needs to hear it, too!
Wednesday—Walk with a close friend and share your experience as you're walking with God!
Thursday—Thankful for one thing that happened this week. Showing gratitude is a huge step.
Friday—Focus on another area in your life that needs improvement; we all have areas that need improvement..
Saturday—Share one significant impact from the week with someone who also needs uplifting.
Sunday—Serve in some capacity in your church or community—connect, serve, and grow.

Trusting God to the Promised Land

A Journey Through the Book of Joshua

BY CARL BARRETT

SERIES: MONDAY BLUES TO SUNDAY PEWS

RESOURCE *Publications* • Eugene, Oregon

TRUSTING GOD TO THE PROMISED LAND
A Journey Through the Book of Joshua
Monday Blues to Sunday Pews

Copyright © 2025 Carl Barrett. All rights reserved. Except for brief quotations in critical publications or reviews, no part of this book may be reproduced in any manner without prior written permission from the publisher. Write: Permissions, Wipf and Stock Publishers, 199 W. 8th Ave., Suite 3, Eugene, OR 97401.

Resource Publications
An Imprint of Wipf and Stock Publishers
199 W. 8th Ave., Suite 3
Eugene, OR 97401

www.wipfandstock.com

PAPERBACK ISBN: 979-8-3852-6009-6
HARDCOVER ISBN: 979-8-3852-6010-2
EBOOK ISBN: 979-8-3852-6011-9
VERSION NUMBER 12/02/25

Scripture quotations are taken from the Holy Bible, New Living Translation, copyright ©1996, 2004, 2015 by Tyndale House Foundation. Used by permission of Tyndale House Publishers, a Division of Tyndale House Ministries, Carol Stream, Illinois 60188. All rights reserved.

Contents

Biography | *vii*

"A Matter of Trust!" | *ix*

Preface | *xxi*

Introduction | *xxxv*

The Book of Joshua—"God's Promise is Fulfilled" | *xliii*

Chapter One	'God's Qualified'	1
Chapter Two	'Godly Hero'	6
Chapter Three	'Godly Reliance'	10
Chapter Four	'Godly Memories'	15
Chapter Five	'Godly Growth'	21
Chapter Six	'God's Opening'	26
Chapter Seven	'Godly Obedience'	32
Chapter Eight	'God's Point'	39
Chapter Nine	'God*less* Appearance'	44
Chapter Ten	'Godly Unity'	52
Chapter Eleven	'Turning Point'	58
Chapter Twelve	'Godly Journal'	64
Chapter Thirteen	'Godly Portion'	69
Chapter Fourteen	'Godly Precision'	74

Chapter Fifteen	'Godly Boldness' | 78
Chapter Sixteen	God*less* Fruit | 83
Chapter Seventeen	'Godly Assignment' | 87
Chapter Eighteen	'Godly Assistance' | 92
Chapter Nineteen	'Godly Honor' | 96
Chapter Twenty	'Godly Seeker' | 106
Chapter Twenty-One	'Godly Rest' | 114
Chapter Twenty-Two	'Godly Understanding' | 120
Chapter Twenty-Three	'Godly Fight' | 128
Chapter Twenty-Four	'Godly Pledge' | 135

In Summary: "They Finally Made It!" \| 143

'The Danger of Distrust' \| 150

Next Steps: 'Trust God's Wisdom!' \| 161

Follow Up: Trust + Obedience = Genuine Faith \| 169

In Closing: "Just Trust and Obey!" \| 179

Bibliography \| 189

Biography

Carl Barrett is the Founder and Executive Director of Monday Blues to Sunday Pews Ministry. In partnership with other Christ-based organizations, they aim to raise more funds to serve the needy, support mission fields, and spread the word of God worldwide by distributing more Bibles. He's the author of impactful books such as God Values Our Daily Steps, God's Guide to Freedom, God's Holiness vs. Man's Lawlessness, God's People Count, and God's Generation of Hope.

But Carl's influence extends beyond his ministry. He also leads the First Impressions Team at Central Tyler Baptist Church in Tyler, Texas. His unwavering dedication to spreading the message of God's love and grace is a testament to his inspiring mission. He has served as a Personal Development Mentor for the Texas Juvenile Justice Department, a teacher and chaplain in multiple state prisons and detention centers, a CASA Representative (Court Appointed Special Advocate) in various counties throughout Texas, and an instructor for the National Fatherhood Initiative.

Carl Barrett's educational journey is a testament to his unwavering commitment to learning and personal development. His academic achievements, including a BSBA from Madison University and studies in biblical and theological studies at Texas Baptist Institute, as well as courses in Critical Issues in Christian Apologetics at Biola University and an Introduction to C.S. Lewis at Hillsdale College, reflect his dedication. His studies at Dale Carnegie, Development Dimensions International, and Personal Dynamics Institute have equipped him with a deep understanding of human relations development, motivational leadership, and the empowerment of engagement. His commitment to personal development is a source of motivation and encouragement for all who follow his work.

Carl's aspiring passion is to help people apply the truth of God's word to their lives so they can live it out for the glory of God, as representatives of Jesus Christ on this earth. He would tell you that it starts in our homes, then throughout our neighborhoods, communities, churches, and abroad. *Our lives as Christlike followers are essential to our Lord and the building of His Kingdom in our everyday lives.*

"A Matter of Trust!"

Did you know that right now, at this very moment, God is working out a plan for you and me on this side of Heaven? As we will come to see throughout this book, it is a plan that we can *trust* to the very end of our life's journey, regardless of all the intense trials and tests that will confront us in everyday life (Jer 29:11–13). In all His sovereign and mysterious ways, our Holy Creator is preparing His entrusted children for a specific event in the future, where we will dwell with Him in a place where there are no more worries, suffering, and pain for the rest of our lives.

Do you ever wonder just how glorious that day will be, where we will dwell with our Lord and no longer have to deal with all the strife this life has to offer? But make no mistake about this statement: In our Heavenly Father's planning process of holiness in our lives, just like the verse in Jeremiah 29:13 states, *it is only if we look for Him wholeheartedly that we will find Him and come to trust His plan in our lives as His devoted children.*

One thing is certain: His plan will come to fruition in His perfect timing! And if you're paying close attention to our current-day events, that day could come sooner than we expect! For some, time is running out. When I ponder more on this, I think of that one generation of Israelites who failed to trust and believe in God to their Promised Land. But there was hope for another generation of followers, like us today. We will surely see if we're truly preparing for that Big Day!

You see, God wants us to stay connected with Him and seek Him above all other things in this life, where we can sincerely know Him and be loyal and faithful to Him (like He is to us). He wants us to commit our lives according to His will, possess a constant faith in all our battles in life, stay the course of obedience, be patient and wait on His timing, and trust Him with all our hearts, souls, minds, and strength. These components must be alive and active in us so we can become all He desires in this life as His chosen ones. (Please read the 3rd chapter of Ephesians & Colossians and

"A Matter of Trust!"

1 Peter 2:9–10). As we prepare for our future Promised Land, we will undoubtedly see that there is still more work to be done in our personal lives and those that we hold dear to our hearts.

Throughout this journey in the book of Joshua, we'll discover that God's children today, just as thousands of years ago, must rely on Yahweh's active work in our lives, both biblically and spiritually, to fulfill our Heavenly Father's long-term plan. Just as in the days of Joshua, God wants all of His entrusted children to believe in His guidance daily because if we're not living by the principles of His instructions, we will not mature and grow in all His ways. And over time, we could find ourselves drifting farther from His presence and glory. And if we get too far off course from the ways of God, like that one generation of Israelites, we may find our lives so entrenched in the perils of evil that we may never discover our Promised Land.

With that, there are some challenging questions for every follower of Christ today, to ensure we're rightly positioned with God's directives, and stay on His course to our future land, and they are: [NL1–7]

1. How many followers of Jesus Christ are genuinely on *every page* (the Bible) of God's working process in their daily lives? (Ps 119:9, Isa 55:11, 2 Tim 3:16–17, Heb 4:12–13)

    a. In other words, is God's project of holiness and righteousness fully operational in us every day?

2. Are we allowing our Heavenly Father and Lord, through the power of His Spirit, to prepare and shape us in all His ways of Christlikeness? (Heb 13:21)

    a. That is, are we yielding more to this unrighteous society and culture, *or more to the power of the Holy Spirit and His Holy Word?* (Rom 12:1–2)

3. Do we have a burning desire for more of His word and Spirit at work in our lives versus the ways of man and this world? (Ps 63:1–7).

4. Are we constantly meditating on His Word (daily) and putting it into action to thwart the enemy's tactics in all of our weakest areas? (Ps 1, Deut 6:5–9, Phil 4:9, Eph 6:17, Heb 4:12, 1 Pet 2:2).

5. How do your friends, family, neighbors, and community really know that you're a genuine believing Christian? Is your life producing more fruitfulness or fruitlessness? Specifically, is there more obedience or disobedience in your life as a follower of Christ? (John 14:15, Col 3, Phil 4:8–9, Gal 5:16–23)

6. Have we completely surrendered (to self) and submitted (to Him) ourselves with a willing and humble heart to God's will and long-term plan? (Prov 3:5–6, Jas 4:7)

7. Finally, is the evidence of our genuine saving faith, hope, and love growing as our days on this earth come to an end? The proof will be in our complete trusting and obeying the Lord, where the world will see that we're walking more by the Spirit. (Heb 11:1, Gal 5:22–23, Romans 8)

These are grave questions and heart-to-heart challenges we should ponder and act on today, because we need to know for sure that we're headed in the right direction and progressing toward our future Promised Land. It is crucial to know that we cannot afford to be sitting idle and complacent in a world that is not moving forward with God's plan (like that one generation of Israelites).

Throughout this book, we will be challenged to implement a constant change in our lives as followers of Christ. And make no mistake: We need this challenge of Christlikeness more than ever today, due to the prevalence of distorted truths swirling in our society and culture. I don't know about you, but in these times of untruths, uncertainty, and godlessness, I yearn more and more for the very first words from the mouth of my Redeeming King and Savior on that Day of Glory.

But in the meantime, as His Citizens of Heaven on earth, if we are in line with those seven steps above, we will be producing the type of life, as His entrusted believers, that is honoring and glorifying God. However, just as significant, our Christian lifestyle should also impact and influence others on this lifelong journey (daily). Our faith, trust, and obedience in our Lord should leave a legacy and heritage that will extend to future generations for the cause of Christ, our King.

One thing is for sure: If we're on the Lord's righteous course to our future Promised Land, it will demonstrate that we are connected and conforming with God's ongoing plan in our everyday lives (Phil 1:6). Here's how we can know because the evidence will be in the by-products of our lives as His fruitful servants below:

- The Fruit of the Spirit will be more evident in His devout children, versus all the vices of the enemy (Galatians 5:16–23). They possess a repentant and contrite heart, mind, and spirit with a willingness to act upon their convictions!

- They are taking Bible reading to actual Bible-Living. In other words, they're doers of His Word, utilizing all their gifts for His glory. (1 Corinthians 12, James 1:22–25).

- The world will see more of Christ (His humility, selflessness, love, grace, and mercy) in His followers vs more of the ways of man and this world (Rom 8:29).

- There will be a supernatural presence of His confidence, boldness, contentment, exultation, and enthusiasm for the Lord in our lives that is second to none (Phil 4:4–9).

- His entrusted believers will be more about building the Kingdom of God and storing up treasures in Heaven, versus acquiring more materialistic things of this world. (Matt 6:20)

- They are never ashamed to proclaim the Name of Christ, no matter where they are or who they are around. But they do it with gentleness, kindness, and with words of God's grace and love. (Rom 1:16, Col 4:5–6, 1 Tim 4:6–9).

- People will gravitate to us because of our fruitfulness, where they want to follow us down God's path because of our righteous living (1 Tim 4:12). Think, because of our portrayal of God's peace and joy in our lives, they want and desire that same feeling (Neh 8:10).

Please also refer to the powerful letter from Paul in the book of Titus, which serves as a profound gauge of the sound teachings in our lives as Christians in a secular world. This book is a brief letter from the Apostle Paul to his associate Titus. It emphasizes the importance of sound doctrine and good works as essential components of the Christian faith. The letter encourages believers to live in a way that reflects the Gospel in public life! And that is a key component missing in Christians today!

As our Heavenly Father prepares to lead us to our Promised Land, here's the crux of the matter: Are we trusting in His guidance in our everyday lives? Today, we must trust God's blueprint more than ever, for that is the only way to progress on this side of eternity. Make no mistake: 'Our complete trust in Almighty God will be evident in our spiritual predisposition (inclined to always believe in His ways), and disposition (the quality of our behavior, attitude, and image of Christ). And this state of spirituality will lead us to possess a more habitual display of Christlikeness in our lives, 24/7/365.' Through the guidance of His Spirit & Word, this is the only way to ensure we're in His lifelong will.'

"A Matter of Trust!"

This is important because if our spiritual lives do not align with the guiding doctrine and solid truths of the Bible, we cannot establish a deep communion with God. Without our steadfastness and wholehearted commitment to our Heavenly Father, we will not be empowered by His Spirit to believe and trust Him at every step of our life's journey. We can never forget what King David tells us in Psalm 37:23: "The Lord directs the steps of the godly. He delights in every detail of their lives."

As we can see, God only directs the future steps of the godly which are those who: a) trust Him wholeheartedly, b) are willing to work with Him as His righteous ones, c) seeks to be continually filled with His Spirit, d) are full of humility, e) possess a repentant heart, f) leads by their Christlike example, g) is a selfless servant, h) and has a desire to please the Lord while bearing more fruit for the Kingdom of God.

When we submit entirely to God's grace and live according to His will (faithfully and obediently), we can trust that God will order our steps in every part of our lives. And when we allow Him to lead our steps in this life, as the scripture above states, He delights in it because it glorifies His holy name.

This is pivotal in today's turbulent times. Why, you may ask? Trusting God in every aspect of our lives sets us apart from those who do not trust or believe in God, and we're talking about millions in this country and billions of people worldwide. It is not only a massive game-changer in our lives as Christians, but when His work is active and productive in us, it can significantly impact others who need godly direction in their own personal lives today.

This is a severe stage of our sanctification process because we live in a society filled with the scars of doubt, fear, anxiety, and uncertainty, compounded by people who are critical, judgmental, divisive, hateful, unforgiving, prideful, arrogant, irreligious, and cynical. Regrettably, these types of people don't trust an ever-loving and merciful God, as the enemy and self guide them more in their everyday lives. You see, God needs His children of godliness today to portray themselves as His entrusted believers in this crazed society like never before.

Don't we realize our Lord implores you and me to be His role models as entrusted believers? Why? They place unwavering faith in God, resulting in peace, joy, comfort, and a life that reflects God's faithfulness and all His truths. An entrusted follower of Christ is wholeheartedly dedicated to Jesus because they trust Him in all things, and they are His true bondservants! They are committed to embodying His character and Word in their daily life.

Just think: You and I can set the example as His trustworthy and faithful servants in the lives of many who struggle with trusting an Almighty God right now in this severely off-course culture. However, and this is important: We cannot display ourselves as His entrusted followers *if His working process is not active and alive in us.*

As His chosen royal priesthood, don't we see and realize the importance of why the world must recognize God's work of holiness and righteousness in us? We cannot forget what Peter tells us in 1 Peter 2:9, where we're reminded that God chose us so we can show the goodness and virtuous ways of God to others by the way we live.

And this is because He knew long ago, before the creation of time, that His chosen ones over time would come to trust and obey Him (Please read Ephesians 1)! This is critical because it demonstrates our genuine saving faith, love for His word, reliance upon His teachings and counsel, a wholehearted commitment to all His ways, and hope for the future. This is all because we believe in the Almighty One with every core of our inner being.

When the unbelieving world sees our Heavenly Father's process thriving in us, they will see His presence and guidance at work in our personal lives. *Examples of God's holy teachings should be clearly seen in all His children, all the time!* Why? So they can identify you and me as His true chosen ones, set apart for a specific purpose and plan for what is to come in the days ahead. We are not talking about perfection, but rather a continuous progression of His acts of holiness and righteousness, which is gradually removing those unholy things from our lives.

But just as important, we must display God's divine handiwork in us, primarily through all life circumstances (the good, the bad, and the ugly), because it can influence an unsaved world that does not trust our Holy God and Lord and Savior. And here's a PowerPoint for believers today: Millions in this country and billions worldwide do not even know what trust and faith in a Higher Power looks like. Never forget that, as His entrusted believers, we're His examples and representatives for a world that needs to trust in an Almighty, Loving, and Merciful God. *That is why we need His working process to always function and flourish in our lives each and every day.*

Look at it this way: When we display God's work in us, the world will know we're God's *living sacrifice* for a reason (Rom 12:1–2). And when we're a living sacrifice for our God and Lord, it means we have dedicated our entire life to God in worship and obedience because we trust Him with all our hearts, minds, and souls. It means surrendering our will, desires, and actions to align with God's purpose and living in a way that glorifies Him daily, proving that our genuine saving faith is active and alive.

"A Matter of Trust!"

I am quite sure many of us have heard this statement over the course of our lives: 'Just Trust the Process.' This expression refers to trusting in the journey and having faith that a structured plan will ultimately work out for the best—despite any obstacles that may arise along the way. But most importantly, within this popular phrase lie some powerful, life-applicable components that every Christ-follower needs today to succeed. They are *1) Persistence (enduring), 2) Perseverance (constant faith), 3) Patience (waiting and trusting in God), 4) Participation (accepting His will and plan), and 5) Production (output of fruitfulness).*

Seriously, consider the spiritual and biblical implications of these words. We will discover that when these powerful words are applied and actively at work in our lives as Christians with genuine determination, they can develop a pattern of significant growth and progress. Yes, there will be 'temporary' setbacks, but our spiritual response to those barriers and minor failings can make all the difference in the world. How?

When these five components above are engaged and enforced in our daily lives, they will reveal where our genuine trust and faith truly lie. We must all realize that we will all face our battles on this side of eternity, which will challenge our trust and faith in the Lord. But never forget this: When we trust God through all the trials of life and firsthand witness our enriched and reconditioned transformation, we get to enjoy those little victories and, eventually, our ultimate triumph at the end of our lives.

Just think: Over three thousand years ago, a generation of God's children failed to incorporate these five components above into their lives, resulting in their shortfall in entering their future Promised Land. Example: They did not endure their trials with constant faith and had trust in Almighty God's leading. They lacked patience in cooperating with Yahweh's work of holiness in their lives, which led them farther away from His plan.

This eventually led to their refusal to participate with God and His appointed leader. They had every resource from our Living God that could have led them to the Promised Land. It was clear that they drifted away from His presence rather than trying to draw near to Him, all because they did not stay connected with Him and had no trust in His long-term plan. Undoubtedly, they were not godly producers.

However, the second generation chosen by God will have the undeniable opportunity to demonstrate their steadfastness by trusting in God every step of the way on their journey to the Promised Land. If they are patient and willing to participate with God wholeheartedly, they will be productive in their efforts toward the land of milk and honey (once and for all). What a great lesson for us today!

"A Matter of Trust!"

Christians, make no mistake about this statement: 'There is no process more critical today, tomorrow, and in the future *than trusting in the work of Almighty God's sovereign plan in our personal lives.*' Trusting the biblical and spiritual process outlined by our Heavenly Creator means believing that the desired outcome will be achieved by diligently following God's plan, despite all the unpredictable difficulties we will confront in this life. We will discover that trust is a significant component that unlocks and exposes our faith, hope, and love in a Sovereign and Holy God! Yes, trust in God is closely related to faith, but it emphasizes our complete reliance and confidence in God's character and His plans.

You see, when we implement and incorporate more spiritual acts of God's ways into our daily lives, we demonstrate that we are holding firmly to God's Word, accepting it, believing in it, trusting it, applying it, and obeying it. If our actions are in step with God's working process, they will be evident in our trust and obedience. Consider this: If we truly trust Jesus as the Lord of our lives and have placed our faith in Him alone, we will naturally obey Him and comply with every precept in His word.[1]

Yes, faith is the assurance of things hoped for and the conviction of things not seen, and we cannot please God without faith (Heb 11:1, 6). However, this is key: Faith is a confident belief *in the truths of God's Word and His promises*, even when they are not immediately visible or tangible. And here's the takeaway: Trust is an extension of our faith, involving reliance on God's Promises and His faithfulness (Prov 3:5-6). Without it, we will not progress in our spiritual walk. If we rewind the clock thousands of years ago, trust was a key component that the Israelites, and even their faithful leader, Moses, were missing, which could have helped them reach the Promised Land.

To validate this, look at the power of God's message to Moses and Aaron, as recorded in Numbers 20:12. For it says, But the Lord said to Moses and Aaron, *"Because you did not trust me enough to demonstrate my holiness to the people of Israel, you will not lead them into the land I am giving them!"* We must pay close attention to this most profound and significant point: Because Moses *did not trust God's most divine instructions*, God told this faithful leader that he could not enter the Promised Land.

In this compelling passage, Moses' leadership faltered when he stopped trusting God and began acting on his own impulses. This led him to misrepresent the Holy One and fail to demonstrate Yahweh's holiness to the nation of Israel. You see, God wanted Moses to illustrate actions of obedience and holiness by simply trusting in Him and not taking matters

---

1. Hilpert, Tom. "1 Samuel #15, Trusting Obedience."

into his own hands. This great and faithful leader was God's representative to the nation of Israel, just like we are today in our homes, communities, and worldwide.

It was apparent that God's nation of Israel was already struggling with trust and belief in Yahweh, and Moses' disobedience did not help the cause. This storyline is significant for faithful followers of Christ today, as disturbing reports indicate that only a third of Americans trust the Church, and this trend continues to decline year after year. [2] What's my point in all of this?

Don't we realize that you and I are the Church, the representatives of the Body of Christ? When it comes to displaying God's righteousness and holiness, we're front and center as His living examples in today's world. The unbelievers, the weaker in faith or immature Christians, and the ones consumed by more of man's ways and this world are looking at you and me as entrusting believers and followers of Christ. For their sake, are we exhibiting more of God's truths than the falsehoods of man? Are we representing acts of His most divine characteristics for the glory of God? Before we reach the end of this book, you and I will see if our faith, trust, and obedience remain steadfast as His devoted servants and if His plan is being achieved in our personal lives.

It's crucial to remember that God's process active in us involves knowing and believing that He's in control of all things and works in a way that brings about His goodwill and glorious outcome. Yes, it may require suffering and persecution, but these times of distress can lead to sanctification, with an extreme focus on our eternal prize, because we trust in the One Who is our Driving Force in this life (Philippians 3).

Here's a tell-tale sign that our Lord and Living God is in the driver's seat of our lives, and we're trusting in His guidance. When children of God have Christ at the helm of their lives, they rely on His understanding and knowledge, long for His wisdom, obey His guiding principles, yield to His Spirit for counseling, act upon their personal convictions, and yearn for more of His word, which leads to a changed heart, mind, soul, and spirit.

Please never forget this powerful takeaway: 'If God's work is active and alive in us, the power of His word and Spirit will unlock the potential for you and me to achieve God's desired destiny in our future lives, for victory is surely on the horizon (Heb 4:12–13). Our trust in God's plan is vital in today's time because it demonstrates that we have faith in our Heavenly Father and believe that following Him will lead to unimaginable promised blessings in the future. Always remember this: *Believing in and trusting*

---

2. "A Third of Americans Trust the Church."

God's reliability and strength is a choice, even when circumstances or feelings suggest otherwise. (Please read Deuteronomy 30.)

To be empowered to choose the ways that are pleasing to God, we must ask ourselves as a daily reminder: Are we more led by the Spirit of God or by the ways of this world? *If we are led more by the power of His Holy Spirit, we will not have those feelings that are not of God.* And when we are led more by God than this world, we will be more apt to choose according to God's will and His desire in our lives. How?

When we trust the Holy Spirit to lead us in our everyday life, it means we are allowing Him to direct our decisions, thoughts, and actions that align with God's will. I cannot stress this enough: It involves submitting our lives to His guidance, trusting that He will lead us down the right path, and enabling us to live in a way that glorifies God.

I keep repeating this because many proclaimed believers do not submit themselves to God because of these dangerous factors below that prevent them from giving their lives entirely to our Heavenly Father. They are: Habitual sins, pride, selfishness, not trusting in God's word and promises, unforgiveness, lack of faith, continual disobedience, no desire for God's word in their lives, and not yielding to the conviction and counsel of the Spirit of God. This is going to be a spiritual gut-punch.

If these vices are constantly at work in your life more so than the holiness and righteousness of God, then you may not be truly born again. We must realize that if we have genuine faith, trust, and obedience in God as His entrusted followers, there must be evidence of a transformed life. That is why we must conduct an in-depth spiritual self-examination of our lives and ensure that our genuine saving faith is centered around Christ alone (2 Cor 13:5)!

Once again, we should ask ourselves this question daily: 'Does the world see tangible signs that we trust in an Almighty God, regardless of life's misfortunes?' Consider this: If we truly know the Truth, believe it, and trust it with all our hearts, minds, souls, and spirits, then we live by it through all the storms and tests of life. And through those trials, we share the powerful message of this Truth with others, which is the Good News of Jesus Christ. *That is when we know we are grounded in our absolute trust in God's ways and that the Truth has set us free because Christ is the Lordship of our lives, and nothing can change that.*

Undoubtedly, trusting God is the most important lesson we can learn as believers and followers of Christ in today's time. Nothing else compares with this; nothing comes close. How? It anchors our faith, hope, and love, leading us to be more obedient to all His ways with a humble and contrite heart. It helps us comply with His words with the guidance of His Spirit. You see, *trusting in our Almighty God and Creator is what we do because of the faith we have been given once we accept Christ as the Lord of our lives.*

Consider this profound point: Approximately half of David's psalms reveal that trust was a prominent and essential aspect of David's life. Throughout the Holy Scriptures, we see the emphasis and examples of our biblical heroes' unwavering trust and faith. A short list of examples for us today: From Abel, Noah, Abraham, Isaac, Jacob, Joseph, Moses, Rahab, Esther, Ruth, Daniel, the Major and Minor Prophets, the Disciples, Mary (mother of Jesus), and Paul (to name a few).

Those who inherently possessed faith in God and had trust and belief in His plan were empowered in their obedience, which enabled them to move forward with God. We must realize that the power of trusting God sparks personal growth today just as it did thousands of years ago. When we trust Him alone, we discover the courage to confront our fears and seek His wisdom and knowledge in every aspect of our lives.

Make no mistake about this statement: "We are not spiritually advancing toward our Promised Land as Followers of Christ if we don't adhere to complete trust and obedience to the biblical truths of God's Word!" If only that one generation of Israelites had genuinely trusted and believed in the power of God's truths! The outcome would have been different, but that was not meant to be. Undoubtedly, God is trying to teach us key lessons from the past failings of His chosen ones as He prepares us for that grand entrance one day soon, where His promise to you and me will be fulfilled. Do you really believe in this promise?

Think about this: If we don't believe and trust in the truths of God's promises, it's as if we're calling our Faithful God a liar. I don't know about you, but that's a severe gut punch for me! You see, our Lord and Creator are searching for wholehearted followers who are committed to Him, trust in His truths, and comply with them in every part of their lives (2 Chronicles 16:9). He's entrusted us with the ability to live the type of godly lives that will empower and sustain us on this earth as we progress and approach our new home (Read 2 Peter chapter 1). Remember: As His entrusted followers, He's endowed you and me with so many of His divine characteristics that should be at the forefront and active in our daily lives. Doesn't this motivate you to be in sync with God's work in your life, knowing that we share so many divine attributes with our Holy Creator?

Isn't it wonderful that God is not a distant or unknowable force—He has made Himself known through His Word (the Bible), creation, and His interactions with humanity (Genesis chapters 2 & 3, John 1:14–18, Romans 1:19). By studying His attributes and applying them to our lives, we deepen that communion with our Heavenly Father that keeps us aligned with His future plans through His Son, Jesus Christ. Undoubtedly, God has given us every reason possible to believe in and trust Him. Is that belief and trust evident in our lives as His children?

Consider this: Those who faithfully follow, love, and obey God's plan and trust Him with all their heart, mind, soul, and strength, in a strong sense, exemplify the greatest commandment in their lives (Matt 22:37-40). And when we live this type of life, there will be a day when we will hear those 7 words from the very lips of Christ, once we enter His Glorious Place. It's that place of unfathomable, eternal blessings He has promised to those who are faithful to His teachings until the end of their lives on earth.

Our everyday trust and faith in our Lord can help us reach that grand entrance so that we can hear Christ's most precious 7 words to His devoted ones. Question: *Do you know what those 7 words are?* As His dedicated servants, hearing those words from our Lord is a matter of our absolute trust in Him, believing in the truths of His Promises, showing the evidence of our genuine saving faith, and obeying all His guiding ways! The choice lies in you and me today!

Jer 17:7, "But blessed are those who trust in the Lord, and have made the Lord their hope and confidence."

2 Tim 4:7-8, "I have fought the good fight, I have finished the race, and I have remained faithful. And now the prize awaits me—the crown of righteousness, which the Lord, the righteous Judge, will give me on the day of his return. And the prize is not just for me but for all who eagerly look forward to his appearing."

Preface

Can we honestly say that we're fighting the good fight for our Lord and King, right now, today? If we know for a fact that we're genuine followers of Jesus Christ, and God's work of holiness and righteousness is active in our daily lives, it should be clearly displayed in our cause for Christ! You see, "I have fought the good fight" (as stated in 2 Timothy 4:7) signifies a life lived with unwavering faith and unshakeable perseverance. It is one who persistently faces challenges and temptations with courage and dedication to their deeply held beliefs. And this belief stems from their love and trust in the One who will ultimately lead them to victory.

Even though we may get knocked down at times, the good fighter of the faith, who trusts and obeys their Lord, in all their determination, does not give up because they keep pressing on toward the goal that awaits them one day (once again, read Philippians 3). They're the Onward Christian Soldier who portrays a solid testament of the Gospel lived out in their lives as they progress from this side—to His Side. And it's all due to their reliance on God's empowering grace, no matter the depths of their tribulations.

This profound statement from Paul in 2 Timothy should be ingrained in every fiber of our being as followers of Christ because this should be our daily challenge: "Have we truly fought the good fight as His servants of faith, trust, obedience, and allegiance to our Lord and King?" If we're in the good fight for our Lord and God, we constantly meditate on and long to hear those *seven most powerful words* from the very lips of our Savior, Jesus Christ, on that Day of Glory: "Well done, my good and faithful servant" (Matt 25:21).

If these most overpowering words are deeply embedded in our hearts, minds, and spirits, they will be evident in our Christian lives as His faithful and fruitful stewards, illustrating that we're on a straight path to glory. These types of servants have indeed fought the good fight until the very end of their lives due to their undeniable commitment and dedication to

Preface

their godly tasks. Their Lord and God is unquestionably first and foremost in their everyday lives, through all the good and bad times in this life's journey; nothing sways their focus from trusting and obeying Him. Why? Because the power of His Spirit leads them.

With that, we must ask ourselves: Does the weight of these seven words truly move us with so much of His power that we put our faith and trust into action more and more each passing day? Good and faithful servants understand that everything they've been given is a gift from God. The key takeaway is this: 'That gift comes with an assignment from God our Father to be fruitful and multiply in preparation for Jesus's arrival (soon).' And here's the beauty of it all: 'You and I can participate and partner with God now as we progress to our future Promised Land, only if we trust and obey His Son—every step of our lives!'

You see, a good and faithful servant is not just morally or ethically good; most importantly, they are *spiritually sound because they are grounded in the truths of the Holy Scriptures.* Consider this perspective and key takeaway: A good and faithful servant is an entrusted believer, as discussed earlier, who is biblically responsible, loyal, sensible, discerning, and trustworthy. They are spiritually clothed with the Whole Armor of God (Eph 6:10–17). They are Kingdom Builders, not kingdom breakers. And through it all, they glorify the Lord in all that they say and do (Col 3:16–17).

Being labeled as a good and faithful servant is more vital than we realize in today's times because, as God's entrusted believers, it reflects the parable of the talents in Matthew 25:21. This parable highlights how faithful servants are rewarded with greater responsibility and a share in their master's joy. The core idea is that being faithful in small things demonstrates our trustworthiness in small matters, which will grow into something larger. And when we're that spiritually productive, it increases opportunities for His glory, leading to greater blessings.

This parable in Matthew from Jesus Christ emphasizes that faithfulness in one's personal life is how one utilizes the gifts, talents, abilities, and resources given to them by God for His glory. It is a key characteristic of a good and faithful servant because our Lord promises to put that person in charge of more things *if they produce what He's provided for them.* To put this in a more robust perspective, how can we multiply and add more to the Kingdom of God if our Lord does not give us more responsibility? If we're not producing, it's because we're not complying, trusting, and being faithful to His ongoing process of holiness in our lives.

This is imperative because when we illustrate and prove the principle of our faithfulness to the Lord, He will grant us more divine responsibilities. Participating in God's plan with a willing heart will produce more of God's

Preface

glory, as we have earned the trust and greater responsibility to expand even further. What an honor, privilege, and blessing to know that we can help our Lord and God build His future Kingdom by being His good, faithful, and fruitful servant. As we will see, God expects us to use our gifts and God-given abilities for His glory, and in the end, He will reward those who are trustworthy stewards of what He has entrusted to them.

Let's conduct a test and compare the Israelites thousands of years ago to us today. The Israelites were considered "good" because they were God's chosen people, with a special covenant and a Promised Land signifying an intimate relationship with God. However, the Bible also depicts many times when the nation of Israel strayed from God's laws and faced the consequences for their actions, highlighting that their "goodness" is contingent on their obedience to God's commands. Does this sound familiar in our lives today?

It was evident that the people of Israel failed to observe the terms of God's conditional covenant because they continued to refuse to obey, believe, and trust in all of God's truths. With that, we must sincerely ask ourselves each day: Am I obedient to the truths of God's word? Am I trusting Him in every aspect of my life? Am I as faithful to Him as He is to me (2 Tim 2:13)? As His chosen royal priesthood in a time such as this, am I serving Him in the manner He desires (1 Pet 2:9)? How can we ensure that we're on the right path of faith, which will portray our wholehearted trust and obedience to the Lord and all His ways? We must challenge our spiritual and biblical growth levels more than ever in today's time! Why?

Unfortunately, today, there is a notable lack of enthusiasm and spiritual growth in God's house, with a general sense of lukewarmness in the church community. To prove this point, a survey conducted by the Pew Research Center titled "In the U.S., Decline of Christianity Continues at a Rapid Pace" revealed this staggering statistic and sad finding: 'The religious landscape of the United States continues to change at a rapid clip.' In their telephone survey conducted a few years ago, only 65% of American adults describe themselves as Christians when asked about their religion, down 12 percentage points over the past decade.

And as we look to today, this number continues to worsen. People are drifting and falling away from the very faith in our Lord that can save them by the droves! What is happening? Undoubtedly it's: 1) the lack of biblical knowledge, 2) not applying the spiritual application of His truths in our lives, 3) the influence of a godless culture, 4) associations with the unbelieving world, 5) personal hardships, 6) unconfessed sins, 7) apostasy (refusing to follow, trust and obey our Lord), 8) the search for real purpose in our lives for the Lord, 9) the doubts, disappointments, and discouragements in this life, and 10) the absence of daily genuine worship and fellowship with our Lord. These vice grips are leading millions away from the faith. Remember, when we've distanced ourselves or lost the very faith that can save us, we will never possess trust and obedience to His ways.

It is evident that the very words from our Lord, as recorded in His first parable in Matthew 13 (Parable of the Four Soils), are coming to fruition before our very eyes. Looking at the ten crutches listed above, which are damaging detriments to our genuine saving faith, it's obvious there is no spiritual discipline and accountability in the lives of Christians. We must all realize that our firm faith is built on a solid relationship with the Lord that will elevate our trust and obedience in all His ways. In other words, we put Him first, above any and all things (Matt 6:33). He should be our Source for everything, and we should live by the depths of His word in our daily lives (Colossians 3).

Unfortunately, and sadly, too many proclaimed followers of Christ seem to be in the middle of the road today, with all the separation of Christianity swirling within our society and culture. What do I mean? For some, the term "middle of the road" may mean being halfway or "sitting on the fence," which can portray a person who is not sufficiently committed to one side or the other. They are more in a state of fleshly perplexity than spiritual clarity; in other words, they are neither hot or cold! From a religious or theological perspective, a person who is not hot or cold could be described as lukewarm. And when you hear the biblical word 'lukewarm,' it should rattle your spiritual cage to the depths of your soul and spirit.

Look at it this way: A "middle-of-the-road" Christian is not extreme about their faith and relationship with the Lord because they do not have 100% trust and dependence in His guiding principles. And this unfortunate position in a person's life will indeed lead to a lack of obedience in all His ways. The gut punch is that they are spiritually tasteless, unflavored, weak, and watered down in their beliefs. When Christians take the middle road position, they do not give their all to an Almighty God. In other words, as stated earlier, they are not wholly committed to His ways, which leads them not to be faithful and trust in all the truths of God! They are not totally unresponsive to Christianity, but neither are they excited about their relationship with God and our Savior.

Consider this alarming fact: In Jesus' final letters to the seven churches, the church of the Laodiceans was in this state (Read Revelation chapter 3). Jesus told them they were neither cold nor hot, and because of this, He would rather spew them out of His mouth. In other words, our Lord was saying to that church that they were not on fire for the Lord, nor refreshing in their Christian Walk. While cold could also mean dead in spirit or lacking enthusiasm, there was still an opportunity for growth, allowing them to be more refreshing in God's eyes. But when a believer is lukewarm, they are so complacent that there is no room for growth.

Undoubtedly, this church was in the danger zone of being lukewarm, middle-of-the-road believers. This leads me to ponder: Is there really such a thing as lukewarm Christians if we're dedicated followers of Christ? Once again, please refer to the very first Parable in Matthew 13, "The Parable of the Four Soils," because this message serves as a reliable measuring stick of our lives as productive followers of Christ—or not!

Regrettably, when many Christians are positioned in the middle of the road, it could be because they are so deep in their road of despair that they don't care about their state of spirituality. They are so entrenched in their world of brokenness that they don't know how to get up and press on as trusting and onward Christian Soldiers. They seem to move more with the waving currents of 'self and this world'—more so than God's empowering promises. It almost seems that in these anxious or impatient moments of waiting, they yearn for something miraculous to save them from all the disheartenments in life. However, in their pattern of spiritual flatness, they don't try to remove themselves from their state of dispirited defeat. Where's their trust in God?

Please realize that as times become increasingly unpredictable in today's world and we navigate our turbulent life experiences, we are called by God to trust in His promises, *which can help us rise from our lowest points of weakness to His highest points of strength*. Always remember this: When Paul opened his letters where he stated that he was praying for believers to have grace and peace, he was telling you and me that God's grace is not just a concept; it's a powerful force that moves us to walk in the Spirit, not the flesh (Please read Romans chapter 8 and Galatians chapter 5).

When we're more in tune with His Spirit, then His peace guards our hearts and minds from the ways of this world (Phil 4:7). And that unbelievable peace of God brings us harmony and calmness of body, mind, and spirit. This will lead us to trust in the power of God's grace and all His assuring promises more and more each passing day. And here's the key takeaway: When we surrender to self and submit to the power of God, yielding to His Spirit during times of uncertainty, worry, anxiety, and fear, we trust God to guide us from the middle of the road to His paths of righteousness and holiness that will lead to the Promised Land.

This could be one of the most serious points in the book, as it pertains to real-life application, because layered within the upcoming commentaries are actual words of challenge from our Lord, Jesus Christ. We will see that there will be some significant punches to our spiritual gut. Once again, we're

Preface

not trying to be too judgmental, but we must be accountable to the power of God's word (Heb 4:12–13, 2 Tim 3:16–17) and never be in a position of grieving the Holy Spirit (Eph 4:30).

I will strive to convey this severe message with words of God's grace and love as much as possible, guided by empathy and compassion. However, I am communicating this passage with urgency because of the lack of genuine and heartfelt spirits and hearts in today's churches, which fail to trust and obey the Lord as He desires. We all must understand that true believers and followers of Christ, as born-again Christians, should show signs of significant change for the Lord, not the ways of man and this world.

To ensure we don't fail like that one generation of Israelites and don't fall from the very faith that can save us, let's return to the first parable recorded in the Gospel of Matthew 13. Why? Because woven in this spiritual lesson is a teaching that we should all pay close attention to and apply today, tomorrow, and in the days to come in order to progress in our everyday Christian Walk.

Here it is: Do we take our Lord's words in the scriptures with such stern conviction when He says that *only one of four soils is productive?* Do we understand the magnitude of this most potent Parable in Matthew 13? If not, we risk remaining stagnant and lukewarm in our spiritual growth and failing to advance toward our ultimate goal. How?

This Parable is one of the most significant teachings found in the Gospels, as it illustrates the diverse responses to the message of the Kingdom of God. Each type of soil represents a distinct condition of the human heart and its receptivity to the spiritual and biblical truths of the Bible. It separates the good, faithful, and entrusting servants from those who are not following God's plan. This may not be exceptionally comforting for many self-proclaimed believers. Why?

In the very first Parable recorded in Matthew 13, we see some compelling words from our Lord, Jesus Christ, that encompass four types of people: 1) Those who are not believers, 2) those who are not growing, 3) those more consumed by the ways of the world and man, 4) and finally to the ones who are genuinely productive. Our Lord is clearly telling you and me that His word has been planted for all, but for that first group, it was quickly snatched from them, for these are the unbelievers.

Then, we see that the words never took root in the second and third groups, for they are not listening and trying to understand God's word. This is because they are not grounded in the truths of His holy scriptures, where there should be real-life application. We must ask ourselves: 'If there is no change in a person's life once they accept Christ as their Savior, were they

Preface

ever 'born again'? This is a harsh question, but, as I said at the outset of this book, we will all be challenged to change for the Glory of God.

To bring this to light, we cannot forget the conversation between Jesus Christ and Nicodemus, as recorded in John 3:1–21. As Jesus talked with Nicodemus, He said, "I tell you the truth, no one can see the kingdom of God unless he is born again.' 'How can a man be born when he is old?' Nicodemus asked. 'Surely he cannot enter a second time into his mother's womb to be born!' Jesus answered, 'I tell you the truth, no one can enter the kingdom of God unless he is born of water and the Spirit. Flesh gives birth to flesh, but the Spirit gives birth to spirit. You should not be surprised at my saying, "You must be born again".

This is what I'm trying to say: While being "born-again" signifies a spiritual rebirth and initial transformation, it's not a one-time event, but a continuous process of growth and internal and external change that weeds out areas of unrighteousness, allowing individuals to mature spiritually. A born-again Christian experiences a change in heart, mind, soul, and spirit, a new love for God and the Lord, and a desire to live according to His will and future plan. Please always remember: When we undergo the stages of transformation into the image of Christ, it is a lifelong journey of sanctification, where the Holy Spirit works to reshape our thoughts, emotions, and actions.

Never forget what Paul says in 2 Corinthians 5:17. As new believers in Christ, our old life and unspiritual ways of living should be gone, and only the new life in Christ should be apparent. Once again, we're not talking about perfection *but the continual progression of spiritual maturity*. You see, this spiritual transformation is a complete departure from the old ways of living, transitioning towards a new life with a renewed mindset, heart, spirit, and purpose. This is imperative because you and I now have a new identity as recipients of God's grace, which should exhibit more of His Son in our daily lives.

I say this because when there's no spiritual growth in a person's life, it is evident that the ways of the world and man consume them more. There is no wholehearted commitment in their life of true prayer, worship, service, and praise to the Lord, because the works of the enemy sway them. Over time, this leads to them not being wholly devoted to applying God's Scripture to their daily lives, which is a significant detriment to their faith, trust, and obedience. However, when one is dedicated entirely to the Word of God and His Spirit, one thing is sure: There will be signs of a transformed life for God's glory. Let's delve more and examine a key takeaway from this profound passage and Parable in Matthew 13.

Preface

Jesus tells us, "To those who listen to my teaching, more understanding will be given, and they will have an abundance of knowledge. *But for those who are not listening, even what little understanding they have will be taken away from them.* That is why I use these parables, For they look, but they don't really see. They hear, but they don't really listen or understand."

Just think: This is precisely what happened to that first generation of Israelites. They saw God's miracles and provisions and heard His voice, but still ignored and did not believe in God's guidance, leading them not to trust and obey Him completely. Instead, they trusted in other things that led them astray and influenced their future course in life. Yahweh wanted them to incline their ears to His ways so He could guide them to their future Promised Land.

And for us today, it is evident in this compelling passage from Christ that only those who truly listen, trust, obey, and apply His guiding principles in their lives will obtain more knowledge. But for the people *who are not* using their ears to hear His word, eyes to see the ways He sees, hearts to receive His message, minds to conform to His ways, mouths to share His Good News, and souls and spirits as a living sacrifice for His glory are in danger.

Seriously, do these words from Christ in this Parable, 'what little understanding they have will be taken away,' resonate within you? We are familiar with the unbelievers in the world and can readily identify them, for they are the first group. But the second and third groups of 'so-called' followers are those in churches today, and are not living out their genuine saving faith for the glory of God. If these two groups of people, at one point, received the message of Christ but fell away, we could infer that unfruitful people in the church are in a state of being lukewarm, which is a terrifying prospect.

With that, we must seriously ask ourselves this question: If God's children are not on board with His plan 100% and the truths of God's word have been taken away from them (like the 2nd and 3rd soils), how can there be spiritual and biblical application in their lives? If we're not productively fruitful for our Lord, why would anyone dare to jeopardize their relationship with Him by testing the threshold of His patience? Let me be clear: The Lord did not give us this parable to cause us to question our salvation. Instead, He gave it to motivate us to produce much fruit for His glory, so that we can hear those seven words from the lips of Christ. That should be our top priority and aspiration every day of our lives as we move forward to our future home.

This is imperative because the parable illustrates how people respond to the Gospel. The second and third soils represent those who initially

Preface

believe but eventually fall away due to personal sufferings, persecution, or worldly distractions. Only the fourth soil, which means those who truly hear, understand, and bear fruit, is considered to be genuinely committed wholeheartedly to our Lord. Never forget what Christ says in Matthew 6:24: We cannot serve two masters. Here, Jesus urges believers to reflect on their priorities, as this passage reveals the more profound implications of Christ's teaching on genuine faith, trust, and commitment to Him or the ways of this world.

As devout Christians, we must understand that faithful followers trust and believe in their leader, Jesus Christ, with all they have. They don't test Him but live by every word of the Bible. Once again, we're not talking about perfection, but progression. Authentic believers live more by God's grace than by their own works. This means that because of their tight bond and relationship with Christ, they are being shaped more like their Lord by the power of His Word and Spirit as each day passes. They are fully committed to God's plan of sanctification and are full-time servants, not part-timers, just one or two days a week. This is because they are more intensely focused on the eternal promises rather than the temporal ways that this world offers.

If you boil this down, you are either a fan sitting in the stands, one who is not contributing to or participating in God's plans every day, or one who follows and trusts the ways of our Lord. Look at it this way: 'You are either following the crowds of people and this world, or Christ (there is no in-between).' And here's the Takeaway: If you're a fan in the stands and not on the field of God's action plan, you're not truly listening, believing, and applying the Word of God to your life. How can we be good fighters of the faith if we're in the stands watching, but not doing? Never forget this: We cannot defend the faith if we're not genuinely living it out!

We should know by now that actual followers of Christ put God's word into practice daily; in other words, as noted several times earlier, they're doers of the Scripture (Jas 1:22). And if we're not productive each day, listening, receiving, understanding, applying, and obeying the word of God in our lives, we could be in danger of having it snatched away (refer back to the 2nd and 3rd soils). Once again, consider the first generation of Israelites who left Egypt during the Exodus and wandered in the wilderness. They did not trust and have enough faith in God's ways and all His truths, which would eventually lead to their death. We cannot live by our feelings and emotions alone, but by faith, where we trust in His divine guidance.

Consider this PowerPoint: What should our faith look like if our Holy Creator is the Author and Finisher of our faith (Heb 12:2)? Here is the answer: As noted earlier in the book, and as our daily reminder, *the writings of His holy words should be reflected in every aspect of our lives.* They should exemplify trusting and obeying Christ, our Lord, in everything we say and do daily. Anything less is unacceptable, and we once again must examine our genuine faith, as Paul instructs us in 2 Corinthians 13:5. We must always ensure that Jesus is the Lordship and nucleus of our lives every step of our Christian Walk.'

Let's go deeper into this most critical topic of faith and trust: In our daily routines, do we fix more of our thoughts on the realities of Heaven or the things of this earth (Col 3:1–2)? Do we focus more on things that are worthy of His praise, or do we think more about the godless ways that disrupt our faith, trust, and obedience? (Phil 4:8)? Do we press on toward our eternal goal, no matter what obstacles that may come our way (Phil 3:12–16)? Do we seriously meditate on the breaths of God's word each passing day and put it into practice (Deuteronomy 6 and Psalm 1)? As Paul, Peter, and Jesus' half-brother (James) underscore in their letters throughout the New Testament, whatever you have learned, received, or heard, put it into action!

With that, are we applying the scriptures to our lives (Jas 2:18, 2 Tim 3:16–17)? How do you know that you're living out your saving faith through the channels of trust and obedience? Here are some indicators! Do we genuinely yearn for more of His word in our hearts and minds than the news of today (Psalm chapter 119)? Do we yield more to His Spirit than the ways of man (Gal chapter 5, Rom 8:5–12)? Are we living out our salvation with trembling and fear daily (Phil 2:12)? In other words, our faith, trust, and obedience are so rooted in our Lord, "We serve the LORD with fear and rejoice with trembling." What does this mean, you may ask?

There should be an absolute reverence and respect for God's ways in our everyday lives. When we're out of sync with His Spirit and Holy Word and know that we're not aligned with all of His ways, there should be such a conviction within us that it leads us to be offended because we're disrespecting His ways of holiness. You see, serving the Lord with fear and trembling means acknowledging His holiness and authority in our lives, and rejoicing with a deep respect and awe for who God is.

It reflects the theme of obedience and reverence towards God, because of our faith and trust in Him and all His ways. But it also involves the unfathomable emotions of fear and joy in the context of worship and devotion to the Lord of our lives. Once again, are we genuinely growing in the ways of the Lord or the ways of this world? Seriously, ask yourself this question: *Are we living a life that matters and makes a difference for the glory of God, one that depicts our daily respect and honor for Him?*

Once again, these are all tough questions for all Christians! But at the end of each day, we must ask ourselves whether the world sees more holiness (set apart and dedicated to God's plan), righteousness (acts of Christlikeness), and godliness (determined to honor God) in all our words and deeds. Again, we're not talking about perfection but a continuous improvement process. Our faith should be so rock-solid that our trust in the Lord remains unwavering and unshaken. Look at it this way: "The world should see such a level of Christlikeness in us that they know we're moving forward to a future land full of unbelievable blessings."

When we live under God's guiding principles of faith through the power of His Word and Spirit, we know that our Father not only desires it, but He also expects it! Just as God chose the second generation of Israelites to help lead His people to the Promised Land, He expected them to adhere to His plans and follow His appointed leader, Joshua, as willing and dedicated partners. No matter the trials and tests they would confront along the way (and there would be many), He expected His children to trust in Him and obey all His ways.

And these same fundamentals that have been in place for thousands of years apply to you and me today, and it's this: "Without trust and faith in a Leader, believing and obeying God's plan, we will not succeed from this temporary life to our everlasting life ." With that, we all must ask ourselves, Who is our Faithful Leader for today—One that we will follow all the way to the end of our life journey? Is Jesus Christ your leader and Lord of life right now? Never forget this key takeaway: 'Whoever our leader is in everyday life will be portrayed in us, inwardly and outwardly.'

Obviously, the first generation of Israelites chose not to follow God's appointed and faithful leader because they decided to follow the ways of the world instead. But the second generation now has a new beginning, emerging from all the past wanderings to a land of enriched promises if they make the right choice to be an entrusted participant in God's plan.

I can only imagine what was going through the minds and hearts of that second generation of Israelites when they were told that they would be counted as righteous if they obeyed God and chose to follow all His ways. After all, they had seen the miraculous work of God's hands, but they also witnessed the destruction of their ancestors. Now, through the rebirth of another generation of followers, there was a newfound hope to finally reach the land of God's unfathomable riches.

As we will see throughout this book, the faith and trust of the second generation of Israelites grew as they drew closer to the Promised Land because they knew God had kept His Promises. However, they still had to enforce obedience in their lives to fulfill all the original plans God had promised to Abraham, Isaac, and Jacob. Make no mistake, their faith and trust would be tested throughout their journey to ensure their reliance was in God alone.

Would they please God as His new chosen ones and follow His appointed leader with loyalty and accountability? If they fail, it will be evident in their disobedience. As a reminder, Christians must ask ourselves this today: Is the evidence of our faith heightened as we get closer to our Promised Land? Does our hope, confidence, contentment, enthusiasm, peace, and joy (in what's to come) enlighten a world that is so off course of God's path to Glory? If we're that excited and connected with our Lord in all His ways, our trust and obedience in our Heavenly Father will make an impact and difference in today's world of confusion.

Once again, in today's society and culture, many churchgoers profess their faith in Jesus Christ and testify to themselves as His devoted followers. Sadly, they are not implementing that genuine saving faith. We must never forget that Jesus set an example for His followers through the teachings He shared and the way He served others. Believers need to remember that faith is not passive; it actively seeks to align with God's vision and will, which springs forth our trust in the promises of His Word.

When our genuine faith is alive and in action, it demonstrates that we trust in God's promises of spiritual blessings (Please read Ephesians 1). As we progress in our spiritual walk, the guidance of His Word and the Spirit will encourage us to bear more fruit for Him. It will bring us great hope, an expectation that is not fleeting but reassuring and can be shared with others. When we do this, it's a testament to our trust in God's word that will move us to assist others in our life journey who need to believe in God's mighty promises today.

We must challenge ourselves daily: "Does our obedience align with our genuine faith and trust in a Holy God who will lead us to our glorious home, once and for all?" As a reminder, please remember this fact: "Obedience is a testimony of our faith." How? It reflects a real believer's trust, love, and commitment to God. Through obedience and trust, faith is made visible, demonstrating the transformative power of a life surrendered to God's will and plan.

And that changed life is awaiting those most precious words from the very lips of our Redeeming Savior, *"Well done, my good and faithful servant"!* If we long to reach our Promised Land, once again, these words should be ingrained in our hearts, souls, and minds each and every day. The world should see that as devoted Christians, we follow the One down His righteous path, leading us to our everlasting place of comfort.

Oh, what a glorious day it will be when we enter His gates of thanksgiving and see Him face-to-face! Hopefully, we're leading others to this remarkable place of eternal rest by being His good, faithful, and entrusted servants who honor and glorify Him in every aspect of their lives! Please remember this key point as we continue to progress: 'Our entrance into His Kingdom can only happen if *we accept and follow God's only Son by faith, obey His word, and trust the leading of His Spirit in our daily lives! There's no other way* (John 14:6, Romans 10:9–11)!

One thing will become apparent before we reach the end of this book. As His faithful servants who are dedicated to following the Way, the Truth, and the Life, those who are sincerely committed to the Lord will surely die to self, embrace Christlike humility, and enrobe themselves with God's love, grace, and mercy. You and I are His entrusted followers, endowed with many of God's beautiful divine characteristics that should be evident in our Christian Walk. But as His children who trust Him with every fiber of our being, *none of this will be apparent if we do not completely surrender and submit it all to Him as the Lordship of our lives.* It is the only way to ensure that we rely 100% on our Savior and King and are grounded on His path to everlasting freedom.

Introduction

Did you know that our Lord and King, Jesus Christ, gave His genuine believers three commands and action plans for following Him today? 1) Deny self, 2) Take up one's cross, and only then can we 3) Follow Him. Following Jesus is to forget oneself and one's personal interests and desires in this life. The Lord calls true Christians everywhere to practice self-denial for the sake of God's Kingdom, which completely goes against our flesh's desires. That is why we need His empowering Grace to reassure us that we're on His path of righteousness. This action plan is so important to Christ that He mentions it in each of the Synoptic Gospels (Matt 16:24, Mark 8:34, and Luke 9:23).

For Jesus says, "Then Jesus said to his disciples, "If any of you wants to be my follower, you must give up your own way, take up your cross, and follow me. If you try to hang on to your life, you will lose it. But if you give up your life for my sake, you will save it. And what do you benefit if you gain the whole world but lose your own soul? Is anything worth more than your soul?"

In today's complex, confusing, and consuming ways of man, this world and the enemy, which are filled with so many distorted truths and deceptions, we must ensure that we genuinely know we're on the righteous path of our Faithful and Trusted Leader, Jesus Christ. We should only follow and be dedicated to His ways, His truths, and His life. As stated earlier, and as our constant reminder: 'What we consistently follow in our daily lives will be reflected in our words and deeds, both inwardly and outwardly.' Our lips and actions will reveal the genuine passions of our hearts and minds in everyday life! (Please read Matt 12:36–37, James 3:5, Psalm 19:14, Proverbs 4:23, Ephesians 4:29, and Colossians 4:6). With that, is it more of the world or the Lord? Who are we truly and honestly following more in our everyday life?

Introduction

Do you remember the game 'Follow the Leader'? It was a popular game in my day, but it is not as well-known as it was over half a century ago. The idea of this game was to mimic the antics of the person in front of you. The rules were fundamental: One person was chosen as the leader, and the rest would line up behind them and copy all the leader's actions. However, there was a consequence for anyone who did not successfully copy the chosen leader's motions: 'If they did not comply or were out of sync with the leader, they were removed from the game.' But the great news is that there was a reward for the one who successfully followed the leader's movements to the letter. They would be the designated leader for the next round.

While the exact date of this game's invention is unknown, it's considered one of the oldest children's games. However, here's what we know: 'Follow the Leader' is one of those traditional games that's still played by some, and it has been passed down from generation to generation. I remember being a follower more often than a leader. In the intense moment of the game, I recall being captivated by the leader's every move, down to the detail. Why? I aspired to be the leader in the subsequent round, but more importantly, I did not want to be removed from the game.

Many of us who recall this game found it rewarding because, if a person followed their appointed leader to the T, victory was apparent, knowing a reward awaited them at the very end of the game. However, the followers had to pay close attention to every movement that the leader made, or they would not be able to proceed. When I failed the test of following the leader and was removed from the game, I remember feeling disheartened while sitting on the sidelines, because I was eager to get back in the game for another chance to redeem myself.

This leads me to ponder: Our Lord, Jesus Christ, gives us numerous opportunities in life to redeem ourselves through His love, grace, and mercy, all because He loves us and is exceedingly patient (please read 2 Peter 3:15 and Hebrews 12). The Bible teaches us that God is gracious and compassionate, offering us opportunities for redemption and new beginnings, regardless of our failings and shortcomings.

For instance, after Peter denied Jesus, He restored him, demonstrating God's willingness to forgive and make all things right regardless of all his wrongdoings. Look at the powerful story of Paul, a man who was out to destroy all Christians. How the Lord transformed His life from an enemy to a conqueror for Christianity should be our model for today. Ultimately, God's love and forgiveness are always available to anyone ready to submit themselves to His empowering grace and follow Him wholeheartedly. It should encourage us to seek Him where He provides personal growth and renewal. What a faithful and loving God we can serve and follow today!

Introduction

When I reflect on this most memorable childhood game, I see so many striking parallels with the Christian Leader-follower relationship. Just think: The Leader-follower dynamically characterizes our role in the field of servanthood as our Lord's chosen ones in practical ways. How? We should be following the example of our trusted leader, Jesus Christ, in every biblical and spiritual aspect of our lives, which should impact and influence others to follow Him, as well, to His home in glory. And here's the profound takeaway:

'If we're not following, living, serving, and growing in the same fashion as our Lord and King, we must ask ourselves this question: Are we in jeopardy of being removed?' When we don't follow our Leader Jesus Christ in every move, according to the holy scriptures, and we are convicted by His Spirit when we get out of line, how disheartened are we that we let Him down? Are we motivated to get back into His game of selfless and faithful service and show our Lord that we are more willing the next time around?

As stated earlier, isn't it wonderful that He gives us more chances in life than we deserve? But we cannot afford to continually test His patience before it's too late and He removes us. Always remember this PowerPoint: When our God and Lord gives us a second chance, it means we are given another opportunity to earn His trust. (Please read 2 Peter 3:9). And we surely can't forget Paul's powerful message in Romans 6:15–16, "Well then, since God's grace has set us free from the law, does that mean we can go on sinning? Of course not! Don't you realize that you become the slave of whatever you choose to obey? You can be a slave to sin, which leads to death, *or you can choose to obey God, which leads to righteous living."*

Look at it this way: We're chosen to be in God's game (His will and plan) of following His Leader and Son, Jesus Christ, all because of His grace, mercy, and love for us. We cannot forget that God's Grace is a gift from Him, as recorded in Ephesians 2:8. But when we sin and drift away from His will, the conviction from His Spirit should be so overwhelming that we will have such a godly sorrow that our response should be evident in seeking His guidance for counseling and correction. (2 Cor 7:10–11)

You see, the Spirit's conviction within us is a movement of love and grace, not an excuse to sin and continue to stray from His purpose and plan (Rom 6:1–2). Here's the power of this: Grace is how we live, how we are saved, sanctified, and how we will be kept in the game that will glorify our Lord in our life journey. With that, we must challenge ourselves as His followers daily with this: 'Why live a sinful life and continually stray from His will when Christ offers to make us whole and right in God's eyes and keep us in His long-term plan?'

Introduction

Undoubtedly, when we're going through this life journey and not following our Lord wholeheartedly in the way He desires, it is mainly due to those stages when we wander aimlessly in the wilderness, take our hearts and minds off His holy word, lack faith and trust in His ways, possess a disobedient and hardened heart because we neglect the counsel of His Spirit. We must remember that if we need clarity, purpose, direction, and a goal of victory in this life, it is evident that we need a faithful and trusted Person to get us through those turbulent times in our lives, and it's in the Name of Christ alone!

That is why we must submit and follow the only One (Jesus Christ) Who can lead us down His path of spiritual freedom. Make no mistake about this: We can trust our Lord and Savior today with any and all matters in life we're experiencing because He always has our best interests at heart, which is leading us to our future Promised Land!

Always remember this: God's word teaches us to follow Jesus Christ as our leader in every phase of our lives. If His Word and Spirit are active and alive in us, they will exemplify our absolute trust and obedience in Him each day. This is important for us today, tomorrow, and in the future. Why? As noted often, and as our reminder, following Christ's example daily is the only way for us to succeed in this life, because He's the only One who can lead us safely to our final destination.

The author in Hebrews 13:6-9 reminds us, "So we can say with confidence, 'The Lord is my helper so that I will have no fear. " What can mere people do to me?" Remember your leaders who taught you the word of God. Think of all the good that has come from their lives and follow the example of their faith. Jesus Christ is the same yesterday, today, and forever. So do not be attracted by strange, new ideas. Your strength comes from God's grace, not from rules about food, which don't help those who follow them."

In this compelling passage, the author reminds us that since the Lord is with us, we can rest assured that He will always be with us and help us. There is nothing in life that you and I must ever be afraid of; no fear, paranoia, worry, anxiety, or stress. Yes, we may lose things, suffer in this life, and endure those stages where people may hurt or disappoint us. Yet, despite all that, there is a God and Lord with us, helping us through it all. Never forget this key fact: Our Lord and Savior is our consistent and constant Guide that we can trust throughout our life journey, all the good, the bad, and the ugly; for He never changes. As reassurance from the power of His word, please read Romans 8:31-39.

In this book, "Trusting God to the Promised Land: A Journey through the Book of Joshua," we will discover that following a leader, appointed by the Almighty One is key to our success in moving forward to a future land.

Introduction

Throughout this journey, we will learn whether our genuine saving faith, hope, and love are evident in our trust in Christ at every step, from this side of eternity to His precious place of wondrous glory, where there will be no more suffering and pain. However, as His entrusted believers, as noted earlier in the book, we have work to do today on this side of Heaven because we will see that faithful followers are needed today more than ever. Why?

1) Followers of Christ do most of God's work. 2) They utilize their gifts to their fullest potential. 3) Christian followers are passionate about God's work and the people they serve. 4) A Productive Christlike follower maximizes their spiritual strengths, minimizes their fleshly weaknesses, and capitalizes on their godly opportunities. 5) Godly followers will defend their leaders when they encounter negative and false complaints. 6) Solid followers of Christ set aside their personal aspirations and ensure that their interests and loyalty align with the leader's and team's mission (according to God's plan), and 7) Genuine followers of our Lord set the precedent for the next generation. Look at it this way: It should be a godly chain of reactions throughout our lives that yields fruitful results, which is not only impacting others, but most importantly glorifying God our Father.

As discussed at the outset of the book, "A Matter of Trust" falls back on us as His entrusted followers, where our faith and obedience engage us with the Almighty One. You see, "A matter of trust" is all about how One (God) relies and depends on others (you and me) to fulfill our long-term obligations and acts in a manner that honors and glorifies Him. This is important because a clear sign that we have entrusted ourselves to God is evident when we submit, surrender, and yield to Him and all His ways.

And when we do this, we believe and trust our faithful God and Lord can and will do what He says, which will be accomplished through us as His vessels! It is essential to understand that entrusting ourselves to God means we make ourselves available so that He can work out His plan through us. Consider the power of that because that's what Jesus did for His Father, which fulfilled God's will and ultimate plan of redemption.

And think: If that one generation of God's children from the Exodus had trusted and believed in God's guidance and plan to the T, it could have been their game-changer in life. But that was not meant to be, because they were not on board with God wholeheartedly! This old storyline remains as our example to this day.

Reflecting on the shortcomings of that one generation of Israelites and the future responsibilities of the succeeding ones, I am led to consider the powerful concept of trust in today's times. You could break the word' TRUST' down into many acronyms. However, I love this one, as it

Introduction

effectively conveys the key points of this profound word of accountability." It is Totally—Relying—Upon Our—Savior—to the T! What does this mean?

Totally means giving the Lord our whole heart, soul, and mind with all our strength, because of our love for Him and His ways (Mk 12:30). Relying means depending entirely on Jesus Christ in all aspects of life, with the guidance of His word and Spirit (Prov 3:5-6). *Upon* is when we have built all principles of faith and trust in our Lord (Isa 26:3, Ps 37:5). When we do this, we know that our *Savior* is saving us from the present to what is to come in our future life (Rom 10:9, Acts 16:31, John 1:12, 3:16-17, Col 1:13-14).

And finally, to the *"T"* means we know beyond a shadow of a doubt that Christ is the perfect and exact model and fit for us to follow today, in order to reach our Promised Land (John 13:14-15, Matt 16:24, 1 Pet 2:21). When we live by these key fundamentals, we know that we're following the One where we don't allow deviations, distractions, disruptions, and disturbances to deter our path. We trust Him 100% and don't question His direction, for we know He has a greater outcome! This would have been another great lesson for that one generation of the Israelites who failed to follow God.

This is critical, and I can't stress it enough because believing in and trusting God is central to our genuine saving faith. You see, belief is the intellectual acceptance of something that is factual and true; and trust is putting that belief into motion. Then you see faith come alive! Consider this: "You cannot have faith without trust, and you cannot have trust without faith; they go hand in hand." Once again, we all know what God's word tells us in Heb 11:6: "And it is impossible to please God without faith. Anyone who wants to come to Him must believe that God exists and that He rewards those who sincerely seek Him." This is important because when our faith and trust are interlocked, it can bring spiritual stability and confidence that will help us in areas such as obedience, growth, and overcoming challenges. It also enables us to stick to God's plan in our lives.

Many are familiar with the well-known passage in Jeremiah 29:11-13, which we mentioned at the beginning of the book, stating, "For I know the plans I have for you," says the Lord. "They are plans for good and not for disaster, to give you a future and a hope. In those days, when you pray, I will listen. If you look for me wholeheartedly, you will find me." The key takeaway from this most memorable and profound passage is for those who diligently pray to align their plans with God's future desires. They truly yearn and search for Him with all their heart, soul, mind, and strength, and trust His plan to the very end. To make this concrete, recall the popular Psalm in chapter 34: 'Those who trust in the Lord will be blessed.'

Introduction

In this journey through the Book of Joshua, we will see that God appointed this great leader for such a time as this, which was so needed for His chosen people. One generation under Moses's guidance failed the test, but because of God's grace, mercy, and love, He would allow another generation to surface and help lead the nation of Israel to its Promised Land. What a striking parallel for Christians today! Our Heavenly Father has chosen you and me as His own for a purpose and plan that will lead us from this wretched life to His place of everlasting comfort. The key is following His Only Begotten Son, Jesus Christ, to the T!

If we know for a fact that He's our Way, Truth, and Life, as noted in John 14:6, then our lives should be adoring Him, learning from Him, serving Him, and becoming more like Him. Once again, we are not talking about perfection but steady spiritual progression. We should know by now that a genuine follower of the Lord is a true representative of everything they say and do that glorifies His Most Holy Name. How can we know?

Once again, they are doers of the word, saying what He says, doing what He does, seeing what He sees, loving as He loves, forgiving others as He forgave us, and becoming what He is. There is no wavering and waffling from our role as His entrusted believers and faithful servants. With that, are we in alignment with His perfect plan?

This journey will indeed challenge the genuine followers of Christ! I hope and pray that you're up for the challenge of change and the application of Christlike accountability, where we truly follow the Only Example that will lead us to our future home of rest and peace. We will see if that new generation of Israelites will live up to God's expectations and standards in every aspect of their lives, just like you and I should be doing today. Yes, they will make it, but will they sustain the power of God in their lives by trusting and obeying Him, which can surely be passed down to future generations? Time will tell!

The Book of Joshua—"God's Promise is Fulfilled"

After over 400 years, God's Promise to Abraham in Genesis chapter 12 is about to be fulfilled. One major takeaway from this powerful book is that when our Heavenly Father assures us He will fulfill His Promises in our lives, we can be confident He will be faithful to His word. While His timing may differ from ours, His faithful commitments will always come to pass for our spiritual good, and in the end, we will not be disappointed. This unwavering faithfulness in God is our source of security and hope we all need today. We must ask ourselves: 'How patient, obedient, faithful, trusting, committed, and willing are we in waiting for His plan to unfold in our lives?'

As we will see in this marvelous book, in God's timing, He eventually took the land from the idolaters and entrusted it to His children. However, as we will come to understand, as God's chosen nation prepared to conquer the land, Yahweh had high expectations of His people. He expected His people to trust and believe in His guidance, obey His laws and regulations, and faithfully govern the land as He saw fit.

This was not a mere request but a weighty responsibility and duty He entrusted to His chosen ones to represent His holiness and righteousness for others to see and follow—a role of significant importance. This same expectation from God also relates to you and me today. However, the question remained: Would they fulfill this responsibility? How about us? Before the end of this journey, we will see the actual measurements of our trust and obedience, rooted in our genuine saving faith! We will see!

Israel had journeyed a long-winded and indirect route through the aimless wilderness for far too long. All because they were pointlessly following their selfish desires and leaning more toward their own wisdom than God's. This led to their lack of faith and refusal to obey God and His leaders, causing them to stray from the path to God's Promised Land. We must

The Book of Joshua—"God's Promise is Fulfilled"

even ask ourselves today: As Christians, do we ever find ourselves in this same predicament as the Israelites? In other words, do we allow meaningless, useless, and unproductive things to take our hearts and minds off the ways and directions of our Lord, which leads us to not trust in Him first and foremost?

As we all know, God has destroyed the generation that failed and has now appointed a new generation of Israelites, who, with their renewed faith and trust, are ready to cross over the Jordan and possess the land God had promised them. God lived up to His word, and this new generation is a testament to His faithfulness. But would His future children live up to the high calling from God? Would they trust Yahweh in the way He desires so they can take possession of all the land God promised centuries earlier?

Now, as God's children's wandering years come to an end and they finish their bewildering stage in the wilderness, they will have the opportunity to trust in God's guidelines for the future and conquer the land that is theirs because of God's covenant. Their fearless leader, Joshua, was committed and ready to obey his Lord because he believed in God's promises and set an example for the nation of Israel to follow. The Israelites were required to do it God's way and choose the One they would serve forever, which was the example Joshua set forth for God's children to follow.

Joshua would be the vessel and channel through which God's children could see the ways of their Lord, so they would come to believe and trust in all His Promises. We must ask ourselves: Are we the vessels and channels of faith where our trust and obedience in the Lord are the example for others to follow? Today, the choice is ours individually to follow God's path of promises and victory, or to forsake it. Whether we obey or forsake, the consequences of our choices are significant because they carry the gravity of eternal impact, not just for ourselves, but also for others. I would pray that no one would choose the latter of forsaking our Lord! How loyal are we to our King and Redeeming Savior today? Our true tests are coming as we journey throughout the Book of Joshua.

Through this great and faithful leader, we will see his complete reverence and respect for the One who would lead him and his people to their Promised Land once and for all. This fearless and obedient leader possessed the faith needed to achieve victory for the nation of God. He believed and trusted in Yahweh, which was evident in his loyalty and wholehearted commitment to fulfill God's plan. And because of his unwavering faith, nothing would stand in the way of his accomplishing this historical feat. Do we have that same type of faith and trust in our Lord and God right now to achieve a feat beyond our comprehension?

The Book of Joshua—"God's Promise is Fulfilled"

God promised His children that they would experience great abundance once they enter His Promised Land, and we can experience that same blessing if we follow the ways of His Son to our future land. We must never forget this: Just like then and even to this day, for God to prove His faithfulness to all His children, He will always align it with the truths and credibility of His word, as recorded in the Bible! Our Lord and God is that trusting! We must rely on the truths of His Holy Word as our daily guide to the Promised Land.

The Book of Joshua could be one of the most overlooked books in the Bible. Many theologians call this powerful book the "Book of Ephesians in the Old Testament." Why? In Joshua, we have the nation of Israel; in Ephesians, we have the church. Both books speak of entering and possessing: You see, while Joshua has an earthly inheritance, Ephesians has a heavenly inheritance. This remarkable book records the only time Jesus is referred to as the Commander of the Lord's Army (Josh 5:14)—a striking parallel to our King of Kings in Revelation 19. It describes the only city in history that was shouted down by its enemies (Josh 6:20) and gives us the account of the most unusual day in history (Josh 10:14). And it's the second of two occasions where God tells a man (Joshua) to take off his shoes, for he is standing on holy ground.

It also contains two of the most memorized passages by millions for years. Josh 1:8–9, "Study this Book of Instruction continually. Meditate on it day and night so you will be sure to obey everything written in it. Only then will you prosper and succeed in all you do. This is my command: be strong and courageous! Do not be afraid or discouraged. For the Lord your God is with you wherever you go."

And then there is Josh 24:15, "But if you refuse to serve the Lord, then choose today whom you will serve. Would you prefer the gods your ancestors served beyond the Euphrates? Or will it be the gods of the Amorites in whose land you now live? But as for me and my family, we will serve the Lord." We will see that Joshua, as God's appointed one, would fulfill Yahweh's long-term plan based on these very words.

Could this be the most exciting Old Testament book, as summarized by one of the most exciting Old Testament verses, as recorded in Joshua 1:11: "Go through the camp and tell the people to get their provisions ready. In three days, you will cross the Jordan River and take possession of the land that the Lord your God is giving you."

Just think, in just three short days, Israel would accomplish that long-term goal, which had eluded the nation for nearly 40 long years. God was about to demonstrate His Mighty Power in His perfect timing as He

The Book of Joshua—"God's Promise is Fulfilled"

prepared to lead His children into the land He had promised the Patriarchs centuries earlier. What a faithful God we serve and can trust to the very end!

However, we surely cannot forget the significant themes in the Book of Joshua, which are: The fulfillment of God's Promises to His chosen people, God's sovereignty and judgment over all evil nations, the miraculous crossing of the Jordan River, the distribution of the land, and God's favor toward His children. Throughout this remarkable book, we are reminded of the Israelites' faith in God, which becomes increasingly evident as Joshua assumes the leadership role of God's nation after Moses' death.

It is when they prepare to cross the Jordan River before God supernaturally parts it that we see the Israelites' faith again. It's as if God had to remind His people of His miraculous power once again, just as He did when He parted the Red Sea. This led me to ponder: 'How many reminders do we need today to trust in God consistently?' While we live in a world full of ongoing disappointments and disheartenments, our Loving Lord and God is always faithful and true to His very words to you and me, which will be for our good!

But here's a central theme of the book of Joshua, even for us today: "Ultimate Victory through our Trust in the Lord." Josh 21:24 reminds us, "Not one of the good Promises which the Lord had made to the house of Israel failed; all came to pass." His promises to you and me today will come to fruition in His perfect timing, so never lose your trust in all His ways. Remember what Paul tells us in Phil 1:6: "And I am certain that God, who began the good work within you, will continue his work until it is finally finished on the day Christ Jesus returns."

Thanks to one of the greatest leaders in the Bible, Joshua, and his unwavering commitment to God and the Israelites, we will see one of the most significant and spectacular Promises in the Old Testament come to fruition before our very eyes in God's Word. Almighty God undoubtedly knew that He had chosen the right man, Joshua, to lead the Israelites to victory in the land flowing with milk and honey. And trust me, you and I will see that we've been chosen for such a time as today to fulfill God's plan as our journey on this earth comes to an end. It will hinge on our guidance by the Power of His word and Spirit.

You see, Joshua was filled with the Spirit, which led to his commitment to Yahweh's call to continue His plan and fulfill it. It was evident that Joshua trusted in God's promises and was utterly dedicated to His Lord because of his faithful obedience to God throughout this journey to the Promised Land. Yes, Joshua had moments of weakness, like all of us, but he did not waver from his absolute belief in God's undeniable truths. And today, we

The Book of Joshua—"God's Promise is Fulfilled"

cannot allow the enemy to prevent us from finishing God's long-term will in our lives!

In time, we will see that this great leader recognized the need for God's strength to help him endure and persevere, one step at a time, as he prepared to lead the nation of Israel to the Promised Land. Isn't it amazing that Joshua's name means salvation and was the man God chose to lead His people out of the wilderness? While Joshua was born a slave in Egypt, in God's timing, he would become a conqueror in Canaan.

Always remember this as we move forward: We were once enemies of the Lord as sinners (Rom 5:10), but once we accepted Christ as our Savior by faith, that leads to our trusting and obeying Him with all our hearts, souls, and minds with all our might, we can become conquerors over the enemy. Yes, victory is surely on the horizon when we allow our God and Lord to prepare us in all His ways and we yield to His leading and guidance in all our battles, where we can attain our victories in life.

Joshua's preparation and planning, guided by God, conquered the future land through three military campaigns. During these campaigns, Israel engaged with more than 30 armies over the course of seven years. The first Military Campaign was focused on the central region of Canaan, as recorded in Joshua chapters 6–8. The second was concentrated in Southern Canaan, as recorded in Joshua chapters 9–10, and the third military campaign in Northern Canaan was recorded in Joshua chapters 11–12.

Through God's guidance and instructions, Joshua devised a plan and employed the "divide and conquer" method, dividing the southern part of Canaan from the northern part. And because of his close counseling with the Lord, the Israelites would overcome all obstacles and, in time, establish victory. Our faithful Yahweh assisted Joshua in enforcing the "divide and conquer" plan, a strategic approach that involves breaking down a complex problem or situation into smaller, more manageable parts, which are then addressed individually.

The purpose of this Master Plan from the Almighty One was simply this: Joshua would prepare the armies of God's children to attack the smaller cities and groups of Canaanites separately, which prevented the enemy from forming a strong coalition against Israel. In doing so, *Joshua could focus on one target at a time, then capitalize on their weaknesses, maximizing his chances of success in overcoming the enemy* and taking the land God had promised.

Sounds like a strategy we need to enforce in our daily lives against our #1 enemy! If we were to focus on and tackle those weak areas in our lives, one at a time, without being overwhelmed and bombarded, we can establish those victories one win at a time. You see, throughout the Bible, we find

The Book of Joshua—"God's Promise is Fulfilled"

many instances where God reminds us that the *battle* is not ours but God's (2 Chr 20:17). The battle is not plural, but singular.

Joshua's job was to lead the people across the Jordan River into Canaan and reclaim the land God had promised Abraham. Undoubtedly, Joshua was well-trained by Moses and God in preparation for leading the chosen nation of Israel to victory and the conquest of the land flowing with enriched blessings from God. But before the fearless, faithful, and obedient leader could take on this enormous responsibility, he would be required to do a few things:

Despite Joshua's lack of internal strength, the Lord commanded him to be strong and courageous three times, to keep the law of Moses, to divide the land among the people (guided by Yahweh), and to continually study and meditate on the word of God. One thing was for sure: Joshua trusted God's word and all His Promises. This courageous leader knew beyond a shadow of a doubt that Yahweh would be with him every step of the way, and victory was surely on the horizon.

From the beginning, God promised to be with Israel and has remained faithful to this Promise throughout their history. We must never forget that God's blessings were not limited to Israel; He intended to bless the world through Israel, a promise that includes all children of God who have accepted Jesus Christ by faith today. We should know that God's promises can bring numerous blessings, such as deliverance from addiction and the bondage of sin, protection and provision, and the strength to endure and persevere through all our trials and tribulations.

Always remember: He will never leave or forsake us because His love never fails (Deut 31:6–8, Heb 13:5–6 and Psalm 136). His grace is sufficient, and He is always there to fight our battle(s) (2 Cor 12:9, Deut 3:22, Rom 8:31). However, our part lies in absolute faith in His word, trusting in all His Promises, and obedience to all His ways, for it is through these components that we receive His spiritual blessings!

Brothers and Sisters in Christ, make no mistake about this today: You and I are qualified servants, just like Joshua, chosen by God to grow in our spiritual maturity, always relying on His empowering truths and assisting others in these trying times of spiritual warfare. Our assigned duty is to embody boldness, confidence, courage, and strength and lead others on this life's journey to the opening of God's entrance—that will one day unite us all in the presence of our Lord, where we will have rest and peace forever.

Our Heavenly Father has already committed to being with us and helping us every step of the way in this life. But we must take on this high calling and pledge to be faithful to Him, as He has been true to His children since the beginning of time. Never forget this: Our faithfulness shows our commitment and dedication to God and all His children. It will clearly demonstrate our 100% trust and obedience to the Truths of God's long-term plan as we move toward our Future Promised Land. Are you prepared to take on this significant responsibility?

2 Tim 1:5–9, " I remember your genuine faith, for you share the faith that first filled your grandmother Lois and your mother, Eunice. And I know that same faith continues strong in you. This is why I remind you to fan into flames the spiritual gift God gave you when I laid my hands on you. For God has not given us a spirit of fear and timidity, but of power, love, and self-discipline."

"So never be ashamed to tell others about our Lord. And don't be ashamed of me, either, even though I'm in prison for him. With the strength God gives you, be ready to suffer with me for the sake of the Good News. For God saved us and called us to live a holy life. He did this, not because we deserved it, but because that was his plan from before the beginning of time—to show us his grace through Christ Jesus."

Chapter One

'God's Qualified'

Josh 1:1–9, "After the death of Moses, the Lord's servant, the Lord spoke to Joshua, son of Nun, Moses' assistant. He said, "Moses, my servant, is dead. Therefore, the time has come for you to lead these people, the Israelites, across the Jordan River into the land I am giving them. I promised you what I promised Moses: 'Wherever you set foot, you will be on land I have given you—from the Negev wilderness in the south to the Lebanon mountains in the north, from the Euphrates River in the east to the Mediterranean Sea in the west, including all the land of the Hittites."

"No one will be able to stand against you as long as you live. For I will be with you as I was with Moses. I will not fail you or abandon you. Be strong and courageous, for you are the one who will lead these people to possess all the land I swore to their ancestors I would give them. Be strong and very courageous. Be careful to obey all the instructions Moses gave you. Do not deviate from them, turning either to the right or to the left."

"Then, you will be successful in everything you do. Study this Book of Instruction continually. Meditate on it day and night so you will be sure to obey everything written in it. Only then will you prosper and succeed in all you do. This is my command—be strong and courageous! Do not be afraid or discouraged. For the Lord, your God, is with you wherever you go."

Moses has died, and God has appointed Joshua as the new leader to guide His children and the nation of Israel into the Promised Land. As the book of Joshua opens, the Israelites are camped along the east bank of the Jordan River. Approximately thirty-nine years earlier, the Israelites had the unbelievable opportunity to enter God's Promised Land; however, despite all of God's promises to provide and protect His chosen ones, they failed to trust Him. As stated so often, and as our constant reminder, the disobedience and disbelief of the first generation prevented them from entering their future land full of God's blessings. Sadly, it led to their wandering in the wilderness, where they eventually died off.

Now, a new generation of faithful followers will have the opportunity to obey Yahweh and rely on His promises and provisions to reach the other side of God's blessings. Can you imagine what was going through the hearts and minds of God's children when they finally realized that their years of frustrations were coming to an end? Undoubtedly, this waiting period required a great deal of patience, as it involved waiting for God's timing to come to fruition.

I love how this passage begins with God saying, "Moses, my servant, is dead." God not only says that His servant is dead, but He also calls out Moses by name. This leads me to ask: Is our level of faithful service, as His entrusted ones, so profound in the eyes of God that He not only recognizes us as His true bondservants but calls us out by our name because we're that loyal to Him? Even though Moses failed to wholeheartedly trust his friend, the Almighty One, God did not forget His faithful friend even at the end of his life.

But what is just as compelling is that God qualifies Joshua as His leader in this very poignant conversation when He tells Joshua that His words of provision and protection are guaranteed, the same commitment He made to Moses. You see, God never wavers from His original promises; they stand true from beginning to end. As stated earlier, our Lord and God never lies, and when He tells us that His promises will come to pass, they will, in His perfect timing!

Our Almighty God reassures Joshua three times to be strong and courageous so that this great leader would know for a fact that God would be with him every step of the way. As God's chosen and qualified ones (you and me), these exact words apply to us today! He is with us in our life journey, and God reminds and reassures us of this through His very word! But also nestled in this compelling passage, which powerfully applies to you and me, is when God tells Joshua that the only way he will be successful is when he not only meditates on God's Word but also *when he obeys it and does not drift away from its teachings.*

As God's new leader, Joshua was responsible for leading millions of His children into a new land. It must have been comforting and reassuring for Joshua to begin with a genuine and personal conversation with God as he prepared to take on this enormous role. His undeniable devotion and obedience to God led to this close and personal talk with God, which is needed (even for us today) to reaffirm that "no matter what," He will be by our side through it all.

However, Moses' legacy is not forgotten, as God reminds Joshua not to forget the godly instructions Moses taught him and the nation of Israel. He tells Joshua to study His book continually and meditate on them day and night so he can be sure to obey everything in it. Most importantly, ingrain them so deeply in your heart, soul, and mind that you will not deviate from its purpose and plan. As noted earlier, if Joshua obeys God according to His guidelines, he will succeed and prosper in everything he does as God's leader.

Yahweh also reminds Joshua multiple times to be strong and courageous, as if God had to remind and reassure this qualified leader that He would be with them, ahead of them, and behind them, and would give them victory. God tells Joshua never to be afraid or discouraged, for He will lead him along the way into the land He promised from the beginning. Joshua is ready for the task as God's qualified leader because He has been prepped for forty-plus years.

Joshua's qualifications are evident, as he was Moses's right-hand man and aide for many years. But in God's eyes, it meant a lot more than that. Joshua proved his godly status by believing in God's promises and having complete confidence that God would help them conquer the land. The evidence is in the story of Joshua and Caleb, who were the only spies to return a favorable report and believed God would aid them in their success. He proved himself to be an obedient and faithful man to God. Joshua's position as a qualified leader for God resonated with the Israelites, as they would later iterate in Chapter 1, "We will obey you just as we obeyed Moses."

As God's qualified servants, is our status as the Lord's appointed so resounding that everyone recognizes us as His loyal and devout followers, and when we speak of God's word, people stop and listen? It's like the old EF Hutton commercial: "When EF Hutton talks, people listen." When others hear you begin to speak about God's word, do they stop in their tracks and turn to listen to your position as a godly servant? Are the people within your sphere so moved by your position as God's chosen one that they are even cautious in what they say and do? In other words, your calling as God's qualified one is so profound that it inspires respect for God due to your position as His appointed one (Please read 1 Peter 3:8–17).

Unfortunately, many so-called Christians are clanging voices talking about their self-accomplishments with nothing substantiating their proper position as bondservants for the Lord. A true bondservant for Christ exemplifies their qualifications in how they conduct themselves spiritually.

A clear indicator of this is the Fruit of the Spirit (Gal 5:22–23). You see more of the spirit alive in their words and deeds than in their fleshly ways. And make no mistake, these types of godly people will display more acts of grace, mercy, love, humility, and selflessness than those who are not genuine followers of Christ.

Regrettably, too many people in the community, school, workplace, and even churches are striving to achieve a different status quo, one that's measured by the world's standards and a constantly changing culture that's not aligned with God's plan. Please never forget this reminder: When we stray from God's word, fail to maintain daily communication with Him, and do not follow His Spirit, we take our eyes off the Lord, which can lead us to disregard God's guiding principles as His qualified servants.

You see, Joshua was qualified in the eyes of God, all because of his humility, belief in God's promises, and trust in Yahweh's guidance. This leader was committed to the cause for God's glory with obedience, boldness, faithfulness, and integrity. He attained his status in the eyes of his Beholder because he was filled with the Spirit of God (Deut 34:9). We can only be qualified in the eyes of our Creator if we strive to please Him first in life, for nothing else matters. But the gut-wrenching question for us today is this: 'How filled are we with the power of His Word and Spirit in our daily lives so we know we've attained the status of His qualified servant in His eyes?'

Joshua knew he was somebody in God's eyes because he possessed the gifts and talents from His Lord to accomplish this monumental task. This great leader inherently possessed unwavering commitment, integrity, and loyalty to God because of his faith, trust, and obedience. And with God's assistance, Joshua knew he could make a difference in the nation of Israel as God's representative. When you read this powerful story about Joshua and all his God-given abilities, it becomes clear that he did not allow anyone to distort his view of God's calling and purpose as a capable servant of his Lord.

Sadly, in today's world, the measuring stick for qualifying people in various positions is based on their a) appearance, b) accolades, c) family heritage or lineage, d) wealth and materialistic possessions, or e) the class of people they're associated with. It's more about the community of cliques they are connected with, rather than one person who is a truly more qualified individual. Isn't it great that our Holy Creator has a different set of spiritual lenses in comparison to the earthly ways of man?

While humans make their final decisions based on the criteria listed above, that is a far cry from God's standards, for He looks at the heart (1 Sam 16:7). God's internal measuring barometer in meeting His specifications and expectations as His chosen one is; 1) how close are we in our relationship with Him, 2) our aim to please Him first and foremost and 3) do we always say yes to His will and plan and trust and obey it to the end?

Trust me when I say this: You are somebody to God, and as His child and follower of Christ, you have the gifts and talents to meet the qualifications as God's servant. You may not think you're ready, but you are, and don't let the enemy tell you otherwise. While the eyes of humans, the standards of this world, and the enemy say you're incapable of handling a godly task, do not allow that battle in the mind to overcome the status of what God has instilled in your heart and spirit.

As His own, we must all realize that we have something to boast about today, tomorrow, and in the future when we allow the power of God's Word and Spirit to empower and enable us to achieve unbelievable feats for the glory of God (2 Cor 10:17–18). Remember that our battle is between the flesh and the Spirit, but they cannot coexist. That is why we must yield to the One that will give us victory and dictate our future as a certified, fit, and equipped servant of the Lord today (Read Galatians chapter 5). It's ours to claim as His qualified servants today!

> 1 Cor 1:24–31, "But to those called by God to salvation, both Jews and Gentiles, Christ is the power of God and the wisdom of God. This foolish plan of God is wiser than the wisest of human plans, and God's weakness is stronger than the greatest of human strength. Remember, dear brothers and sisters, that few of you were wise in the world's eyes or powerful or wealthy when God called you. Instead, God chose things the world considers foolish in order to shame those who think they are wise."
>
> "And he chose things that are powerless to shame those who are powerful. God chose things despised by the world, things counted as nothing at all, and used them to bring to nothing what the world considers important. As a result, no one can ever boast in the presence of God. God has united you with Christ Jesus. For our benefit, God made him to be wisdom itself. Christ made us right with God; he made us pure and holy, and he freed us from sin. Therefore, as the Scriptures say, "If you want to boast, boast only about the Lord.""

Be proud of who you are in Christ as His qualified one, where you can serve Him with all your heart, soul, mind, and strength. And then, He will receive all the honor, praise, and glory to His Most Precious Holy Name for all you do for Him as His child!

Chapter Two

'Godly Hero'

Josh 2:1–14, "Then Joshua secretly sent out two spies from the Israelite camp at Acacia Grove. He instructed them, "Scout out the land on the other side of the Jordan River, especially around Jericho." So, the two men set out and came to the house of a prostitute named Rahab and stayed there that night. But someone told the king of Jericho, "Some Israelites have come here tonight to spy out the land." So, the king of Jericho sent orders to Rahab: "Bring out the men who have come into your house, for they have come here to spy out the whole land." Rahab had hidden the two men, but she replied, "Yes, the men were here earlier, but I didn't know where they were from. They left the town at dusk, as the gates were about to close. I don't know where they went. If you hurry, you can probably catch up with them." (She had taken them up to the roof and hidden them beneath bundles of flax she had laid out.)

"Before the spies went to sleep that night, Rahab went up on the roof to talk with them. "I know the Lord has given you this land," she told them. "We are all afraid of you. Everyone in the land is living in terror. For we had heard how the Lord made a dry path for you through the Red Sea when you left Egypt. And we know what you did to Sihon and Og, the two Amorite kings east of the Jordan River, whose people you completely destroyed. No wonder our hearts have melted in fear! No one has the courage to fight after hearing such things. For the Lord, your God, is the supreme God of the heavens above and the earth below.

"Now, swear to me by the Lord that you will be kind to me and my family since I have helped you. Give me some guarantee that when Jericho is conquered, you will let me live, along with my father and mother, my brothers and sisters, and all their families." "We offer our own lives as a guarantee for your safety," the men agreed. "If you don't betray us, we will keep our promise and be kind to you when the LORD gives us the land."

We all know the fascinating story of Rahab, but we must recognize Joshua's wisdom in sending out spies secretly. Just like Moses, Joshua demonstrated his qualifications as a leader appointed by God, as he needed strategic information about the city for the upcoming battle. Although he knew God was with him and that He would fight their battles, Joshua heeded God's wisdom and took proactive steps by sending out two spies to gather the necessary information as they prepared. No doubt, Joshua exercised his wisdom as a godly man; after all, he was filled by the Spirit of God. As we will see in this storyline, God had his Almighty hands on every person involved in this remarkable tale.

As stated, in preparation for their famous battle with Jericho, Joshua needed more details about this city, so he sent two spies to scope the territory. However, another incredible aspect of this story—that clearly illustrates God's hand in the entire matter—is that Rahab's home is situated within Jericho's walls, making it accessible for the spies to hide, providing a better view of the city, and offering a perfect escape route. God had already begun preparing Rahab as His own for this most crucial event; He positioned her both physically and spiritually at just the appointed time. God would eventually use her in mighty ways, not just for the aid of the nation of Israel but for the future lineage of our Savior, Jesus Christ.

Rahab was a young Canaanite prostitute and, as such, not a very likely candidate for a heroine of the faith. She was recognized in her pagan community as a harlot. Still, God will use her miraculously, and she will now have a new identification in the eyes of her Heavenly Father. Because of her belief, courage, and faith in Almighty God, her one-act would lead her to gain a position in the Hall of Faith, as recorded in Hebrews 11, alongside many other Saints. Even Jesus' half-brother James would acknowledge Rahab in the second chapter of his epistle, in the classic theme, "Faith without works is dead."

Jericho was one of the principal seats of idol worship, mainly devoted to Ashtaroth, the goddess of the moon. Undoubtedly, a paganist culture surrounded Rahab, which influenced her lifestyle, but that would not define a woman who rightfully feared the Almighty God. And because of this awe-inspiring reverence for her Lord, she would choose to follow Yahweh rather than an evil community.

Rahab had heard about the Almighty God leading His children into their land by word of mouth. He had performed miraculous things in providing for the Israelites and conquering one king after another east of the Jordan. The news had spread and caught the attention of one believer in a town consumed by sinful ways.

In this astonishing story, Rahab misleads the king's men to protect the two spies sent by Joshua. Through this one action, Rahab decides to protect God's people instead of giving them over to evil authorities. This solidifies that her heart has chosen to be faithful and obedient to her new God, following His ways rather than her earthly king.

Her flesh was still at work despite Rahab's courage and boldness in aiding God's children. If we look at the end of the passage above, we see that there was still a manmade fear in her because she pleaded for the two spies to remember her actions of helping them, for no doubt, she feared for her life and her family. She adamantly told the two spies to "Swear to her by the Lord that they would remember her when Jericho falls."

And as godly servants, they promised her (by their life) and guaranteed she would be saved—if she lived up to her commitment. This is a profound passage because when you swear by God's name, it's as if you're standing in front of God, serving as your own witness and the other party, assuring them 100% by your word that it will happen. What is so powerful about this is that God guarantees anyone who faithfully believes and accepts His Son, Jesus Christ, as their Savior and Lord that He will provide them with eternal protection.

In time, Rahab would leave behind her wicked ways and her old name as a harlot to take on her new role as God's chosen and faithful one. The family of God accepts her with open arms, and this Gentile lady marries a Jewish man named Salmon, and they would have a son named Boaz. Over time, Boaz would marry Ruth, and they would bear a son named Obed. Obed would become the father of Jesse, and he would be the father of David, laying the path to the lineage of Jesus Christ. Rahab's one act of faithful heroism paved the way for you and me to our eternal Savior.

By the world's standards, a hero is admired or idealized for courage, outstanding achievements, or noble qualities. Over time, they are elevated to the human pedestal as megastars and revered as models for all people to follow. Over time, their earthly status is so elevated and exposed that they become celebrities in their own right, where human pride consumes them. And without exception, the earthly hero will disappoint us over time. Many of us fail to realize that there will always be a moral failing of humans on this side of eternity.

'Godly Hero'

However, throughout scripture, we see countless examples of godly men and women who served in powerful ways when they relied upon God's strength to help them exercise their faith and courage. One of the most profound points is that they all possessed physical limitations and needed supernatural spiritual strength and power to help them. And they acknowledged this fact: It all starts with complete surrender and submission to God's ways, not the ways of man.

When we set self aside and yield to the power of God, we can handle God's succession plan for the glory and honor of His name. A godly hero is simply someone who obediently, willingly, and faithfully follows God's will for their life. They humbly and selflessly sacrifice for the well-being of others and assist the weaker ones in their faith. When the world is crumbling down before our very eyes, a godly hero stands at the entrance of God's gate, waiting to help and lead others who need a Savior today. They are not seeking the goal of pleasing themselves or trying to bring fame to their name; instead, they are in it to achieve a status that matters only in God's eyes.

> Romans 15:1-6, "We who are strong must be considerate of those who are sensitive about things like this. We must not just please ourselves. We should help others do what is right and build them up in the Lord, for even Christ didn't live to please himself. As the Scriptures say, "The insults of those who insult you, O God, have fallen on me." Such things were written in the Scriptures long ago to teach us. The Scriptures give us hope and encouragement as we wait patiently for God's Promises to be fulfilled. May God, who gives this patience and encouragement, help you live in complete harmony with each other, as is fitting for followers of Christ Jesus. Then all of you can join together with one voice, giving praise and glory to God, the Father of our Lord Jesus Christ."

Chapter Three

'Godly Reliance'

Josh 3:1–11, "Early the next morning, Joshua and all the Israelites left Acacia Grove and arrived at the banks of the Jordan River, where they camped before crossing. Three days later, the Israelite officers went through the camp, giving these instructions to the people: "When you see the Levitical priests carrying the Ark of the Covenant of the LORD your God, move out from your positions and follow them. Since you have never traveled this way before, they will guide you. Stay about half a mile behind them, keeping a clear distance between you and the Ark.

"Make sure you don't come any closer." Then Joshua told the people, "Purify yourselves, for tomorrow the LORD will do great wonders among you." In the morning, Joshua said to the priests, "Lift up the Ark of the Covenant and lead the people across the river." And so, they started and went ahead of the people. The LORD told Joshua, "Today, I will begin to make you a great leader in the eyes of all the Israelites. They will know that I am with you, just as I was with Moses. Give this command to the priests who carry the Ark of the Covenant: 'When you reach the banks of the Jordan River, take a few steps into the river and stop there."

So Joshua told the Israelites, "Come and listen to what the Lord your God says." Today, you will know that the living God is among you. He will surely drive out the Canaanites, Hittites, Hivites, Perizzites, Girgashites, Amorites, and Jebusites ahead of you. Look, the Ark of the Covenant, which belongs to the Lord of the whole earth, will lead you across the Jordan River!"

'Godly Reliance'

What a powerful chapter! After years of preparation, God's promise is beginning to materialize and become a reality for the nation of Israel. Can you envision some of the Israelites saying, "The time has finally come; we are here, and it's going to happen; everything God said is coming to life before our eyes." However, their trust and obedience in God will still be required every step of the way, from their old past to His new path.

God instructed the people of Israel to wait three days at the shore of the Jordan River (Joshua 1:11), and during their waiting, they had a perfect view of the mighty power of the rushing river before them. After all, at its widest point, the Jordan River is 15 miles wide and 223 miles long! They must have asked, "How can we all (and we're talking about at least a couple of million people) ever cross this mighty, flowing river?" You see, relying upon God's provision and promises and being faithful to Him was not over. Even today, "with God on our side, nothing is impossible if we genuinely believe." (Phil 4:13, Rom 8:28)

What also lies within these powerful passages is the requirement of spiritual preparation before one can cross over this mighty river, when God tells His children to purify themselves. This is imperative because when God instructs us to purify ourselves, it means cleaning ourselves from all sin and impurity, both physically and spiritually. This process signifies becoming holy and acceptable before God, emphasizing the importance of holiness in the lives of believers as they pursue a godly plan.

God's children were required to sanctify and purify themselves, which means they were to separate themselves from everyday things, focus on the LORD's provision, and watch Him do miraculous things among them again. God knew that His children were still weak in their trust, faith, and belief in the Promises of His word, so He continuously had to prove Himself. This leads me to ask: How much does it take for us to finally rest in God's assurance and believe in His words 100%? It would even take great faith in their fearless leader, Joshua, to lead the entire nation of Israel into the Promised Land, but he was up for the task as God's qualified leader.

As a leader (Joshua) who relied on his Lord for all things, God reassured him in the passage above when He said, "Today, I will begin to make you a great leader in the eyes of all the Israelites." They will know that I am with you, just as I was with Moses." This must have given Joshua a strong sense of comfort, knowing that God would do great things through him as a qualified servant. Here's a key takeaway that applies to us today: "Joshua's success relied on following God's commands precisely!"

We also see in this chapter where God commanded the Ark of the Covenant to be raised above the height of man, as it represented the presence and power of Yahweh, which was what they needed to help them move forward to God's Promised Land. They had to rely upon God to get them across to the other side because man's ways would be futile. So, the priests, God's representatives, were called upon to take the Ark of the Covenant, hoist it up, and prepare to cross the river, but there were more specific guidelines for them to follow.

God told them to stop after they had taken a few steps into the Jordan River so God could perform His powerful work before their very eyes. It's as if God wanted them to feel the power and force of the rushing river so He could show them that His Almighty Power would carry them safely to the other side. Then, God stopped the mighty river's flow and backed it up so they could cross over without harm.

A river has symbolic meaning, such as flowing freely, being connected to nature, and having lengths, widths, and depths that can seem overwhelming. Our lives are like a river; they are constantly flowing and have means of connection with the ways of the world or God. It can flow slowly or quickly and change courses over time, but nothing can stop the river from flowing. Too often, our river of life is in the fast lane of this society and culture, moving expeditiously at a lightning pace, altering our spiritual course in life because we're not relying on the truths of God's guidance in everyday life.

No external circumstances can prevent it from flowing, and one thing is sure: "Life always goes on." However, when the rivers of life seem too mighty, full of rapid emotions that swing from one extreme to another, we need something to rely upon to get us through the vigorous rapids of life. Just as physical rushing waters can damage things in their path, spiritual rushing waters can create anxiety and fear and even misdirect our path in everyday life.

At one point in our lives, we will face mighty rushing rapids in our paths, an overwhelming obstacle in the form of a personal battle, spiritual warfare, wandering in the wilderness, or the blow of a personal loss. But in all of God's empowering grace, when we rely upon Him wholeheartedly, He can assist us from the side of brokenness to His promise of comfort and peace. God is that reliable!

Like us today, the Israelites needed spiritual strength, focus, faith, and complete reliance on being led by God's power, as His presence was in their midst, which was the Ark of the Covenant. Did you know that God's presence is amongst all His children right now at this very moment? Through the power of His Word and Spirit, He constantly reminds us that we can rely upon Him for any and all matters in our lives, regardless of whether they're massive or tiny!

Today, we cannot overcome a physical obstacle so towering before our very eyes (like a mighty rushing river) that we lose hope and feel helpless;

we must rely upon God's spiritual strength and believe He can move us from one point to His destination of purpose. God's power is always available to anyone willing and ready to connect with Him, where He can strengthen us to navigate the other side of life's incredible journey.

In Isa 43: 2–3; 10–13, God's word reminds us, "When you go through deep waters, I will be with you. When you go through rivers of difficulty, you will not drown. When you walk through the fire of oppression, you will not be burned up; the flames will not consume you. For I am the Lord, your God, the Holy One of Israel, your Savior."

"But you are my witnesses, O Israel!" says the Lord. "You are my servant. You have been chosen to know me, believe in me, and understand that I alone am God. There is no other God—there never has been, and there never will be. I, yes I, am the Lord, and there is no other Savior. First, I predicted your rescue, then I saved you and proclaimed it to the world. No foreign god has ever done this. You are witnesses that I am the only God," says the Lord. "From eternity to eternity, I am God. No one can snatch anyone out of my hands. No one can undo what I have done." What powerful words from our Holy One. He is telling you and me today, as He did then, that all His children are under the exclusive care of the one and only God, our Savior.

God's word is full of comfort and reliance; for instance, Joshua's passage in chapter one, verse eight, was a testament to His strength. And it can be ours today, tomorrow, and in the years to come if we would only apply it. God reminds us in Josh 1:8, "Study this Book of Instruction continually. Meditate on it day and night so you will be sure to obey everything written in it. Only then will you prosper and succeed in all you do." When we rely upon God for all things, it is only then that we can say, "What an awesome God we serve!" He is not a part-time God; He's an all-the-time God!

Many have heard the saying, "Let Go and Let God." Some people frown upon this comment, but it lies at the heart of a powerful game-changer in what we rely on most: the flesh or the Spirit. Relying on God is not a matter of mental willpower; it's a spiritual lifestyle, a choice to change for the better in all His ways (consider that). It's a holistic shift in daily focus involving the heart, mind, body, and soul, with the aid of His supernatural spiritual strength. If we have sound spiritual habits rooted in the Lord alone, we will be adept and able to rely on Him during our life's most challenging times.

This lesson is crucial because self-reliance is an area of caution for you and me; it must be avoided at all costs. We must never think we can resolve all of life's issues; that is a perilous path. When we are more self-reliant, it's all about conquering life's problems in all our ways—without the help of God. However, when we let go of ourselves, we no longer rely on our abilities and resources; we will yearn for more of God's gracious guidance, yield to His power, and lean upon Him. Godly reliance is when we pursue a relationship with God, walk in all His ways, and trust in Him for our every need and desire that aligns with His purpose. It is a complete submission and surrender to the power of His presence in our lives with the help of His Spirit.

A person who relies entirely on God is a diligent student of His word, connected with their Lord daily. In this divine process, they are growing, maturing, and attaining sanctification—a result not of their efforts alone but of God's continuous guidance and support. Just as God is not a part-time God, our reliance on Him, as His children, cannot waver in the slightest. It must be 100% reliant upon our Lord so He can accomplish His will in our lives today, tomorrow, and in the future.

Always remember that relying on God brings humility, obedience, faithfulness, commitment, and 100% dedication to His will and plan. This complete reliance on God, rather than on ourselves, leads to a profound sense of Christ-like freedom—a privilege and right that liberates us from the worries and fears of life's rushing currents.

> Prov 3:1–8, "My child, never forget the things I have taught you. Store my commands in your heart. If you do this, you will live many years, and your life will be satisfying. Never let loyalty and kindness leave you! Tie them around your neck as a reminder. Write them deep within your heart. Then, you will find favor with both God and people, and you will earn a good reputation. Trust in the Lord with all your heart; do not depend on your own understanding. Seek His will in all you do, and he will show you which path to take. Don't be impressed with your own wisdom. Instead, fear the Lord and turn away from evil. Then you will have healing for your body and strength for your bones."

Chapter Four

'Godly Memories'

> Josh 4:1-7, "When all the people had crossed the Jordan, the Lord said to Joshua, "Now choose twelve men, one from each tribe. Tell them, 'Take twelve stones from the very place where the priests are standing in the middle of the Jordan. Carry them out and pile them up at the place where you will camp tonight.' So, Joshua called together the twelve men he had chosen—one from each of the tribes of Israel."
>
> "He told them, "Go into the middle of the Jordan, in front of the Ark of the Lord your God. Each of you must pick up one stone and carry it out on your shoulder—twelve stones in all, one for each of the twelve tribes of Israel. We will use these stones to build a memorial. In the future, your children will ask you, 'What do these stones mean?' Then you can tell them, 'They remind us that the Jordan River stopped flowing when the Ark of the Lord's Covenant went across.' These stones will stand as a memorial among the people of Israel forever."
>
> "So, the men did as Joshua had commanded them. They took twelve stones from the middle of the Jordan River, one for each tribe, just as the Lord had told Joshua. They carried them to the place where they camped for the night and constructed the memorial there. Joshua also set up another pile of twelve stones in the middle of the Jordan, at the place where the priests who carried the Ark of the Covenant were standing. And they are there to this day."

After the nation of Israel had safely crossed the Jordan River, one might think God would keep them on His path to conquering the Promised

Land. However, that is not the case because God knew that His children would soon forget His promises and provisions. This was a crucial step for God's chosen ones because Yahweh wanted the Israelites to remember this milestone in their historical and unbelievable journey. Why? So that they would not forget all the things God had brought them through before they would conquer their new land. At this moment, it was as if the Almighty One was telling His children to be still in all their anxiety and hurrisome ways—and know that I am your God (Ps 46:10)!

After this remarkable feat was accomplished, most of us would have wanted to press on and take care of Jericho. After all, the Canaanites and other nations had already heard what God was doing for the Israelites and were in fear. This fear was not just a reaction but a recognition of God's power and authority. Hence, God's children had all the physical momentum on their side, and after crossing the mighty Jordan River, they were ready with God's help to take over the land.

However, God, in His infinite patience, never rushes. This is one of His divine attributes that we, as His children, often struggle to emulate. While we might have been tempted to let our eagerness drive us forward, this was not God's plan for His children. He wanted them to do something that would honor Him and remember what had just happened. This pause was not a delay but a divine strategy that would set the stage for all future events in their new land. So, God calls for a spiritual time-out for Israel before they press on and physically conquer Jericho.

This reminds me of this fact: Way too often in life, when our flesh is so consuming, and we're caught up in the 'hustle and bustle' of life, and we feel like everything is going our way and nothing can stop us, we need to take a spiritual break to put God's ways in perspective before moving forward physically. In other words, we must ensure that our Lord controls and guides every step we take. The Israelites had no choice but to take this brief pause because they needed God's guidance before pressing on to overcome the enemy—the same guidance we need today in every step of our life's journey.

After crossing the Jordan River, God directed them to build a memorial from twelve stones from the river. What is significant about this is that God wanted each member of all twelve tribes to collect a stone from the middle of the river, not a tiny pebble, but stones that would have to be carried on their shoulders. It was apparent that Yahweh wanted them to apply all their hearts, minds, souls, and strength in this significant undertaking.

Here's the beauty of this: God wanted this accomplished before the Ark of the Lord (His presence), so He could witness all their efforts in complying with His command. Why is this so important, you may ask? Today,

'Godly Memories'

our Lord wants you and me to make every effort possible to set milestones in our lives that will remind us of everything He has done for us on our life's journey. And never forget this fact: He knows if our efforts will honor Him or not because our Holy Creator knows our every desire and motive (Ps 38:9, 139:2–23)!

Not only did a representative from each tribe place a stone on the side of the river where they camped, but their leader, Joshua, even placed a memorial of twelve stones in the middle of the riverbed. These memorials, which traced the nation of Israel's journey from wandering to settling, were not just for the present generation. They were a means for the people of Israel to pass down the memory of God's marvelous deeds to their children, ensuring that His work would not be forgotten among future generations.

The pile of memorial stones, strategically placed by Joshua in the river Jordan, serves as a comforting reminder of God's greatness and fulfilling promises. When the river lowers in a season of drought, these stones stand as a testament to the time God dried up the Jordan, offering reassurance even in our times of spiritual drought. What a profound sign of knowing that no matter if we're in a weakened state of our heart, mind, and spirit, if we will reminisce and remember all the things our Lord has done for us and trust Him each step of our Christian Walk, He will surely let us know that He's with us to the very end.

Even today, we often fail to trust God because we forget the great things He has done in our lives. Our childlike faith is usually weak because we overlook the greatness and goodness of God. We mainly forget God's goodness and provisions in life because we are not as close to our Lord as we may think. When we're so consumed with the ways of the world and our earthly life, we can easily drift away from our Lord when we're not aligned with Him through the power of His word, prayer, worship, fellowship, and our connection to His Spirit. When this happens, we rely more on our desires and self-work, leaving us entirely out of sync with His will. Never forget that the evidence of God's real work in our lives is living proof that others need to see active in us daily.

Godly memories can be personalized in various ways. For example, our Heavenly Father wants us to remember His lovingkindness so that we can teach these lessons to our children, enabling them to realize how good God is and become more thankful. We can also say that our godly memories involve retaining all our powerful experiences with God, such as how He brought victory in our new lives through Christ, rather than dwelling on our old past of bondage. For many, it is all about recalling specific instances of how our God has guided, provided for, and redeemed us, which fuels our faith and hope for the future.

Godly reminders are vital in our lives as Christ-followers because only those who sow seeds of God's love, mercy, and grace in their minds and hearts will reap godly memories of His righteousness and holiness. They will focus their thoughts on the realities of Heaven rather than the things of this earth. They focus on things worthy of His praise, versus those not of God (Phil 4:4–9). They will set out to renew their minds in the ways of Christlikeness rather than conforming to the mindset of the ways of man and this world (Rom 12:1–2, Col 3:2–10). Conversely, those whose minds are full of impurities and unholiness are not aligned with God's will, for their lives will be fruitless and spiritually dead. That is scary!

This is crucial in our Christian Walk because when we forget God's wondrous works in our lives, we can feel entitled, as if we deserve His grace and mercy, when, in fact, we don't deserve anything at all. When we fall into this detrimental state, we lose our humility and taste of God's goodness because we have fallen prey to prideful ingratitude. And think: This is the very sin that got Satan kicked out of Heaven. When we forget the godly memories of all He's done in our lives, we risk losing our gratitude to a Loving, Merciful, and Gracious God. This cautionary warning echoes Romans 1:21: "Yes, [people] knew God, but they wouldn't worship Him as God or even give Him thanks." *And they began to think up foolish ideas of what God was like. As a result, their minds became dark and confused.*"

Yet, a true believer in Christ, having witnessed His work and tasted His goodness and lovingkindness, understands that God desires us to remember His miracles and turnarounds, for they define us as His children. When the world sees His indelible imprint in our lives, they witness the profound inner and outer changes of Christlikeness coming to fruition. This underscores the importance of living a life that honors God, a life filled with meaning and purpose, which will ultimately come to the surface for His glory.

Why is our remembrance of God's activity in our lives so crucial? Remembering God's goodness inspires us to respond to our world with hope and faith rather than fear. It enables us to recall God's love, which ignites our genuine passion for others. The discipline of remembering inspires us to act out genuine fruitfulness that will glorify and honor our Lord today, tomorrow, and in the future. Throughout the Bible, numerous examples of God's people being called to trust and join Him as He restores their lives for the sake of Godly remembrance are there for us to observe to this day. And this is not just for their own benefit but also for the benefit of others, which should spread from one era to another.

However, when we get caught up in the busyness of everyday life and are not grounded in the sound truths of His word and Spirit, we risk

'Godly Memories'

forgetting all the little and big things in life that He has brought us through over our lifetime. God wants us to store His godly memories in our lives because they are spiritually healthy for us and others. It allows us to share our life-changing, godly experiences with others, fostering a sense of community and mutual support. This sharing elevates our joy and brings us peace, contentment, victory, and comfort because we have something productive and good to talk about with others.

This is a key takeaway: When we yield to the power of His word and Spirit, God can help us overcome sinful feelings and desires, enabling us to stop unhealthy thinking. His word is a powerful tool that helps us to gain more self-control over unrighteous spiritual thoughts or actions. Once again, it's all about complete surrender and submission to His empowering authority and control. Don't we realize that God does not want us to dwell on getting revenge for something that happened in the past or think about an event that brings us into a rut of complacency, shame, regret, or depression? The key to this is applying God's word and living by it.

In chapter four of Philippians, God's word reminds us to always be full of Christlike joy, to let everyone see that we are considerate in all we do, and to remember that the Lord is coming soon. He tells us not to worry or be anxious but to pray about everything, and then the peace of God guards our minds and hearts. The operative statement here is, "Always be full of joy in the Lord, attentive and compassionate in how you live out your joy, and remember He is coming soon. Don't worry; tell God what you need and thank Him for all He has done." Living by God's word is the key to finding peace and joy in our lives, and it reassures us that He is always with us.

Our Lord has provided us with every resource to help us establish our thoughts more on Him and not the things of this earth. As stated earlier, when we get too fixated on the things of our earthly life, we quickly forget God. Once again, our Lord reminds us in Phil 4:8-9, "And now, dear brothers and sisters, one final thing. Fix your thoughts on what is true, and honorable, and right, and pure, and lovely, and admirable. Think about things that are excellent and worthy of praise. Keep putting into practice all you learned and received from me—everything you heard from me and saw me doing. Then the God of peace will be with you."

Here are some memorable idioms that may be helpful today:

"When we fix our thoughts on godly memories and all His goodness and Promises, by His Word and Spirit, God can conform our thoughts that will align with His good will and plan."

"We must call on our minds to focus on God faithfully, diligently, and with tranquility, more often than wandering away from His presence."

"De-focus from all the negatives, re-focus on godly thoughts, and stay focused on His righteous ways."

"Take a break from the battleground in the mind and rest in the meadows of God's peacefulness."

"Godly thoughts lead to a righteous purpose; righteous purpose goes forth in Christlike action; Christlike actions form pure habits; pure and clean habits can lead to a character of holiness; and His holiness alive in us fixes our path on His eternal destiny."

"If we consciously learn from our spiritual convictions and counseling, we can find comfort, guidance, and peace in His wisdom and guidance."

"Our attitude in the morning can control our entire mindset throughout the day."

"Don't be anxious about the things in this world, for they only lead to an uneasy and worrisome spirit."

"The fleshly mind may be a beautiful thing to behold—but it can be a beast that is too often out of control."

"Reel in your old line of ugly thoughts and cast out a new line of godly images in your mind and heart daily."

"When we pile up spiritual milestones in our life's journey, as a token for others and God's glory, it displays our genuine faith and belief in all His promises and truths."

Ps 77:11, " But then I recall all you have done, O Lord; I remember your wonderful deeds of long ago." Prov 10:7, "We have happy memories of the godly, but the name of a wicked person rots away." It is so essential for us to plant, nurture, and grow our godly memories!

Chapter Five

'Godly Growth'

Josh 5:2-9, "At that time the LORD told Joshua, "Make flint knives and circumcise this second generation of Israelites. So, Joshua made flint knives and circumcised the entire male population of Israel at Gibeath-haaraloth. Joshua had to circumcise them because all the men who were old enough to fight in battle when they left Egypt had died in the wilderness. Those who left Egypt had all been circumcised, but none of those born after the Exodus, during the years in the wilderness, had been circumcised. The Israelites had traveled in the wilderness for forty years until all the men who were old enough to fight in battle when they left Egypt had died. For they had disobeyed the LORD, and the LORD vowed he would not let them enter the land he had sworn to give us—a land flowing with milk and honey."

"So, Joshua circumcised their sons—those who had grown up to take their fathers' places—for they had not been circumcised on the way to the Promised Land. After all the males had been circumcised, they rested in the camp until they were healed. Then the LORD said to Joshua, "Today I have rolled away the shame of your slavery in Egypt." So that place has been called Gilgal to this day."

The Israelites spent almost forty years unnecessarily in the wilderness because they did not fully grasp the power of God's Promises. The enemy seemed invincible in their eyes, and most were paralyzed by fear, unable to move forward. It was obvious that their lack of faith and trust led them to underestimate God's ability and power to protect and provide for His children, which could have led to their victory in the land He promised they would conquer and dwell in. Sadly, they would not trust or believe in Yahweh's future plan. It was very apparent that the old generation lived more by the flesh than by the Spirit of God, so God had to put forth a new generation of dedicated followers.

Now, a new generation of God's children is emerging, and what a dramatic shift in this story! The fear has now shifted from the Israelites to the Canaanites. They have heard of all the things Yahweh has done for His children, and now the enemy is struck with fear as His new generation of believers will march on to the Promised Land. This shift in fear is not a cause for alarm but a source of empowerment. It should remind us of our own victories when we stand firm in our faith in God's Promises, encouraging us in our spiritual journey.

When God made the original covenant with Abraham, He required that each male be circumcised as a sign of cutting off the old life and beginning a new life with their Lord. This religious rite was not a sign of entering adulthood, as was the case with the pagan nations. The difference for God's nation was a sign of following and committing their lives to God, *and it was performed only once.* As we see in the passages above, Joshua would circumcise the sons of this new generation, and they would rest in the camp, taking time to heal in preparation for their battle.

Circumcision was always a powerful act of consecration to God. In it, an Israelite said, "I'm not like the other nations. I listen to God and do what He says I should do." It was stepping out in faithful obedience and identifying yourself as one of the LORD's people, renouncing the flesh and the world. It was a personal statement and commitment to dying to self and living for God. When they came of age, they had the conscience (inner sense of right and wrong) and consciousness (internal responsiveness) to know what pleased their Almighty God and respond diligently.

Joshua makes it very clear why a new generation was born in the wilderness, and it was this: The old generation did not obey the voice of the LORD and take the Promised Land flowing with milk and honey, as God commanded. Now, a new era was ushered in to replace the older generation that did not believe in God's truths. God's work would go on with a generation of people who were more responsive and compliant with His will and plan. Unfortunately, the people of God who were unbelieving would not share this glorious promise.[1]

It is easy to identify an unbeliever because you see no significant pattern of Christlikeness or godly growth in their daily life; you see more of the world active in their words and deeds. Sadly, what we're seeing in churches

---

1. Joshua 5. "Circumcision and Passover at Gilgal."

today is people who are not obedient and faithful to God because there is no growth in their Christlike Walk. This is tough to say, but the challenge applies to me as much as you, and it's this: If we don't hold ourselves accountable as Christians and we continue to live in a state of stagnation as believers, we won't see the body of Christ performing to the level that will win souls over for Christ.

So, this leads me to ask: What does it mean to grow in Christ? It means increasing your knowledge of our Lord and Savior, deepening your love and yearning for His word, and strengthening your obedience to His will. It is leaning more on His wisdom and trusting all His ways in your life! It is weeding out our areas of unrighteousness and incorporating more of His Righteousness. Displaying every element of the Fruit of the Spirit is seen more in their lives as they grow (Gal 5:22–23).

It is a faithful commitment to not just reading God's word but seeing the evidence of godliness in our sanctified lives as believers. There is more yielding to His Spirit versus the ways of man and this world. Peter reminds us in his second epistle that God provides us with all the resources to live a godly life, so there are no excuses or scapegoats. We should know by now that our Heavenly Father wants us to demonstrate more of His Grace, Mercy, and Love in our daily lives. So, what is holding us back if we're not living as Christ longs for us to be?

Once we accept Jesus as our Lord and Savior and commit our lives to Him, the journey does not stop there; it is a continuous process of growth, maturation, and sanctification through the power of His word and Spirit. Sadly, I've been around teenagers exhibiting more godly growth than a fifty-year-old Christian. How can this be? The key lies in this: I call this the 5 C's of Christlikeness, a profound guide that can enlighten and direct us in our spiritual growth.

Godly growth is a Christ-follower *who is committed daily to communicating with their Lord, while consistently demonstrating the conviction and counsel of God's word and the* Holy Spirit in their life; it's active and always at work. Not just once a week, but throughout the week! God's word reminds us in Heb 6:1–3, "So let us stop going over the basic teachings about Christ repeatedly. Let us go on instead and become mature in our understanding. Surely, we don't need to start again with the fundamental importance of repenting from evil deeds and placing our faith in God. You don't need further instruction about baptisms, the laying on of hands, the resurrection of the dead, and eternal judgment. And so, God willing, we will move forward to further understanding."

If this activity is not alive in us, the one thing holding us back, which will hurt, is our genuine love for His word in our daily lives. Remember, His words are not burdensome (1 John 5:3), but He has the power to help us accomplish His will once we give it all to Him. The master key is when we trust and obey. You may ask: What should our stages of godly growth look like? It's biblically sound and grounded in the truths of the Holy Scriptures. When we're growing in Christlikeness, these godly qualities are evident as we:

1. Bear with the shortcomings of others (exemplifying gentleness, Rom 15: 1–21).
2. Use our words more carefully (conveying words with grace and love, Col 4:6).
3. Give and serve cheerfully (it's not forced; it's a willing and joyous commitment, 2 Cor 9:7, Ps 100:2).
4. Resist temptation and, when we sin, repent quickly (possessing a humble and contrite heart, 1 Cor 10:13, Jas 4:7, 1 John 1:9).
5. Keep our promises to God and others (embodying genuine godly integrity and trustworthiness, Num 30:2, Eccl 5:4–5).
6. Respond to challenges with peace (be a peacemaker, not one that creates division and discord, Matt 5:9, Rom 12:18, Heb 12:14).
7. Let others see more acts of His lovingkindness in our lives vs selfishness and cruelty (1 Cor 13:4–7, Col 3:12–14, Eph 4:32).
8. Forgive (for God has forgiven us, and he implores us to do the same, Matt 6:14–15).
9. Be low to speak, quick to hear, and slow to anger (displaying more spiritual self-control in our lives, Jas 1:19).
10. And whatever you do, in word or in deed, do everything in the name of the Lord Jesus, giving thanks to God the Father through Him (Col 3:17).

If these steps are actively alive in us, we have the Fruit of the Spirit at work in us (Gal 5:22–23). And that's a beautiful sign to know that we're abiding in Him and Him in us as His children to ensure we're truly growing (John chapter 15). It's a tell-tale sign that we're hearing the word of God, which is receiving, accepting, obeying, and applying it (a sign of His wisdom, discernment, and faithfulness, Rom 10:17). Always remember: The divine characteristics of God should be increasingly evident in those being transformed by the Holy Spirit. If not, it's not the lack of God's power! It's the shortage and deficiency of His word and Spirit active in our daily lives!

'Godly Growth'

And this shortage of His power is because we're too focused on our own selfish deeds more than the Grace of God. And when this happens, when we're not living under the freedom of Christ as His faithful servants, as Paul profoundly reminds us in his letter to the church of Galatia. This is very important because when we rely more upon ourselves to grow, we forget that God's grace is sufficient (2 Cor 12:9).

And here's the danger zone: When we "fall from the Grace of God," we depart from complete reliance on God's undeserved favor and turn towards self-effort or legalism to achieve salvation or righteousness. This shift from genuine trust in the Lord and all His ways can potentially lead to a separation from Christ, where we will never grow or bear real fruit.

Col 1:6, "This same Good News that came to you is going out worldwide. It is bearing fruit everywhere by changing lives, just as it changed your lives from the day you first heard and understood the truth about God's wonderful grace." Godly growth leads to a complete transformation within us, individually, that impacts others for the glory of God.

Chapter Six

'God's Opening'

> Josh 6:1–5, "Now the gates of Jericho were tightly shut because the people were afraid of the Israelites. No one was allowed to go out or in. But the Lord said to Joshua, "I have given you Jericho, its king, and all its strong warriors. You and your fighting men should march around the town once a day for six days. Seven priests will walk ahead of the Ark, each carrying a ram's horn. On the seventh day, you are to march around the town seven times, with the priests blowing the horns. When you hear the priests give one long blast on the rams' horns, have all the people shout as loud as they can. Then the walls of the town will collapse, and the people can charge straight into the town."

At the end of chapter five, we see the great leader Joshua approaching the city of Jericho, where he faces a Man with a sword in His hand. In all his boldness, Joshua approached Him and asked Him if He was a friend or foe. This mysterious Man did not reply to Joshua's question with either or, but instead, conveyed to Joshua that He was the Commander of the Lord's Army.

What a powerful point and stage in Joshua's tenure as the leader of God's nation! What would occur is similar to what happened in Moses' life when he approached God, as described in the incident of the burning bush at Mount Horeb (Sinai). The main difference was this: The "Commander of the LORD'S Army" was a manifestation of God Himself, which would be the presence of Jesus Christ.

God wanted to make Himself visible before His great leader, before this essential and significant task would be achieved. And this is key for us today because we must remember that Jesus is the Lord of hosts, and we must submit to His power and control so He can fight all of our battles so we can win (just like Joshua in this story), all for His glory. He wanted to let Joshua know from His very lips that His Lord was with him. When Joshua realized Who he was talking with (just like Moses), he fell to his knees on the ground in reverence and said to the Lord, "What do you want your servant to do?" And it was then that God replied with the exact words He did with Moses, "Take off your sandals, for this is holy ground."

What a decisive moment! The stage has been set, and God is opening the door for the leader of God's chosen nation to take the city of Jericho. Joshua's total submission to the Lord shows us that he knows Who is in charge. It is also a virtual guarantee of victory for Israel because a humble servant and leader allows God to take control, especially since it's His battle. When we follow the Commander of the army of the LORD, how can we lose? This should remind us of the passage Paul mentions when he says, "If God is for us, who can be against us?" (Romans 8:31).

You see, at this moment, God had come to instruct Joshua in the plan to capture Jericho, and the appointed leader knew God was with him. We will see that this great commander and servant will carry out a plan that is so improbable it could *only* have been initiated at the direct command of God. It was all about Joshua submitting himself willingly to the Almighty's leading.

What is critical for us to understand is that Joshua's relinquishing power to Almighty God demonstrates to us, as Christians, that the missing element in our lives of victory will not occur unless we allow the Mighty Conqueror to govern them. When we humbly submit to Him, it opens our lives to God's hand, allowing Him to do miraculous things. We will see that when we enable our hearts, minds, and spirits to the power of God's word and His Spirit, He will accomplish unfathomable feats in our personal lives as He did for the nation of Israel!

Jericho was one of the world's oldest cities, deeply rooted in paganism, which was not pleasing to God. In this opening passage in chapter six, God shows us just how tightly shut the door was because of their absolute fear of the Israelites, but it was really the fear of Almighty God. No one was allowed in or out of the gates of this city, as they wanted to ensure that the Israelite army could not enter through the slightest opening. In their feeble minds and all-out physical efforts, the enemy thought they could prevent the power of the Israelites, with the backing of God, from breaking through their walls!

However, God has already predetermined the outcome of this impending battle because He tells Joshua, "I have given you Jericho, its king, and all its mighty warriors." What a level of confidence and comfort Joshua must have had when he heard God say, "It's done; the battle is won!" Do we have that same confidence, comfort, and boldness just knowing what God's word tells us in Revelation when Jesus Christ returns? "Victory belongs to the Lord! Death and sin have been defeated, our King is alive and well, and He has secured a place of eternal rest and peace!"

This pagan city (Jericho) had soldiers standing guard day and night on top of the walls, and they could see for miles. It symbolized their military power and strength, leading the Canaanites to consider their city invincible. But the improbable, in the eyes of the worldly man, is about to take place. But even after God had told Joshua that the battle was already determined and was won, why did the Israelites have to go through all these complicated instructions and gyrations for seven days?

First, it was what God commanded, and it was to be taken seriously and followed to the T. Second, it was God's battle, not man's. Third, it was to fulfill the truth of His word and covenant about the Promised Land to the Patriarchs back in Genesis, and this was imperative because God is always faithful to His word. Fourth, following His commands, in detail, clearly shows us that the battle would depend upon His power, not man's weapons. Fifth, God's method and strategy for the Israelites would heighten the enemy's terror. Sixth, following God's specific and exact plans was a test of the Israelites' faith in God's instructions.

And seventh, adhering to God's guidelines, whether they thought it was foolish or not to make all these physical maneuvers, would establish their wholehearted obedience to Yahweh. It was about yielding to His leading and not allowing their flesh to take over. By trusting in God's way, the Israelites would see the fruits of their labor come to fruition, no matter all the gyrations. And in God's timing, they would establish the ultimate victory for the glory of God!

Don't we all realize that our enemy today, Satan, has been defeated by our Lord and Commander, Jesus Christ? However, he continues his onslaughts of spiritual warfare in our lives because he wants to shut tight any opening of the Lord coming into our lives and doing great things. Our adversary continually tries to lead us down a destructive path, rather than the victorious one we can possess in Jesus Christ. The enemy will do everything in his power to strain our spiritual lives, so we will not open our hearts and minds to the power of God's work.

As a Mentor, Instructor, and Chaplain in the prison ministry, I would often tell inmates that when they shared their life-changing testimony about how the power of God had transformed their lives, they had just upset the enemy. They would ask why. It was because the enemy of God wants to

'God's Opening'

silence us and close any openings of God's mighty work in our lives. However, we cannot disappoint our Lord to the point where we do not open our hearts, minds, and spirits to His Almighty Power so He can do wondrous and the most unbelievable things in our lives.

God's word reminds us in Rev 3:20–22, "Look! I stand at the door and knock. If you hear my voice and open the door, I will come in, and we will share a meal together as friends. Those who are victorious will sit with me on my throne, just as I was victorious and sat with my Father on his throne. "Anyone with ears to hear must listen to the Spirit and understand what he is saying to the churches."

If you feel like your spiritual life and heart are pinched off and hardened by the ways of this sinful world, and you are not allowing God to open up and come in, the willful sin in our lives prevents God from entering because sin separates us from God's will. However, when we confess our wrongdoings with a humble and repentant heart, this opens the door to a willingness to let Him come in and call us friends, rather than enemies.

Our Lord and Savior, Jesus Christ, knocks at the door of our hearts because He wants to come in and have fellowship with you and me. He wants to draw us closer to Him through the power of His word and Spirit and show us the plans He has in store for us in the future. He will always be patient and, at times, persistent because He loves and cares for us that much. Never forget what God tells us in 2 Pet 3:9, "The Lord isn't really being slow about his promise, as some people think. No, he is being patient for your sake. He does not want anyone to be destroyed but wants everyone to repent."

Our Lord will not force or break down that door because He wants us to open our hearts, minds, and spirits willingly and freely, so He can show you and me the promises and provisions for His faithful followers. You see, we can only hear that gentle knock and soft voice when we willfully stay close to Him through His word, prayer, worship, fellowship, with the guidance of the Holy Spirit.

But sadly, like Israel, most people today ignore God's most gracious and open invitation. They pay no more heed to the Good News of Jesus Christ than the Israelites did to the message of the prophets, leaders, and especially God Almighty. Why? Because they, too, are captivated by this temporal world and all its evil offerings. Unfortunately, it still holds more sway and power over societies worldwide than all the glorious realities of Heaven.

Always remember: There are two sides to every door: the one where we are by ourselves, relying upon ourselves for all the answers in life, or the other side where our Lord is ready to come in and help when we respond to that knock and voice and open His door of invitation. Are we intentionally staying close to the sound of that soft knock and loving voice?

The door God wants to open for you and me will be consistent with His word and validated by the power of the Holy Spirit. This is important because God is not the author of confusion, unlike the enemy; He is full of clarity. Our closeness to scripture and real-life application of His truth is life's game-changer. It will let us know when God is knocking so we can allow His Truth to come into our lives and give us the necessary victory in all the battles we endure. The key to this is what we saw in Joshua's response earlier in this chapter: His total submission to the Commander-in-Chief!

As James reminds us in the fourth chapter of his epistle, when we submit ourselves to God, we can better resist the devil, and he will flee from us. Submitting ourselves to God means we listen to Him, obey Him, serve Him, and follow Him faithfully. When we submit ourselves to God's power, we acknowledge His Lordship in our lives. However, it comes with a cost. And that's relinquishing our selfish desires, earthly hopes, and worldly wants. Instead, we choose Jesus and go wherever He leads.

Taking up our selfish cross and following Jesus means we obey Him and put His words into daily practice. The Lord tells us, "If you love me, keep my commands" (John 14:15). We cannot serve God wholeheartedly if we have not submitted ourselves to Him 100%. It's not possible. That's why it is so critical that we deny ourselves and choose to abide in all His ways. When we choose to serve our Lord through all our words and deeds, it demonstrates Who the Victor is in our lives. What does this lead to? A more joyful, peaceful, and reassuring life of Christ in control of our lives, not us.

Never forget this key takeaway: When we open our hearts, minds, and spirits to the truth of God's word and sincerely accept Jesus as our Savior and Lord, we experience the profound transformation of becoming a child of God. This life-altering change reminds us that a genuine surrender of our hearts to Him brings about our salvation, marked by faith, love, and hope in Christ alone. Opening our internal life's portal to our Lord is a true sign of humbly dying to self and giving it all to Him.

This is so important because Peter reminds us in the fifth chapter of his first epistle that God opposes the proud and gives grace to the humble. This is essential because spiritual humility opens the door to God's power. When we do this, it enables us to give all our worries and issues to Him. In this powerful chapter, our Lord reminds us to stay alert and watch out for the enemy's strategies. He tells us to stand firm in our faith and realize that other believers are going through the same battles we are. You see, in all His lovingkindness, God called you and me to share in his eternal glory through Christ Jesus—all because we opened our lives to His Son. So, after we have suffered a little while, He will restore, support, and strengthen us and place you and me on a firm foundation.

God's Opening is simply an invitation to His righteous ways of living if we accept, trust, and obey His guidance. Yes, this applies to everyone, no matter who you are or what you've done. God's love, mercy, and grace are immeasurable and boundless, so it is available to anyone willing to dedicate their lives to Him wholeheartedly. When we allow God to come into our hearts, minds, and spirits, we will no longer conform to the ways of the world, but instead enable Him to renew and restore us (Rom 12:1–2). In doing this, we consent to His ways where He can counsel, teach, equip, correct, and train us in His ways of righteousness and holiness (2 Tim 3:16–17).

Always remember God's open invitation in His holy word, recorded in the following passages. Isaiah, chapter 55, tells us, "Anyone who is spiritually thirsty, come and drink because it's free." And never forget what Christ our Savior tells us in Matt 11:28–30, "Come to me, all of you who are weary and carry heavy burdens, and I will give you rest. Take my yoke upon you. Let me teach you, because I am humble and gentle at heart, and you will find rest for your souls. For my yoke is easy to bear, and the burden I give you is light."

These are profound passages of comfort in the power of God's assuring Promises for you and me today. If we don't open our hearts to all our Creator's ways and allow Him to perform His extraordinary accomplishments in our spiritual lives, we are truly missing out on unfathomable blessings for today, tomorrow, and the future.

Please know that when we open our lives to the Lord, we will focus more on His will, become more assertive in our faith and trust, love more than hate, become more adept at obeying and applying His word in our lives, possess more of His joy and peace, elevate our hope in what's to come, establish more contentment, and rely more on His grace to help us endure and persevere through it all for His glory.

Remember what the author tells us in Heb 12:1–2, "Therefore since we are surrounded by such a huge crowd of witnesses to the life of faith, let us strip off every weight that slows us down, especially the sin that so easily trips us up. And let us run with endurance the race God has set before us. We do this by keeping our eyes on Jesus, the champion who initiates and perfects our faith. Because of the joy awaiting him, he endured the cross, disregarding its shame. Now he is seated in the place of honor beside God's throne." This open invitation to be with Him in this place of honor is available for anyone who chooses to accept and believe, by faith, in Christ as their Savior and Lord!

Chapter Seven

'Godly Obedience'

Josh 7:1–13, "But Israel violated the instructions about the things set apart for the Lord. A man named Achan had stolen some of these dedicated things, so the Lord was very angry with the Israelites. Achan was the son of Carmi, a descendant of Zimri, son of Zerah, of the tribe of Judah. Joshua sent some of his men from Jericho to spy out the town of Ai, east of Bethel, near Beth-aven. When they returned, they told Joshua, "There's no need for all of us to go up there; it won't take more than two or three thousand men to attack Ai. Since there are so few of them, don't make all our people struggle to go up there."

"So approximately 3,000 warriors were sent, but they were soundly defeated. The men of Ai chased the Israelites from the town gate as far as the quarries, and they killed about thirty-six who were retreating down the slope. The Israelites were paralyzed with fear at this turn of events, and their courage melted away."

"Joshua and the elders of Israel tore their clothing in dismay, threw dust on their heads, and bowed face down to the ground before the Ark of the Lord until evening. Then Joshua cried out, "Oh, Sovereign Lord, why did you bring us across the Jordan River if you are going to let the Amorites kill us? If only we had been content to stay on the other side! Lord, what can I say now that Israel has fled from its enemies? For when the Canaanites and all the other people living in the land hear about it, they will surround us and wipe our name off the face of the earth. And then what will happen to the honor of your great name?"

"But the LORD said to Joshua, "Get up! Why are you lying on your face like this? Israel has sinned and broken my covenant!

'Godly Obedience'

They have stolen some of the things that I commanded must be set apart for me. And they have not only stolen them but have lied about it and hidden the things among their own belongings. That is why the Israelites are running from their enemies in defeat. For now, Israel itself has been set apart for destruction. I will not remain with you any longer unless you destroy the things among you that were set apart for destruction. "Get up! Command the people to purify themselves in preparation for tomorrow. For this is what the Lord, the God of Israel, says: Hidden among you, O Israel, are things set apart for the Lord. You will never defeat your enemies until you remove these things from among you."

What a turn of events in this one chapter for the nation of God. Just when they thought all was going their way with God on their side, everything in their little world came tumbling down—all because one man ignored God's instructions. His disobedience cost the Israelites physically, emotionally, and spiritually. However, we will also see that there was something the great and faithful leader Joshua failed to do.

At the end of chapter six, we witnessed the beautiful story of how God fulfilled His promise by saving Rahab and her family from the destruction of Jericho. But we also see these specific guidelines from God in this same chapter where He says, "Do not take any of the things set apart for destruction, or you yourselves will be completely destroyed, and you will bring trouble on the camp of Israel. Everything made from silver, gold, bronze, or iron is sacred to the Lord and must be brought into his treasury."

However, one faithless and disobedient man, Achan, failed to comply! What a compelling contrast in just a few verses. We must never forget that God will keep His promises aligned with His word when others are faithful to Him (like Rahab). However, God does not forget when others do not obey Him, as there will be repercussions for those who do not comply with His guidelines.

Achan's sin was not only a detriment to the entire nation and its leader, but also led to God threatening to withdraw His presence from the nation. But the ultimate fatality at the end of this story is that it cost the lives of Achan and his entire family. All because he did not "set apart" the items God instructed them to destroy. Achan could have had all his heart desired if he had only waited on the LORD for it. Sound familiar? A critical takeaway message for you and me today is that we must eliminate any disobedience in our lives so we can comply with all of God's guidelines.

God was crystal clear in His command because He did not want His children to keep anything from the wicked city of Jericho for themselves. Only the things made from silver, gold, bronze, or iron were kept for the treasury of the Lord's house that could be dedicated for sacred uses. It's not that He was ever going to use their items for a particular use; it was all about the children of God complying with His commands, in other words, absolute obedience to Yahweh.

You see, Jericho was to be a dreadful sacrifice to God's justice because the people had filled the measure of their sins with worship of other gods and their own self-indulgence. It was evident that God commanded the complete demolition of anything made into false idols. This was important because God did not want anything associated with the hands of corruption to be mixed with His people of righteousness. Obviously, Yahweh wanted the Israelites to be set apart for His holy use, and that could not happen when idolatry was present in any shape or form. Always remember: Our portion of blessings comes from God Almighty, not from the hands of sinners.

Achan's one act of defiance cost him dearly. After he and his entire family were burned, the Israelites piled a great heap of stones over Achan, which remains to this day and is called the "Valley of Trouble." The Lord was no longer angry after Joshua and the people removed the family where the act of rebellion occurred. However, there is something Joshua failed to do as the leader of God's nation. When Joshua went against the Canaanite city Ai (Josh 7:3), he did not consult God but relied on the strength of his army to defeat this small city. You can even sense arrogance in the replies of his soldiers when they said, "Don't make all our people go up there and struggle; there are only a few of them."

It's as if they're saying, "We don't need God, and we can take them easily because they are small and a less formidable opponent—we can do this in our own strength." Nowhere in this passage do you see Joshua talking with God and seeking His guidance and wisdom before taking on the city of Ai. We must always understand that it is a grave mistake, regardless of the size of our confrontations in life, if we don't consult with the Lord on the right course of action.

Too often in our daily lives, we rely on our own skills, abilities, and knowledge to tackle a seemingly minor tasks without consulting the Lord first. How easily we forget what God's word tells us in Proverbs 3:5–6, Psalm 32:8, Psalm 37:23, and Proverbs 16:3,9, where He tells us to involve Him in every step of our plan. He requires us to commit our work and all the details to Him, and then, He will establish our plans. It all boils down to our absolute reliance and obedience to the Lord!

'Godly Obedience'

God clearly reminds us that He will instruct, teach, and counsel us on how to proceed in life. If we do, His eyes and guidance will be upon us. Who wouldn't want to aspire to these simple commands, especially if we're going to avoid headaches and heartaches daily? But most importantly, if we allow Him to direct our paths, we have the great opportunity to glorify Him because we obeyed Him through every step of the process.

As genuine Christians, don't we realize God wants to be part of our daily plans? When we include Him, it shows that we've submitted to Him wholeheartedly. It also illustrates that we rely on His sovereign power, not ourselves. It demonstrates that we depend more on His knowledge and wisdom so that we can learn from His teachings in preparation for future plans.

When we involve God in all things, it demonstrates our genuine love for Him and His word. This deep involvement brings to fruition our absolute trust, humility, and obedience when we align with His purpose and plan. Our closeness with Him is paramount; each step of the way through the power of His word, prayer, and Spirit. When we allow Him to guide us, He prepares us spiritually. His timing is always perfect, and the end result, though not always what we expect, is always for our good, according to His divine plan.

We all know this scripture so well in Romans 8:28–29, where God's word reminds us, "And we know that God causes everything to work together for the good of those who love God and are called according to his purpose for them. For God knew his people in advance, and he chose them to become like his Son, so that his Son would be the firstborn among many brothers and sisters." These passages suggest that God is at work in everything, but they do not imply that every event that happens to us will be beneficial. Why? Because evil is prevalent in this world, and we're consumed with a sinful nature.

But often, we fail to grasp the full context of this passage. We tend to focus on parts of Scripture that align with our comfort zone or self-expectations. However, it's crucial to consider the entire message, especially when God says, 'for those who genuinely love Him and are called according to His will.' God can turn any circumstance around for His glory, but His goal is not to make us happy and content in our own little world. His goal is to fulfill His purpose and plan in us, which is to be more Christlike, leading an obedient and holy life that honors Him. Ultimately, He chose us to become more like His Son, Jesus Christ.

Obedience is not just a choice; it's a matter of spiritual life and death in the Christian faith. It's a clear demonstration of our love for the Lord—or the absence of Him in our lives. Jesus reminds us in John 14:15, "If you love Me, obey My commandments." The Bible is clear: we show our love for Jesus by obeying Him in all things. As we've seen in the Israelites' journey, disobedience creates a distance from God's presence and leads to consequences. We cannot be in God's will and plans if disobedience is prevalent in our daily lives. Therefore, obedience is a crucial responsibility that we must uphold. But it's not just a duty; it's a transformative power that can lead us to a more Christlike life, inspiring and motivating us to walk in His ways.

This is crucial for us today because a Christian "Who is not obeying Christ's commands can rightly be asked by the Lord, 'Why do you call me, 'Lord, Lord,' and do not do what I say?" (Luke 6:46). That is powerful and should be a gut punch for many so-called Christians who are dabbling in the area of disobeying all His commands. You cannot have part of the world's ways in your life and the Lord's, too. He wants all of our obedience. Yes, we will still have sin and struggle with disobedience, but that's why sanctification and striving for more of His holiness are crucial in our everyday lives.

This reminds me of all the conversations I had over my ten years of ministry as a mentor, instructor, and chaplain in the prison ministry. In all their internal battles within the walls of those compounds, and even for us outside those walls, I realized some root issues regarding the power of the word O–B–E–Y. See the breakdown below. Christians who struggle with obedience often lack these critical elements in their Christian Walk. This was a gut punch to me.

- Obsessive passion is missing in the everyday Christian life. In other words, they don't have a daily hunger, longing, or appetite for His ways of holiness. If we saw a more consistent pattern of His Holy Word in Christians today, we would see more evidence of godly behaviors and a greater predisposition to Christ in our lives every day. Obsessive passion drives Christians to live a life that is pleasing to God.

- "*Believe in what you truly believe in.*" What does this mean? Although almost every Christian claims to believe in Christ and His word, their faith is often more superficial. You see, in the spiritual realms, the content of our genuine saving faith affects all areas of life, and we cannot do anything pleasing to the Lord without "genuine faith." Heb 11:6. *It must be real and active, and this is evident when we trust and obey Him in all areas of our lives! As stated earlier, and as our daily reminder, belief is the intellectual acceptance of something you know is factual and true. Trust is putting that belief into motion. And then our faith comes to life!*

- Eagerness has dried up in the Christian's life. The ambition, desire, and motives of living according to God's word have almost evaporated from the very life around us. There's a severe lack of zeal, willingness, and readiness to defend our faith as Christians daily! We must initiate and implement the eagerness of His word and Spirit in our daily lives; if not, there will be a great chasm between us and His very presence!

- Yielding to all His ways! This means we surrender and submit to the power of the Holy Spirit in our daily lives, with no trace of the world remaining in us. Consider this: If I were in a major city preparing to merge onto an eight-lane corridor moving at the speed of light, *one split second of improper yielding could lead to disaster.* Not just for me but for others, as well. It's a domino effect of consequences.

Without these simple components in our daily lives, as Christians, we will struggle with obedience to God's word, which will lead us far from His purpose and plan. A young lady shared a powerful example of how a degree can make a significant difference as we move further from the original point. In other words, if we allow one slight era of misguidance in our life's journey, we will be severely off course. And that is precisely what disobedience can do in our lives. See below:

If I were traveling toward a specific destination and were off by a single degree for every foot of my journey, I would be off target by ninety-two feet after a mile. That is not very significant. But to put this in a more robust scope, I would miss my origin point by 435 miles if I were traveling around the world. And if that does not strike a chord, if I were on a straight-line course from the Earth to the sun and I were off one degree, that journey would miss its target by 1.6 million miles. What's the point?[1]

When we fail to obey God at every point in our daily lives, it reveals a massive gap in our trust in all His ways. Our walk with Christ will suffer unless we address it. It's not just reading and listening to the power of His word; it comes down to you and me being doers of His word. Christians, we cannot draw closer to the Lord if we're not in line with His word and will in every moment and step of our everyday lives; we will always be off course and never attain His ultimate destination.

> Jas 4:4–10, "You adulterers! Don't you realize that friendship with the world makes you an enemy of God? I say it again: If you want to be a friend of the world, you make yourself an enemy of God. Do you think the Scriptures have no meaning? They say that God is passionate and that the spirit he has placed within us should be faithful to him. And he gives grace generously.

---

1. Roundy, "A Mere One-Degree Difference."

> As the Scriptures say, "God opposes the proud but gives grace to the humble." So, humble yourselves before God. Resist the devil, and he will flee from you. Come close to God, and God will come close to you. Wash your hands, you sinners; purify your hearts, for your loyalty is divided between God and the world. Let there be tears for what you have done. Let there be sorrow and deep grief. Let there be sadness instead of laughter and gloom instead of joy. Humble yourselves before the Lord, and he will lift you up in honor."

Always remember this: When we're obedient to the Lord, it brings forth our genuine state of humility and love!

> Deut 30:19-20, "Today I have given you the choice between life and death, between blessings and curses. Now I call on heaven and earth to witness the choice you make. Oh, that you would choose life, so that you and your descendants might live! *You can make this choice by loving the Lord your God, obeying him, and committing yourself firmly to him. This is the key to your life. And if you love and obey the Lord, you will live long in the land the Lord swore to give your ancestors Abraham, Isaac, and Jacob.*"

Chapter Eight

'God's Point'

> Josh 8:1-2, "Then the Lord said to Joshua, "Do not be afraid or discouraged. Take all your fighting men and attack Ai, for I have given you the king of Ai, his people, his town, and his land. You will destroy them as you destroyed Jericho and its king. *But this time,* you may keep the plunder and the livestock for yourselves. Set an ambush behind the town."

What a significant contrast between the opening of chapter eight and chapter seven. This shows us that when we involve God first and foremost in all things, He not only brings us those victories in our lives, but in all His graciousness, He allows us to enjoy those beautiful blessings at every point in life's journey. And when we lean upon Him for all things, even in all our blunders, He will encourage us to get up and back on track. But it's only when we yield to Him first.

The Israelites prevailed only after God's nation of Israel cleansed their camp from the unrighteousness of Achan's sin, all because they leaned upon Yahweh's guidance. And in all of God's mercy, He gave His children another chance to redeem themselves, even after God had threatened to withdraw His presence from them because of Achan's rebellion. Did they learn from this horrific experience?

It was evident that the great and faithful leader, Joshua, learned some invaluable lessons from that first defeat at the hands of Ai, and it was this. 1) Confess your sins when God has revealed them to you because He loves a humble, repentant, faithful, and obedient heart. We must never forget that God knows all, and we cannot keep anything from Him; He wants us to be honest and come clean (Heb 4:12-13, Psalm chapter 139). 2) Even though we fail God the first go around, in all His mercy, grace, and love, He will give us another chance when we incline upon Him and His ways. That's when we refocus on God's will and plan, deal with the sins and shortcomings in our lives, and press on with the guidance of Almighty God; He will then point us in the right direction.

The beautiful portrait in this passage shows us that even with all the sinfulness in our lives, there is a point to which God wants to bring us back. When we go through the cycles of sin, He loves it when we come to the fact of this matter: "We cannot move forward to His next spiritual point in our Christian Walk until we repent, seek His forgiveness so He can strengthen us and set us back on the course that He desires in our life."

However, we must remember that we cannot attain those little victories if we 'recycle' the same sins daily. If that is the case, we're not in His will and plan, which means we're not leaning upon the guidance of His word and Spirit. We often fail in our Christian lives when we repeatedly indulge in those old, sinful traits. God wants us to convert our habitual sins into acts of godliness that honor Him.

When we have failed at some point in our Christian lives, we need to know how to get back on track. We must deal with it before God by repenting and dying to self, and then look forward to what He has for us without delay. Our enemy wants us to dwell on our past and not focus on God's direction in our Christian life. However, we must remember that what is past is past, because we're no longer that old person; we're now a new creation, pointing in a different direction (2 Cor 5:17).

Paul gives us a powerful illustration in Phil 3:12-17,

> "I don't mean to say that I have already achieved these things or that I have already reached perfection. But I press on to possess that perfection for which Christ Jesus first possessed me. No, dear brothers and sisters, I have not achieved it, but I focus on this one thing: Forgetting the past and looking forward to what lies ahead, I press on to reach the end of the race and receive the heavenly prize for which God, through Christ Jesus, is calling us. Let all who are spiritually mature agree on these things. If you disagree on some point, I believe God will make it plain to you. But we must hold on to the progress we have already made. Dear brothers and sisters, pattern your lives after mine and learn from those who follow our example."

In this passage, Paul directs us toward the path God wants us to follow, which is pressing on toward our eternal goal.

'God's Point'

Never forget this: Even in all our shortcomings and failures in life, God can use them as a foundation for a significant victory in the LORD, if we submit to His empowering grace. You see, God has a plan to move us forward one victory at a time, for His glory. However, too often, we find ourselves going down a path of no return, one that is opposite God's destination point. God ultimately wants to point you and me to live by His biblical principles of life, His original intention when He created humankind.

We must repeatedly remind ourselves that He wants us to be more like His Son, Jesus Christ, which points our lives upward, not downward. When all may seem to be going bad in life, our Loving God wants you and me to enjoy His wondrous spiritual blessings in this life by fixing our thoughts on His realities, not the fictitious things of this earth (Colossians chapter 3).

Many Christians fail to understand this: God wants us to succeed in this life, especially when it glorifies His Holy Name and points the unbelieving world to Him, not the enemy. God does not care whether we think (in our eyes) that something will end badly or be good. He wants you and me to rely upon His power at work in us, with patience and perseverance, so the world will see that our Heavenly Father is capable and able to do all things. In other words, we must always allow the Holy Spirit to counsel and lead us into all His truths!

Here's a PowerPoint to ponder: "God has never had a qualified person serving Him to be disqualified in His eyes." Yes, they may stumble at one point in their life's journey, but they will never fall to the point where they cannot continue their work for the Lord. A genuinely qualified servant of the Lord always depends upon the power of God's direction, and that's why it's easy for them to get up and back on God's course of holy action. All because they know who their Victor is in life, as they press on as 'Onward Christian Soldiers.'

God's word reminds us in Deut 20:4, "For the Lord your God is the one who goes with you to fight for you against your enemies to give you victory." And in Ps 18:32, "God arms me with strength, and he makes my way perfect." God's presence and power are with us in times of conflict. He fights for us and leads us to victory over our enemies. We can trust in His ability to deliver us and grant us triumph. Why? Because, as His faithful and entrusted children, we know that they will bring honor and praise to His name during these times, and we strive for those stages of victory and glory that point our lives to Him.

The Psalmist reminds us in Ps 37:24–28,

> "The Lord directs the steps of the godly. He delights in every detail of their lives. Though they stumble, they will never fall, for

the Lord holds them by the hand. Once, I was young, and now I am old. Yet I have never seen the godly abandoned or their children begging for bread. The godly always give generous loans to others, and their children are a blessing. Turn from evil and do good, and you will live in the land forever. For the Lord loves justice, and he will never abandon the godly. He will keep them safe forever, but the children of the wicked will die."

In this passage, God makes a powerful point: He delights in those who follow His ways and points others to Him in their daily steps. What is so comforting and encouraging in this passage is that God watches over us and will make firm the godly person who is pointed in His direction. His ultimate point in our daily life is that we desire His will and plan, which brings us joy—because the "Joy of the Lord is my strength" (Neh 8:10). It is so evident in our everyday life that it will lead others to Him.

As we stated earlier, God wants you and me to be successful and experience His spiritual blessings, but what comes with those blessings are fights, battles, and trials. We refer to these as 'spiritual warfare,' the struggles we will face in our faith journey. However, in this excursion, we must acknowledge our Father at every step so that He can guide and direct us down the righteous path He has destined for us.

God can direct all believers if they possess a vibrant prayer life, read His word, be doers of His word, submit to Him wholeheartedly, and trust Him in complete faith and obedience. Acknowledging God and recognizing His presence is the first step. However, we must trust in God and entirely depend on Him, not on our own ways. We're on a distorted path if we think we can point ourselves in His direction without His Help.

God is always ready to hear from you and delights in helping His children. If we seek Him out first, He will direct our paths and point us in the right direction. God's word reminds us in Jer 29:11–14, "For I know the plans I have for you," says the Lord. "They are plans for good and not for disaster, to give you a future and a hope. In those days, when you pray, I will listen. If you look for me wholeheartedly, you will find me. I will be found by you," says the Lord. "I will end your captivity and restore your fortunes. I will gather you out of the nations where I sent you and will bring you home again to your own land." This passage emphasizes the importance of seeking God wholeheartedly, motivating us to commit fully to Him in our faith journey.

God's point in this passage is that He has a good plan for His children, one filled with great hope. This plan is not about material prosperity but about spiritual growth and fulfillment. It's a plan that promises a future and a hope, *specifically for those who seek Him with all their heart, mind, soul, and strength.* Many people misinterpret this key passage, but God is conveying to His children this fundamental fact: He has a plan to prosper His people amidst the hardships of this world. We must remember that He encourages obedience to His words, highlighting that anyone who turns away from His plan can prevent themselves from receiving His best for their future. The weight of our decisions is evident in the importance of obedience to God's plan, a concept that should fill us with hope and optimism as we navigate our faith journey on this Side of Heaven.

> Phil 1:6, "I am sure of this, that he who started a good work in you will carry it on to completion until the day of Christ Jesus."

Chapter Nine

'God*less* Appearance'

Josh 9:1–6, "Now all the kings west of the Jordan River heard about what had happened. These were the kings of the Hittites, Amorites, Canaanites, Perizzites, Hivites, and Jebusites, who lived in the hill country, in the western foothills, and along the coast of the Mediterranean Sea as far north as the Lebanon mountains. These kings combined their armies to fight as one against Joshua and the Israelites. But when the people of Gibeon heard what Joshua had done to Jericho and Ai, they resorted to deception to save themselves. They sent ambassadors to Joshua, loading their donkeys with weathered saddlebags and old, patched wineskins. They put on worn-out, patched sandals and ragged clothes. And the bread they took with them was dry and moldy. When they arrived at the camp of Israel at Gilgal, they told Joshua and the men of Israel, "We have come from a distant land to ask you to make a peace treaty with us."

This is a lengthy chapter, but one that is so needed as a daily lesson and guide, given the numerous mistruths and godlessness swirling through society and culture today. Equally important is the challenge for all Bible-believing, church-going students of the Word and Christ followers to ensure we're aligned with the Truths of God's word. We will all obtain some great nuggets in this chapter that will surely equip and prepare us against all the enemy forces around us. It's vital to our lives as God's children.

The surrounding nations were petrified of the Israelites, but it was because of what Almighty God was doing in protecting and providing for His children in their blaze of glory to reach the Promised Land. But when the people in the city of Gibeon heard what was happening to the other nations, they resorted to means of deception to protect themselves from complete destruction. Their fear of God and His wrath was so great that it led them to devise tactics different from those of other cities. This unique plan of cunningness and trickery may evoke a stroke of commendation and applause for their creativity from the reading audience. However, it serves as a stark reminder of the importance of aligning with the truths of the Holy Scriptures to avoid such desperate measures of fakery.

While the other cities throughout the region started to unite their armies to physically combat the nation of Israel in a head-to-head battle on the field, the people of Gibeon had another method in mind. Would their strategy of trickery work in their favor and lead Joshua and the nation of Israel to fall for their cunning efforts? We will see if Joshua and the leaders will use their wisdom and discernment and take the approach of these deceptive people to Yahweh and seek His divine guidance, or fall prey to their fraudulent and deceitful lies.

The Gibeonites hatched a cunning plan, presenting themselves as ambassadors from a distant land to the nation of Israel. They aimed to deceive Israel into a peace treaty, convincing them they were not part of the neighboring nations destined for God's wrath. This was a crucial ploy, as Israel was forbidden to make peace with any Canaanite tribes (Exodus 23:23–24). In verse seven of this chapter, we see, "The Israelites replied to these Hivites, 'How do we know you don't live nearby? For if you do, we cannot make a treaty with you." Why was this?

God did not want His children to be part of anything in these wicked cities because they lived contrary to His laws and holy ways. The Almighty One knew that if His chosen ones fell prey to just one inkling of sinful deception, they would fall farther away from His divine way of living. This is a crucial reminder for us today: With so many people living in a world of prevalent evil and mistruths, God's children should never be part of their culture and lifestyle. Remember what Jesus Christ tells us: "We are called to be in the world, BUT not of the world" (John chapter 17, Col 1:13).

Notice the methods of deception used by the Gibeonites. They were clever when they misrepresented themselves (pretended), and they even gave false "evidence" as part of their deception by using old sacks, old wineskins, old and patched sandals, dry and moldy bread. Even beyond their deceptive appearance, the Gibeonites *lied*. They said, "We have come from a far country," when that was not true. All of their self-concocting devices were to support and persuade God's children of the false deceptions they offered in this fictitious front.

Even today, isn't it amazing that we see and hear all the untruths and self-made theories of man? However, I firmly believe that if we're genuinely close to the "Bread of Life" (Jesus Christ), we will not get duped by a world of people who are stale and spiritless. Regrettably, today, we are being fed a plethora of lies because humans are not on the same agenda as God! If we're close to the Lord's guidance, through the power of His word and Holy Spirit, He will help us sort through all the deceiving ways of counterfeiting people in our paths.

Undoubtedly, the Gibeonites' intent, motive, and desire were clear: To mislead Joshua and the leaders, which would protect themselves from God's wrath. Yet, in all their deceptive ways, they showed proper admiration and honor for the God of Israel when they stated, "Because of the name of the LORD your God; for we have heard of His fame." This fear was real, *as* they knew God was fighting and defending His children and nation in the conquest of the Promised Land.

When the Israelites discovered they had been deceived, they deliberated on their response. The leaders of Israel concluded, "We have given them our oath by the Lord, the God of Israel, and we cannot touch them now. This is what we will do to them: We will let them live so that God's wrath will not fall on us for breaking the oath we swore to them."

The Gibeonites, though enemies, teach us a crucial lesson. Their deception was effective because Joshua and his people did not seek God's wisdom and guidance, nor did they ask for a discerning spirit. This lack of seeking God's wisdom and advice was a critical mistake, as it would have enabled them to proactively assess the Gibeonites' deceitful ways. This incident underscores the importance of seeking God's wisdom and knowledge in all our decisions and actions.

The Gibeonites knew it would be useless to oppose this most powerful nation because of the aid of the Great and Powerful God. The Gibeonites' understanding of God's power was profound, as they recognized that no human force could withstand the might of the Almighty.[1] Even though their acts of deception temporarily saved them, they schemed because of their fear of God. Their fear of God was a recognition of His power and a deep understanding of His judgment. You see, for the unbeliever, the fear of God is the dread of His judgment and eternal death, which is everlasting separation from our Heavenly Father (Luke 12:5; Hebrews 10:31). When the faithless sense the wrath of God, they will squirm in all their fleshly ways.

However, for the believer, the fear of God is much different. The believer's fear is complete reverence for God and all His truths. Hebrews 12:28–29 is a good description of this: "Since we are receiving a Kingdom

---

1. Joshua Nine. "The Gibeon Deception."

that is unshakable, let us be thankful and please God by worshiping him with holy fear and awe. For our God is a devouring fire."

Fearing God means having a reverence for Him that profoundly impacts how we live our lives in accordance with His word. The fear of God is respecting Him, obeying Him, submitting to His discipline, and worshiping Him in awe. But isn't it amazing how God protected the Gibeonites because they feared His Mightiness? It should have taught the leaders of God's nation to be more diligent in seeking the Holy One's advice first on how to deal with this matter.

You see, as His genuine children, when we fear God the right way, we rely upon His word and the guidance of His Spirit because we aim to please Him by living out the truth of His scripture. For Christ-followers, a biblical fear of God encompasses understanding how much God hates evil, its falsehoods, and hypocrisy, as well as fearing His judgment on sin.

And here's the danger zone: If we allow any distortion opposite of His word to creep into our lives, we can easily get sucked into lies and deception. When we're surrounded or confronted with lousy information, He will always reveal the "Truth" to His children. If we lean upon His knowledge, wisdom, and discernment, He will surface any falsehoods trying to tell us otherwise.

As we read this unbelievable and powerful tale in Joshua chapter nine, many would ask: "How could they have been so easily deceived after all the preparation God had taught His children?" He even told them about all the wickedness that would confront them in the land they would dwell in. As you read more in this chapter, you will discover the root cause of their deception, which applies to many today.

And here it is: "They did not seek the counsel of the LORD!" The Gibeonite deception was so suave, clever, and influential in all its presentation—that it worked. Even the great and faithful leader of Israel was hoodwinked (outwitted). As discussed earlier, and as a daily reminder, the enemy's plan succeeded because Joshua and the leaders of Israel failed to seek the Lord's guidance in dealing with this matter. We even see where the men of Israel took some of the provisions from the Gibeonites. To tamper with a taste of deception shows that they trusted their fleshly senses instead of the LORD, and it's all because they did not go to God first.

Look at this one example in Josh 9:12 when the deceivers said, "This bread was hot from the ovens when we left our homes. However, as you can see now, it is dry and moldy. It's as if the Israelites were saying, "Look at this bread; feel and taste how stale it is. Surely, they must have come a long way, and that's why it is moldy." Wow! This is a classic example of God's children walking by sight, not by faith. Today, how much trouble do we find ourselves in for this very reason when we do not ask or seek the counsel of the LORD and self-examine our genuine faith, as Paul tells us in 2 Cor 13:5?

Are we easily shamed and humiliated when clever acts of phoniness are presented to us, only to discover that we fell for a lie? Here's another gut punch! If we're close to our Lord through His word and fervent prayer, His Spirit will convict us. This is our reassuring guide in our journey of faith. Why? So He can counsel, correct, and communicate His truths to us. But this will not happen if we don't act upon those convictions. Never forget this: If we're not in the truths of God's word, applying and obeying them, praying for His divine guidance, yearning for more of His righteousness in our lives, and yielding to His ways of holiness, we will, in time, get duped by the enemy!

The main reason why Christians are so easily swayed or led astray from the Truth of God's word is that they are not genuine students of His Holy Word (refer back to the Parable of the Four Soils in Matthew 13). It's time to take responsibility and empower ourselves as actual Bible students. We should seek the Lord's counsel, asking and praying for wisdom, knowledge, and discernment to ascertain God's insight and know when to test the spirits. Remember what the great Apostle John tells us in 1 John 4:1, "Dear friends, do not believe everyone who claims to speak by the Spirit. You must test them to see if the spirit they have comes from God. For there are many false prophets in the world."

The key is staying grounded in God's Word, led by the Holy Spirit, and praying for His divine wisdom and guidance daily, not just one or two days a week. Then, we can tell the difference between true and false and right and wrong. Being genuine students of God's word illustrates our "real love" for Him and demonstrates our faithfulness and obedience to His word alone.

This is so critical today because an evil façade and front are swarming this country and the world in epic proportions, in the form of a false teacher. These phony leaders are after one thing: their own selfish desires, and they will stoop to all means of deception in their presentation, offering us something that may seem true but conveys a misleading message. They are out to lead you to believe their word of self-savviness—when, in truth, *they don't know the True Word Himself.* These individuals are experts at employing subtle, concealing, and deceptive acts and words in manipulative, scheming ways that are so convincing that people actually receive and accept them like an evil charm.

They will be sly in their choice of words and present it as factual, authentic, and genuine in all its content. They are defined as "Wolves in Sheep's Clothing," a term that describes people who play a role contrary to their true character, with whom spiritual contact is extremely dangerous.

'Godless Appearance'

Their visible exterior is so convincing in their conspiring acts because they want to attain their "personal" achievements in life. It is apparent that they seek the ways of their worldly gains versus the truth of God's teaching. Their pursuit of worldly desires portrays them as individuals who lack a genuine fear of God deeply ingrained in their hearts and minds. It's all about them and no one else!

Still, some say, "Oh, their words are accurate and spot on, and they seem so innocent, caring, loving, and pure." Christians, wake up, for these people are that good at their fake appearances and acts of hypocrisy! Many people today are failing the genuine test of faithfulness. Please understand this key takeaway: If you want your ears tickled by words that fit your worldly comfort zone—or hear a message that plays on your emotions of self—or even want to listen to teachings that portray and convey a way of more treasures on this earth, this is not putting God and His word in the proper light! If you're more tied to the ways of the physical matter than the spiritual outcome, you're not aligned with God's overall message!

Sadly, people are falling for this trickery of lies because they are not paying attention to God's word, which leads them to fall prey to the false teachings of people I call "Smooth, Silver-Tongued, Sophisticated Solicitors of Satan." Peter warns us in his second epistle about the danger of these false teachers. The only way to discern their appearance of godlessness versus godliness is by adhering to God's word and praying for His wisdom and discerning spirit to guide you and decipher through all their devious acts.

These false teachers call themselves God's representatives and ambassadors; when the truth be known, they represent their own glory of doom. They do not care about anyone but themselves and will take any drastic measures to get what they want out of life because they are out to devour you and me by giving them what they want, and that's our wealth! This is a danger zone because millions of people are falling prey to their lies and evil deceptions.

But the only way to filter through all their evil intent is to know the Real Truth and be a spiritually sound student of the Holy Word. Today, more than ever, it is imperative that the very breath of God's holy scriptures is ingrained in our hearts, souls, and minds to combat these principalities of darkness with the Sword of God (Read Eph 6:10–20). If we don't have the Whole Armor of God as our daily protector, we are not spiritually equipped to ascertain their falsehoods. Instead, when we're in that delusional state of mind and we've put our guard of holiness down, we find ourselves entertaining their lying ways. Danger Zone!

However, just as alarming are those who proclaim to be Christians but bear no fruit and are more of a stumbling block than a stepping stone to Christlikeness. A fake Christian is simply someone who professes to be a Christian but lives a life contrary to the Bible or that of Jesus Christ. How will we know? By their fruit or lack of (Matt 7:16–20). Christ even tells us that if anyone who causes a young and weaker in the faith to stumble, they are better off to have a millstone tied around their neck and tossed into the sea (Matt 18:6).

People, this is a severe danger zone of being a so-called lukewarm Christian and in jeopardy of being spewed out of the mouth of our Lord. Who in the world would play with their salvation in this manner and tamper with God's justice? This is so important because, sadly, a counterfeit Christian will be very religious on the outside or even go to church every Sunday, but will be just like the deceiving people of the world without any fruit of righteousness. In other words, fake Christians are those who have chosen a saved appearance rather than a saved heart. In reality, their inner being does not sync with their outer appearance. How? The flesh and Spirit cannot co-exist, for they constantly fight (read Galatians chapter 5). One of these forces has more influence on our lives than the other. Do you know which one is reigning and ruling you the most?

Never forget this: The one thing that a person loves the most and dominates their lives, whether the flesh or the Spirit, will supersede in their daily life for the world to see. If you want to know if the flesh is controlling you more than the Spirit, perhaps the list below will help us determine if we are genuine and faithful followers of Christ or *too consumed by the works of the enemy!* If we are more deceived by the enemy, man, and the ways of this world, and these bullet points hit straight to the heart, it's time to make things right with the Lord!

- They talk about religion, but there's no evidence of a Christlike relationship (Tit 1:16).
- They are disobedient and neglect God's word; they cannot even quote scripture. There is no witness to the spiritual manifestation of God's word in their life. In other words, there is no life-changing testimony. (Isa 44:18, Matt 22:29).
- They possess more doubt and fear about the uncertainties in life than genuine faith and trust in the Lord. (Prov 3:5–6, Isa 41:10, Phil 4:6–8).
- They bear no fruit for the glory of God. There is no confirmation of their saving faith (John chapter 15).
- They listen to more false teachings than participating in a Bible-believing body (2 Tim 4:3)! They possess no discerning spirit where they

- can tell the difference between spiritual right or unspiritual wrong (read the five chapters of James).
- Their interpretation of God's word is always confusing, muddied, and inconsistent with the Truth (Matt 13:1–23).
- They live a life of hypocrisy and phoniness (Gal 6:3).
- They exhibit more of the world and man than the Spirit of God (1 John 2:15–16, Jas 4:4, 2 Tim 3:1–5).
- They are unloving, unforgiving, and unrighteous (Gal 5:19–21).
- They are part-time (lukewarm) students, not full-time participants in God's word (Rev 3:15–16). They are so complacent that there is no room for spiritual growth.
- They consistently tell lies and mislead people. They gossip, backstab, and belittle others while always elevating themselves (Prov 19:9, John 8:44).
- They do not possess a repentant heart (Luke 13:3, 1 John 1:9).
- They are full of pride or narcissism rather than Christlike humility (Prov 11:2 and 29:23).

> John 10:1–5, "I tell you the truth, anyone who sneaks over the wall of a sheepfold, rather than going through the gate, must surely be a thief and a robber! But the one who enters through the gate is the shepherd of the sheep. The gatekeeper opens the gate for him, and the sheep recognize his voice and come to him. He calls his own sheep by name and leads them out. After he has gathered his own flock, he walks ahead of them, and they follow him because they know his voice. They won't follow a stranger; they will run from him because they don't know his voice." "Jesus replied, "I have already told you, and you don't believe me. The proof is the work I do in my Father's name. But you don't believe me because you are not my sheep. My sheep listen to my voice; I know them, and they follow me."

Are you truly following the Real Shepherd (Jesus) versus the godless people of today?

Chapter Ten

'Godly Unity'

Josh 10:1–14, "Adoni-zedek, king of Jerusalem, heard that Joshua had captured and completely destroyed Ai and killed its king, just as he had destroyed the town of Jericho and killed its king. He also learned that the Gibeonites had made peace with Israel and were now their allies. He and his people became terrified when they heard all this because Gibeon was a large town, as large as the royal cities and larger than Ai. And the Gibeonite men were strong warriors."

"So, King Adoni-zedek of Jerusalem sent messengers to several other kings: Hoham of Hebron, Piram of Jarmuth, Japhia of Lachish, and Debir of Eglon. "Come and help me destroy Gibeon," he urged them, "for they have made peace with Joshua and the people of Israel." So, these five Amorite kings combined their armies for a united attack. They moved all their troops into place and attacked Gibeon."

"The men of Gibeon quickly sent messengers to Joshua at his camp in Gilgal. "Don't abandon your servants now!" they pleaded. "Come at once! Save us! Help us! For all the Amorite kings who live in the hill country have joined forces to attack us." So, Joshua and his entire army, including his best warriors, left Gilgal and set out for Gibeon. "Do not be afraid of them," the Lord said to Joshua, "for I have given you victory over them. Not a single one of them will be able to stand up to you."

"Joshua traveled all night from Gilgal and took the Amorite armies by surprise. The Lord threw them into a panic, and the Israelites slaughtered great numbers of them at Gibeon. Then the Israelites chased the enemy along the road to Beth-horon, killing them all along the way to Azekah and Makkedah. As the Amorites retreated down the road from Beth-horon, the Lord destroyed them with a terrible hailstorm from heaven that continued until they reached Azekah. The hail killed more of the enemy than the Israelites killed with the sword."

"On the day the Lord gave the Israelites victory over the Amorites, Joshua prayed to the Lord in front of all the people of Israel. He said, "Let the sun stand still over Gibeon, and the moon over the valley of Aijalon." So the sun stood still and the moon stayed in place until the nation of Israel had defeated its enemies. Is this event not recorded in *The Book of Jashar*? The sun stayed in the middle of the sky, and it did not set as on a normal day. There has never been a day like this one before or since, when the Lord answered such a prayer. Surely the Lord fought for Israel that day!"

In this most memorable chapter, we will see the records of the most unusual day in history. Here, the fearless and faithful leader, Joshua, prayed to Yahweh in front of all the people of Israel and asked Him to make the sun stand still so they could achieve ultimate victory over the evil Amorite kings. And because Joshua trusts in the Almighty One and his undeniable unity with Him, it is then that we see where God granted Joshua's request. This event is seen as a testament to God's sovereignty and His direct intervention in the affairs of His people, demonstrating His power and faithfulness. But the key is that when His people rely on His power and provision, and they know and believe that He will deliver and supply all their needs.

We see that the king of Jerusalem (Adoni-zedek) was rightly alarmed when he heard of the conquests of Jericho and Ai. He understood that the armies of Israel would soon come against all the Canaan cities, so he devised a seemingly grand plan to unite with the other southern armies. What else concerned this king was the surrender and subordination of the Gibeonites to Israel. This caused Adoni-zedek to be afraid because Gibeon was a great city, and their men were mighty, but now they were in unison with the Mightiness of God's Army.

Since the great city of Gibeon surrendered to Israel, this sent a message that things were not looking good for the other Canaanite armies. And this is the reason why! When an Israelite army fights for the glory of God, united as a mighty force and utilizing their unique instruments with God's assistance, it would rightly make any enemy afraid. You see, even though they conspired in their acts to join the nation of Israel, the Gibeonites had the spiritual insight to unite with God's force, because that is the only victorious army that will get anyone through the battles of life!

As mighty as the Gibeonites were, they did not submit to Israel a position of weakness because all their men were dominant. Yet it was because of their fear and honor of the God of Israel that they submitted to perpetual service in His Tabernacle. This may lead us to believe that, over time, their hearts have shifted, and they now possess the right and proper fear of God. Now that they are united with the Israelites and are experiencing the Mightiness of Almighty God, do they have more reverence and love for Yahweh?

However, the wrong fear did not make the other Canaanites surrender. It made them organize and fight, and Adoni-zedek became the leader of the southern Canaanite kings. The king of Jerusalem asked the other kings to join him and attack Gibeon. So, the armies of Jerusalem, Hebron, Jarmuth, Lachish, and Eglon all joined together and attacked Gibeon. But remember the powerful passage above. Joshua is told by God to be rest assured, for I have given you victory over them—not even one of them will be able to stand against you.

The enemies of Israel feared greatly, but like our spiritual enemies today, they did not retreat but launched even more bold attacks, as a wild animal might fight when it feels threatened. It's a battle of the proper fear vs. the wrong fear. [1] Little did these southern kings realize that they were assisting Joshua and God's army in all their mischievous plans. These Canaanite forces thought they could unite as one earthly force against the Mighty One, Who would eventually destroy them. It was evident that God had His hand in this entire plan devised by the other Canaanites.

Here's how God can work when we allow Him to lead us. Instead of Joshua drafting separate campaigns against each of these cities, God ensured victory over them simultaneously. They killed many evil nations with one act of God's Sovereignty. This power and divine control should reassure us and give us confidence in our own spiritual battles today. How?

What a beautiful portrait that shows us there is no amount of evil we may confront in our lives that can overcome us when God is with His children. He will assist us in attaining victory over all of them (one at a time, with the authority of His word); He's that Powerful. However, the key is not just leaning upon His guidance, but also our obedience to His commands, and trusting Him through it all. Our faith and obedience are not just passive responses; they are active choices that empower us to face the adversaries we will inevitably encounter in this life's journey.

Remember what Paul tells us in Rom 8:31–34, "What shall we say about such wonderful things as these? If God is for us, who can ever be against us? Since he did not spare even his own Son but gave him up for us

---

1. Joshua 10. "The Southern Kings Conquered."

all, won't he also give us everything else? Who dares accuse us, whom God has chosen for his own? No one, for God himself, has given us right standing with himself. Who then will condemn us? No one—for Christ Jesus died for us and was raised to life for us, and he is sitting in the place of honor at God's right hand, pleading for us."

When God's word reminds us that our Lord is "for us," He is telling you and me that He is on our side, working on our behalf, and for our good. He has proved His lovingkindness by adopting us as His own (Romans 8:15). In this unity, He has given us His Spirit, so we're adjoined with Him through all our intense warfare (Romans 8:16–17, 26–27). Regardless of the circumstances, He has determined to save us (Romans 8:29–30). And here's the summation of it all in Romans 8:31–39: We're told once we're united with His Son in genuine faith and obedience, nothing can separate us from God's love. You see, when we're rooted solidly in the grace and love of our Lord, nothing can sever that bond from Him.

In today's time of severe trials and temptations, we are constantly in a battle against evil forces. With that bombardment, we often feel spiritually immobile and incapable of achieving those little victories. However, we can always recollect what Jesus said in Matt 10:28, "Dear friends, don't be afraid of those who want to kill your body; they cannot do any more to you after that. But I'll tell you whom to fear. Fear God, who has the power to kill you and then throw you into hell. Yes, he's the one to fear."

What a powerful promise of truth because Jesus is conveying to you and me that no matter what may happen to us here on earth, there is a higher reality upon which we need to focus and fix our thoughts, and it's this: There is a bigger war than the one we face, and never forget this—God is the ultimate winner (Ephesians 6:12). Here's the wonderful news. If we are on His side, united with Him through it all, then we will win, too (Revelation 21:7–8, 27).[2]

Christians, it is so crucial for us to understand this critical point today more than ever: We all must ensure that we're united with the Right One on this earth because the Bible paints a pretty grim picture of what all the prevailing evil practices can do if they are incorporated into our lives (like the ones in the nation of Canaan) —they will separate us from a Holy God. Leviticus and Deuteronomy contain detailed and lurid lists, including the worship of demonic idols, taboo sexual acts, and even the sacrifices that were not aligned with God's design. God never wanted His children to dabble with any of their wicked deeds. And this applies to you and me today.

---

2. Got Questions. What does" If God is for us, who can be against us mean?"

When a Christian starts to allow an inkling of evil to come into their lives, it can break their union with the Lord, which is a dangerous place to be, because it can sever our relationship from the will of God. That separation brings disunity in people's lives, leading them apart from God's purpose and plan. They are now drifting through perilous currents because of their disjointed ways. It is so vital today, more than ever, that we do not attempt to join or connect with anything ungodly—because if we do, there will be dire consequences—sooner or later!

What a compelling story when the other kings and armies confronted the city of Gibeon because they had now joined God's army—the nation of Israel. The 'God's army' here refers to the people of Israel who were under God's divine protection and guidance. Even though these other leaders had heard of all the victories the Israelites had accomplished, they did not fear God's nation, its leaders, or especially God Almighty Himself, because they did not surrender to His reign. Little did they know that their self-arrogance and not possessing complete reverence and respect for God would be their demise. However, the Gibeonites had a discernment to unite with the nation of Israel, on God's side. Today, if you feel a firm conviction that you need to part ways with those who are not of God, flee and unite with God ASAP (Jas 4:7)!

Have you ever felt like the unity of arrogant, wicked, and worldly people is so heavily stacked against God's children that it overwhelms our hearts and spirits to the point of frustration, anger, or disheartenment? And so often, it feels like we're in this all alone, which is nothing but a delusional thought cast by the enemy. I love the passage in Peter's first epistle, where he wrote to the believers in Asia Minor to encourage and reassure them of the spiritual blessings of grace and peace, because they had believed and obeyed the gospel. Powerful!

Always remember that if you and I are united in the heart of God's word, grounded in His truths, adhering to His every command, trusting and obeying Him through it all, no number of enemies can overcome us when we're in sync with God. Our proper fear and respect for God will enable us to rest in His empowering arms of grace and protection. When we yearn for more of His ways into our lives and yield to the power of His Spirit, this is a tell-tale sign that we're in unity with Him!

However, when we become too entangled and grounded in the illusory ways of an evil society and culture driven by their own selfish desires, we can easily become sucked into their world of deceitful ways. This will cause people to start forming fleshly ideas about their own personal values, which are more in line with the ways of man and this world. These types of arrogant people have a warped sense of themselves, lack empathy, and place themselves in a superior position to others; it's the same as narcissism. They are more united with the ways of the world and humans *than with God*.

But for believers in Christ, union with God involves being one with Him always; it cannot be broken apart. We never want to be separated from God or do anything contrary to His will, because our unity with Him involves a different aspect of life compared to the ways of the evil world. Evidence of a person in harmony with God is a quiet heart, mind, and spirit that is still and available to God so He can show them His ways of righteousness and holiness.

God's word reminds us in Josh 10:25, "Don't ever be afraid or discouraged," Joshua told his men. "Be strong and courageous, for the Lord is going to do this to all of your enemies." With God's help, the nation of Israel's army won the battle against five Amorite armies. We have seen many examples of God's victories throughout the Bible. He never failed then, and He doesn't fail us today!

Don't we realize that the same God Who provided and protected the nation of Israel with one victory at a time can also attain and sustain our victories in life? If we genuinely believe He's the same yesterday, today, and tomorrow, His empowering strength is not lacking because it's always sufficient (2 Cor 12:9)! Stay united with His Empowering Grace daily, where you can experience one victory at a time on this side of Heaven!

Chapter Eleven

'Turning Point'

> Josh 11:1-6, 23, "When King Jabin of Hazor heard what had happened, he sent messages to the following kings: King Jobab of Madon; the king of Shimron; the king of Acshaph; all the kings of the northern hill country; the kings in the Jordan Valley south of Galilee; the kings in the Galilean foothills; the kings of Naphoth-dor on the west; the kings of Canaan, both east and west; the kings of the Amorites, the Hittites, the Perizzites, the Jebusites in the hill country, and the Hivites in the towns on the slopes of Mount Hermon in the land of Mizpah. All these kings came out to fight. Their combined armies formed a vast horde. And with all their horses and chariots, they covered the landscape like the sand on the seashore. The kings joined forces and established their camp around the water near Merom to fight against Israel.
>
> "Then the Lord said to Joshua, "Do not be afraid of them. By this time tomorrow, I will hand all of them over to Israel as dead men. Then you must cripple their horses and burn their chariots. So, Joshua took control of the entire land, just as the Lord had instructed Moses. He gave it to the people of Israel as their special possession, dividing the land among the tribes. So, the land finally had rest from war."

The fear of God's army conquering the Promised Land (one stage at a time) has now reached the northern troops. God has already provided victories at each juncture from the East to the West, from the South, and now to the North. What a powerful illustration that shows us that God has our back at every point in our lives and will never forsake us at any stage—He's always there (Psalm chapter 46)! As we read these storylines at each geographical point, these battles for God's children intensified at each phase, en route to their possession of God's Promises. However, it would still require due diligence and effort for God's children to spiritually lean upon Yahweh for their eventual victory over the enemy.

As the passage above shows us, once these northern armies joined forces, they covered the landscape like the sand on the seashore. Can you imagine looking out over the horizon and seeing the enemies against us that seemed impossible to overcome? However, we have the Almighty One behind, beside, and in front of us—He's genuinely Omnipresent (everywhere), Omniscient (all-knowing), and Omnipotent (all-powerful).

Once again, the vastness of the earthly forces pales in comparison to the Sovereignty of God. As we see in God's precious and gracious words, He will hand over the enemies to Joshua and His children, no matter how intense the enemy has concocted a plan to bring His children down. The contrast between human forces and God's sovereignty is awe-inspiring and amazing. Do we ever stop in our daily lives and reflect on His mighty domination when we yield to His empowering ways?

This was a turning point for the nation of Israel. Now that these four geographical points had been defeated, the land was at rest from war. However, each of the twelve tribes had more of the Promised Land to occupy. Yahweh set the stage and showed His children that if they relied upon His guidance and obeyed His commands, He would enable them to conquer their respective lands for their future possession.

Unfortunately, all the tribes' absolute disobedience prevented them from attaining God's enriched blessings. The weight of their choices was significant. While God was leading them to possess a land of milk and honey, they would choose otherwise. Sadly, for you and me today, many of us miss out on those spiritual blessings in our lives because of our disobedience and failure to rely on the Lord's guidance every day. We often seem to be prone to choosing our own path in life, rather than God's.

The end of this phase of conquest was a greater invitation to the tribes of Israel to cooperate with God. Even though this was a time of rest, as mentioned, much more territory was to be taken. This time of rest was crucial, for the nation needed to recuperate, refocus, regroup, renew, and reinvigorate itself by taking on the godly possessions God had promised. What a striking parallel for Christians today.

When we're caught up in the fast lane of life and have lost touch with God, we need to stop, be still, be quiet, take a spiritual rest, and listen to God's guidance; then we will make better choices in life. However, it was left up to each tribe to possess their portion of the land, just like it's up to you and me individually to possess our spiritual blessings when we give our all to Him!

You see, if each tribe of the nation of Israel was to possess its inheritance in its respective portions of the Promised Land, it was essential for them to apply (individually) the lessons they had learned from God during their war, which was this: "In their unity with Him, simply Trust & Obey God's ways and He will lead them to victory." However, if the tribes failed to comply, it was not a reflection on the power of God but on the people's failure to claim what God told Joshua to allot to each one of them.

In the same sense, Jesus has already defeated the enemy and conquered our spiritual possessions, but He also calls us into battle to gain what is ours: Our state of eternal rest from the worries of this world. [1] Just like the Israelites, it comes down to our willingness to choose God's ways and the blessings He desires in our lives. That is why it's imperative that we 'work out our salvation daily on this side of Heaven—with trembling and fear,' as recorded in Philippians 2:12-13. When we do this, there will be a significant shift in our lives from the ways of the world to the ways of God. You may ask, what does working out our salvation with fear and trembling mean?

A significant turnaround in our lives as genuine believers and followers of Jesus Christ occurs when we demonstrate reverence and respect for God through obedience to His Word. This shows our genuine love for the scriptures as we faithfully adhere to His teachings. The Greek verb "work out" means "to continually work and bring something to completion or fruition. We achieve this by actively pursuing obedience in sanctification, which involves growing spiritually and becoming more like Christ.

Paul helps us to better understand by describing himself as "pressing on" toward the goal of Christlikeness (Philippians 3:13-14). The "trembling" he experiences is the attitude Christians are to have in pursuing this goal, which is a healthy fear of offending God when we're out of line biblically and spiritually. And it's also a sense of awe and respect for His majesty and holiness. Ultimately, it assures us we're on the right path to Glory!

This is particularly important for all Christians today because a turning point is a junction, location, or time in a person's life when a choice for change occurs. It's that life-changing moment when we shift and respond differently, like switching from our old way to our new nature in Christ. As a child of God whose hope and confidence are in Him, our divine encounter with our Lord should bring forth a turning point with unbelievable opportunities to live in the rest and comfort of His provisions in life. It should

---

1. Joshua 11. "The Northern Canaanites Armies Defeated,"

'Turning Point'

yield a flowing life of His blessings that reflects the changes He's made in you and me because we chose Him and not the ways of the world.

This point in our lives is when something has changed its course of direction. It could have taken a severe breaking point in your life to occur, leading to a climactic milestone for God's glory. However, this turnabout and conversion will be a game-changer for us individually, which will undoubtedly impact others. However, a key takeaway is that a godly turning point is only defined when our Christlike character has developed into something unique, where transformation is revealed. If not, the same old story keeps dragging on in our old worldly life; we're still stuck in the same old rut, and nothing is happening fruitfully.

Once we come to genuine saving faith in Christ, the power of God's indwelling Spirit is there, ready and willing to help us through each stage of our lives. However, it boils down to this: We're fed up and tired and have finally reached that 'moment of truth" of complete surrender and submission. In other words, we die to self and give it all to Someone Who has all the authority and power to change us!

When this happens, we realize we're not pleased with our old way of doing things because it wasn't producing any spiritual blessings and, most importantly, it wasn't honoring our Lord. And now, we yearn to renew our minds and hearts because what we want in the future is the opposite of the old—we desire something spiritually refreshing (Rom 12:1–2). And when we make that decisive change, we know and feel it in our spirit, heart, and mind. It impacts our lives and others, but most importantly, it glorifies God. However, one of the main reasons we don't reach that spiritual turning point in our lives and miss that beautiful opportunity is that we're not in God's rest. What does that mean?

His rest is when we're under the liberty of Jesus Christ, where we've given our lives wholly to Him, and we're free from the worries of the world and the heavy burdens and sorrows that plague us. We are free from the death of sin and anything that enslaves our lives and holds us in bondage. Because of our new life in Christ, we now have the freedom to choose our own path. But the course He wants us to follow is the one that guides us from our old past to His new life, as Paul reminds us in 2 Corinthians 5:17.

When we do this, we're more focused on our unwavering faith, trust, and obedience in Him, and are liberated from the works that we do to make ourselves acceptable to Him. We fully recognize His grace and understand that genuine saving faith will bear fruit (Jas 2:14–26). This is crucial because the enemy does not want those turning points in our lives for the good of God. He wants us to get entangled in the hustle and bustle of life and focus on ourselves rather than on the Lord. This is perilous because it will lead to a person who has lost that state of intentional change.

We must realize that, as God's children, we should all experience a turning point in our lives. And this is when God speaks to us and shows you and me His grace, mercy, love, and patience. When we possess that open heart, mind, and spirit to His voice, we come to understand that faith comes by hearing, and that is hearing the Word of God (Rom 10:17). This is when we willingly receive His word, truly accept it, diligently apply it, and fervently obey it.

And here's the beauty of that juncture in our lives: It proves and reassures us that He has not cut us off from His desired blessings, because God wants to bless us. Why? When He blesses us, and we acknowledge His blessings, it creates an attitude of gratitude and draws us closer to Him. He also wants His blessings in our lives to be a witness to others in fruitful ways. But when we ignore Him, we will miss this unbelievable opportunity. Never forget this: Neglecting and ignoring His blessings can lead to disobedience and disrespect for our Heavenly Father. Our classic example is that first generation of Israelites.

Regrettably, man's fall disrupted and shattered God's rest, and we've been astray for millennia. In the second chapter of Genesis, God planted a garden in Eden, a harmonious paradise of tranquility, rest, and solace. He appointed Adam as His caretaker and was there with His servant, walking and conversing with him. They were companions and lifelong friends, albeit temporarily due to one erroneous choice humans made, which was not part of God's plan. Adam and Eve had the option to remain in the peace of God's presence and be liberated from the chaos of life, but that was not to be.

God's rest is a state or place where God rules and manages His creation, free from the mayhem and disorder brought about by sin and rebellion. Just think: God gives us a choice today to enter His resting arms if we surrender and submit to His will, for that is the ultimate game-changer in life. You see, surrendering to God requires letting go of control, trusting in His plan for your life, complying with His commandments, following His will through prayer, the study and application of Scriptures to your life, being more led by the Holy Spirit, and acts of faith and service.

A great example of that turning point for you and me is when Christ came to this world and gave us a chance to make Him Lord over our lives. Jesus reminds all of us to come to Him, those who are weary and heavy laden (burdens), recorded in Matt 11:28–30. He offers us relief from life's pressures, stresses, and earthly chains that have weighed us down for years. Trust me, we all need Him as our turning point in this life's journey!

'Turning Point'

Remember, we're the caretakers of our hearts, souls, minds, and spirits, and it's up to you and me to choose the spiritual change that will turn our lives from the point of earthly disaster to heavenly prosperity, with our Lord in control to lead and guide us. It comes down to you and me making that life-changing choice to move our lives in a different direction for God's glory!

God's word reminds us in Mark 8:22–25,

> "When they arrived at Bethsaida, some people brought a blind man to Jesus, and they begged him to touch the man and heal him. Jesus took the blind man by the hand and led him out of the village. Then, spitting on the man's eyes, he laid his hands on him and asked, "Can you see anything now?" The man looked around. "Yes," he said, "I see people, but I can't see them very clearly. They look like trees walking around." Then Jesus placed his hands on the man's eyes again, and his eyes were opened. His sight was completely restored, and he could see everything clearly."

Many may ask why Jesus touched the man's eyes twice before he could see clearly. So often, at our turning point as Christians, our Almighty One chooses to perform His greatness one stage at a time, just like He did for the nation of Israel when they were freed from bondage. However, in the end, the Lord wants us to have those building blocks of faith and to have complete trust in Him. In that life-altering stage of our lives, His spiritual truth is not always clear at the beginning, but as we undergo the sanctification process, it becomes clearer day by day. But what a turning point in this blind man's life. He was once blind, but now he can see! Come out of the darkness and let His Light be your life-changer, one day at a time!

As noted before, *our chance in life to turn from our old plan to God's will hinges on our choice to change, for His glory!*

Chapter Twelve

'Godly Journal'

Josh 12:9–24, "These are the kings Israel defeated: The king of Jericho. The king of Ai, near Bethel. The king of Jerusalem. The king of Hebron. The king of Jarmuth. The king of Lachish. The king of Eglon. The king of Gezer. The king of Debir. The king of Geder. The king of Hormah. The king of Arad. The king of Libnah. The king of Adullam. The king of Makkedah. The king of Bethel. The king of Tappuah. The king of Hepher. The king of Aphek. The king of Lasharon. The king of Madon. The king of Hazor. The king of Shimron-meron. The king of Acshaph. The king of Taanach. The king of Megiddo. The king of Kedesh. The king of Jokneam in Carmel. The king of Dor in the town of Naphoth-dor. The king of Goyim in Gilgal. The king of Tirzah. In all, thirty-one kings were defeated."

Chapter 12 provides a detailed summary of the kings conquered by Joshua and the nation of Israel, with the assistance of Almighty God. The key to these victories was based on this: "If God's children trusted and obeyed Him and heeded His guidance, one evil nation after another would fall in defeat at the hands of Yahweh!" In total, Joshua's army of God defeated 31 kings in Canaan.

What I find fascinating is that before Israel could establish unity in God's Promised Land, God helped them conquer 31 kings. After the kingdom of Israel split, there were 39 kings between the two nations, but only eight good kings, resulting in 31 wicked kings after the division. The number of evil kings remains the same before and after the kingdom's unity. Think: In over 400 years from the time they entered the Promised Land to the divided kingdom, it was apparent that wickedness still prevailed amongst

God's children. It's as if God is telling us that if we don't remove that one evil thing from our lives, *there will never be unity with Him*; we will always be divided in our loyalty to whomever we serve.

While this list of kings may initially seem lengthy and unimportant, it holds profound relevance for us today. Just as these matters were pivotal to the everyday life of the Israelites, they also touch our lives, answering the question: "What land belongs to Israel?" In other words, what God has given His children as His promise and provision belongs to them, not the enemy. This is a powerful reminder that anything recorded in God's word has real-life application for you and me today. It demands our unwavering obedience and trust in Him. Let's explore some of the compelling parallels in this narrative.

The details of these stages of victory for the nation of Israel are crucial because they make it clear that these events occurred in real time and in real places. These are not fairy tales that begin with "once upon a time"; this is history that starts with specific places, people, and rulers. However, it was also a way for Israel to remember forever the great things God had done for them and to fulfill the truth of His covenant. "Sometimes, in the course of human experience, it is good for you and me to sit down and reflect on what has been conquered at each stage of our lives by the grace of God." Reflecting on our personal experiences and faith is a crucial part of our spiritual journey.

It may seem strange that there were so many kings in a country so small, but in those times, kings were only lords of cities or areas with a few villages within their domain. However, the key takeaway for us is that conquering so many towns and places in such a short time demonstrates that the Israelites were marvelously and wonderfully protected and assisted by the power of God. And when our Almighty One fulfills the truth of His word and commitment to His children, the evidence of those victories brings forth this: "The Promised of His word will come to fruition. And in His timing, it will certainly be accomplished, and no obstacles can get in His way!"

Another significant point for you and me in our battles today is that each of these kings was different, demonstrating that we will have various fights to overcome in our life's journey. It may be in the form of an addiction, a time in the wilderness, a personal loss, a clash with family or friends, spiritual warfare, loneliness or depression, discouragement, frustration, anger, forgiveness, moments of hopelessness or helplessness, no sense of direction (at a crossroads), confused, financial and personal strains, lack of faith and trust in God or a private sin. The list could be longer than 31 kings. Still, the point is this: "No matter the number of adversaries in our lives, when we surrender them to our Lord and submit ourselves humbly to Him—with complete trust and obedience, watch our Lord do His work of perfection in His timing!"

And what a beautiful time to journal those little victories at each point of our life's journey. Making physical notes of all the things God has done in each stage of our lives helps us to remember His lovingkindness and taste the goodness He's provided. Why is it important to remind ourselves of God's work in our personal lives? Because it keeps our spiritual lives fresh and anew of His workings. It helps us to know that He's present and close, and to understand that His words and faithfulness are valid and accurate, both yesterday, today, and in the future. But it also opens a massive door to share our life-changing testimonies with others. When we do this, we glorify and honor our Lord for the impact of His future Kingdom.

A godly journal can mean different things to different people. For some, journaling is a written prayer, a prayer request, or a record of answered prayers. Some people keep a journal of compelling spiritual truths, such as insights from a sermon, quotes from spiritual books, or a collection of Scriptures from the Bible. Some may write accounts of meaningful encounters with God where they had a victory over a particular sin or event in their life.

For some, a journal is a diary, a place to record occurrences in their daily activity and a few thoughts or recollections of various personal trials, maybe a positive turnaround. Some might keep a "gratitude" or "joy" journal that lists one or more things each day, small or large, for which they are thankful and grateful for a turn of events for the good. [1]

The key to writing a godly journal of our life's journey on this earth is that when God is our focal point, we slow down and put the life He desires for us in real perspective. It encourages us to fix our thoughts on His word and heed the guidance of the Holy Spirit. It is then that we become spiritually still and quiet, feel His presence, and come to know our Lord more personally. It helps us to meditate more on His holy word, focus on things that are worthy of His praise, and allow Him to transform and renew our minds and hearts.

I firmly believe that a genuine follower of Christ who has a burning desire for God's presence in their daily life will always yield to the Holy Spirit. When the Spirit of God prompts them, they act immediately. They pause, take a spiritual break from the busyness of this worldly life, incline their ear, tune in to God's subtle and most powerful voice, and take action!

---

1. "What Value is There in Christian Journaling."

'Godly Journal'

God's word beautifully reminds us in Hab 2:1-2, "I will climb up to my watchtower and stand at my guard post. There, I will wait to see what the Lord says and how he will answer my complaint. Then the Lord said, "Write my answer plainly on tablets so that a runner can carry the correct message to others." Habakkuk, a minor prophet for God, was a man who actively sought answers. When troubled by what he was observing, he boldly asked God difficult questions. The pivotal moment in this passage is when God instructs Habakkuk to "Write my answer 'plainly' on a tablet so God's message is 'correctly' conveyed to others." This is a powerful example for us today!

The point was this: Habakkuk was witnessing a dying world, and it broke his heart. We even ask ourselves today: "Why is there so much evil in the world?" "And why do the lawless people always seem to be winning and getting ahead in life?" This minor prophet did not sit idle; he took his complaints to Almighty God with boldness and confidence. But here's the key: God answered with a flood of proof and prediction.

Think about this. So often, we have so much to take to God's throne that our spirits and hearts are overwhelmed. And sometimes, we walk away from the foot of His throne and forget something. It was unintentional, and the great news is that the Lord knows our hearts. But He also knows our flesh is weak—because we always fail when we try to do things in our own strength.

How do we keep track of our prayers when God starts to answer them in many ways? We often forget what God did miraculously in our lives because we do the "life thing" and forget His blessings. It's vital that when God responds in favor of a prayer, we mustn't forget His gracious provisions; that's why it's beneficial to not only take mental and spiritual notes but also to record them in a physical form as daily reminders. These physical reminders are crucial in helping us maintain a grateful and faithful mindset, serving as a testament to God's constant presence in our lives.

If most of us went to the store to buy five items, we would need to write them down to avoid forgetting and to prevent having to go back, which would waste gas and time. And to think, if we have a long list of items to get us through the week, I would venture to say that 100% of us need a detailed checklist to ensure we get everything, and most importantly, the correct items. Consider this: We take the time to write an email or a text message to friends or family (sometimes daily), keep track of our family genealogy, or put together a photo album or scrapbook to recollect those times in our lives that bring back fond memories of joy and happiness.

Why would we not take the time to do the same for all the mighty things Almighty God has done throughout our lives? Our Heavenly Father and Creator took the time to give us a daily journal that helps us to live a life pleasing to Him every day. Not once a week or once a month, each day! I believe God has provided us with a roadmap of remembrance and as a daily guide in the power of His word (2 Tim 3:16-17, Heb 4:12-13). Consider some of the profound passages below that God has laid out in His Word for our daily reminders.

Acts 21:19, "After greeting them, Paul gave a detailed account of the things God had accomplished among the Gentiles through his ministry." After the people heard these things in detail, they praised God!

Ps 77:11-12, "But then I recall all you have done, O Lord; I remember your wonderful deeds of long ago. They are constantly in my thoughts. I cannot stop thinking about your mighty works."

Prov 3:1-4, "My child, never forget the things I have taught you. Store my commands in your heart. If you do this, you will live many years, and your life will be satisfying. Never let loyalty and kindness leave you! Tie them around your neck as a reminder. *Write them deep within your heart.* Then you will find favor with both God and people, and you will earn a good reputation." Take some time to make daily notes on the great things God has done for you!

Chapter Thirteen

'Godly Portion'

> Josh 13:1, 6–7, "When Joshua was an old man, the Lord said to him, "You are growing old, and much land remains to be conquered." "I myself will drive these people out of the land ahead of the Israelites. So be sure to give this land to Israel as a special possession, just as I have commanded you. Include all this territory as Israel's possession when you divide this land among the nine tribes and the half-tribe of Manasseh."

Joshua was old at this stage of his life, but God told him there was more land to be conquered in their quest for this inheritance. So, as God's leader and faithful servant, Joshua and the nation of Israel had more work that needed to be accomplished. God helped them reach this stage, but they had to press on for more of their godly portion. And here's the beauty of serving a gracious God: He would assist them if they would trust and obey Him. He wanted His children's hearts and mindsets to align with His plans; if so, they would be richly blessed.

Let's roll back the clock in time. Remember when Moses deployed the twelve spies to scout the land God had promised? Ten faithless spies measured the giants against their own strength, but Joshua and Caleb measured them against God's. Since the majority did not believe in God's promise, this was the cause of Israel's forty years of wandering in the wilderness.

God would not allow that generation of unbelief to enter, so He waited for them to die in the desert (Numbers 14:26–38). If they had all believed in God's Promises and provisions from the beginning, they could have gained their inheritance (portion) of God's blessings without wandering in the wilderness. The only ones of age who entered the Promised Land at the time of the rejection were Joshua and Caleb, the two faithful spies.

These two devout spies were filled with the Spirit of God and believed in His commitment to His children. They were so convinced of this inheritance from Almighty God that they came back with such enthusiasm and confidence and told the entire nation of God's people, it's ours for the taking because this has been endowed to us by the word of God. The difference between these two men of faithfulness and the other ten is that Joshua and Caleb were filled with the wisdom of God and had no doubt in God's promised inheritance.

For God's children to enjoy the richness and fullness of the Promised Land, they had to make an extra effort and go above and beyond the call of duty to attain their portion of His blessings. This powerful illustration should tell us that our work for the Lord never ends, regardless of age. We must understand that there is much more work to do as the Lord's servants in building His Kingdom today, tomorrow, and in the future. Never forget this passage from Paul in Phil 1:6 as our daily reminder, "I am sure of this, that he who started a good work in you will *carry it on to completion until the day of Christ Jesus.*"

This is crucial because if we ignore our service to the Lord, we can miss out on our portions of God's blessings. Remember what Jesus tells us in Luke 12:48, "When much has been given, much more will be required." However, a self-ambitious person does not understand this because Jesus also reminds us in Matt 6:24, 'We cannot serve two masters; in other words, one has more control over us than the other.' Sometimes, we must conduct an in-depth spiritual examination and determine this: Who controls us more in our life endeavors today?

As His Citizens of Heaven on earth, as His salt and light in a tasteless and darkened world, as His ambassadors and representatives, as His employers of His spiritual gifts, and as His trusted and faithful servants, our service does not cease as long as we can live and breathe! When believers stop serving Almighty God after He has called them, they may open the door to the enemy's traps, which can lead to a rut of complacency.

Our lives as His chosen servants on this side of Heaven are not a time of selfish ambitions, with the wrong intent and motive of attaining our earthly portions of claim and fame. Our life journey was intended to portray us as selfless and humble servants of God and to lead others down His path of righteousness *for His glory*. Always remember, there are no deviations from God's path as His devout servants! If we allow any variation in His calling, we can miss undeniable portions of His blessings.

'Godly Portion'

When followers of Christ cease their service for the Lord, it's as if they're saying: 1) 'I don't like Who I'm serving. 2) My efforts weren't reasonable enough. 3) I fear I will offend someone, which signifies the wrong type of fear. 4) God's not pleased with 'my' fruitfulness. 5) My rewards in this field of service are not fulfilling or self-gratifying. 6) I want to open the door for someone else to serve in my place so I can have a break. And 7) I am called to do something in the secular world.

Firstly, all these mindsets are the enemy's work, because he does not want anyone to serve the Lord faithfully for His Kingdom—he's doing his best to put up every barrier and blockage possible. Trust me; he does not want you or me to receive blessings from God because he wants us to ignore God's goodness and lovingkindness. As God's chosen royal priesthood, we cannot allow that to happen.

But what's alarming is this: If you look at this list above, you see a lot of "me, myself, and I's" and nothing that refers to God's counseling, guidance, and His will. If someone was indeed called to serve the Lord and backed away from God's service, they completely ignored His calling. What a danger zone that could lead to the absence of His blessings in a person's life. When people put God on the shelf, it's all about themselves because they underestimate or undervalue the life of a servant for the Lord.

Here's a sobering truth that may resonate with many of us: When we stray, drift, or lose our way from serving God, we not only fail Him but also risk losing His blessings. In today's society, the allure of worldly possessions often overshadows our pursuit of God. It's a stark reality: Without striving for Christlikeness, we can never genuinely taste God's goodness.

After God helped the Israelites establish themselves as His nation, He still desired His children to do their part and take their portions of the entire land He had promised from the beginning. However, in their journey and battle, the Israelites failed to obey God's command to drive out the land's inhabitants. This disobedience is a powerful reminder of the importance of following God's will.

When they left these pagans in the land unchecked and unchallenged, the unending difficulties of living a life according to God's ways would be entirely difficult. How in the world can God's children take their portion of His blessings when they constantly allow wickedness in the presence of their lives? But most importantly, they separated themselves from His holy presence.

God's word reminds us in Neh 9:35–36, "Even while they had their own kingdom, they did not serve you, though you showered your goodness on them. You gave them a large, fertile land, but they refused to turn from their wickedness. So now, today, we are slaves in the land of plenty that you gave our ancestors for their enjoyment! We are slaves here in this good land."

So often, we forget all the blessings God has poured on us and all His gracious provisions in each stage of our lives. Why? Because we become too fixated on worldly things and start living a lifestyle that is contrary to His ways. You see, when we "forget" our grounded spiritual roots and life of service for His glory, we can easily be tempted to focus on the earthly matters of life, and we then start to rely more on our own wealth, provisions, and security rather than God's. We are here to fulfill His perfect will, not ours. When we focus too much on our way of this earthly life, we will leave God out of the picture and do more harm to the blessings He desires for you and me.

David's psalm in Ps 16:1-6 beautifully reminds us,

> "Keep me safe, O God, for I have come to you for refuge. I said to the Lord, "You are my Master! Every good thing I have comes from you." The godly people in the land are my true heroes! I take pleasure in them! Troubles multiply for those who chase after other gods. I will not take part in their sacrifices of blood or even speak the names of their gods. Lord, you alone are my inheritance, my cup of blessing. You guard all that is mine. The land you have given me is a pleasant land. What a wonderful inheritance!"

It is our fleshly nature to establish our personal goals and then ask God to bless them, *even after we leave God out of the plan.* The only way we can attain His purpose and perfect plan is by doing as David did, recognizing God as the Master of every aspect of our lives and acknowledging His blessings, protection, and provisions at every step. If we leave God out of our aspirations and seek success in our own eyes, we will forget the One Who blessed us with that so-needed portion of our lives. Isn't the Lord the One Who got us to that point of favorable results? Think about that!

When we prioritize our own selfish desires over God's blessings, we can become discontent, which can lead to many selfish and godless behaviors. Remember what David tells us in God's word, recorded in Ps 37:23-24: "The Lord directs the steps of the godly. He delights in every detail of their lives. Though they stumble, they will never fall, for the Lord holds them by the hand." It's the godly who are genuinely led by God and all His ways, and it pleases Him.

Always remember this: When a writer in the Bible says, "God is my portion," he means that God is the source of happiness and blessing. In other words, His children are content with all the Lord has provided in their lives (it's second to none). Why? Because we have the best inheritance imaginable, and we do not seek worldly possessions or comfort outside of God. Nothing is as valuable as the Promises of God in comparison to all the personal riches, honor, and fame. Don't we genuinely believe in our heart of hearts that we need nothing else if God is our portion? Why? We have the richest inheritance of all, Heaven! And here's excellent news: The presence of the Holy Spirit at work within our lives is the guarantee of this "eternal inheritance" we have received.

> Ps 73:21–28, "Then I realized that my heart was bitter, and I was all torn up inside. I was so foolish and ignorant—I must have seemed like a senseless animal to you. Yet I still belong to you; you hold my right hand. You guide me with your counsel, leading me to a glorious destiny. Whom have I in heaven but you? I desire you more than anything on earth. My health may fail, and my spirit may grow weak, but God remains the strength of my heart; he is mine forever. Those who desert him will perish, for you destroy those who abandon you. But as for me, how good it is to be near God! I have made the Sovereign Lord my shelter, and I will tell everyone about the wonderful things you do."

Chapter Fourteen

'Godly Precision'

Josh 14:6–13, "A delegation from the tribe of Judah, led by Caleb son of Jephunneh the Kenizzite, came to Joshua at Gilgal. Caleb said to Joshua, "Remember what the LORD said to Moses, the man of God, about you and me when we were at Kadesh-barnea. I was forty years old when Moses, the servant of the LORD, sent me from Kadesh-barnea to explore the land of Canaan. I returned and gave an honest report, but my brothers who went with me frightened the people from entering the Promised Land. For my part, I wholeheartedly followed the LORD my God. So that day, Moses solemnly promised me, 'The land of Canaan on which you were just walking will be your grant of land and that of your descendants forever because you wholeheartedly followed the LORD my God.'

"Now, as you can see, the LORD has kept me alive and well as he promised for all these forty-five years since Moses made this promise—even while Israel wandered in the wilderness. Today, I am eighty-five years old. I am as strong now as I was when Moses sent me on that journey, and I can still travel and fight as well as I could then. So, give me the hill country that the LORD promised me. You will remember that as scouts, we found the descendants of Anak living there in great, walled towns. But if the LORD is with me, I will drive them out of the land, just as the LORD said." So, Joshua blessed Caleb, son of Jephunneh, and gave Hebron to him as his portion of land."

The Promised Land was divided precisely as God had instructed Moses years earlier, and Joshua did not change one thing from God's original plan: what a man of faithful precision. He obeyed God's commands to the detail with perfection, care, and clarity. This was vital then, and it remains so for us today. Why? Because God is searching for leaders and servants who can follow His guidelines, according to His Holy Word, thoroughly and accurately. He wants His servants to speak and share the truth of His word with exact clearness, not adding or removing anything from its original message.

We often discuss Joshua because of his role as a leader, but his partner, Caleb, was also faithful from the beginning. When he and Joshua scoped the Promised Land at Moses's request, he saw greatness in the land God had promised, and he believed beyond a shadow of a doubt in God's help in conquering this area. But what I love about Caleb's request for his portion is when he states, "I am as strong now as I was when Moses sent me on that journey, and I can still travel and fight as well as I could then. So, give me the hill country that the Lord promised me." He was eighty-five when he made this request, but was as strong as ever.

Caleb was indeed an example of God's faithful servant when he scouted the land of Canaan and returned with the assurance that God's promises were real. What a powerful illustration of how we can use our times of God's favor to show others just how precise God is in working out His plan in our lives. In other words, His promises to each believer will be perfected in His timing. But just as important, this beautiful portrait shows how a follower of the Lord grows in spiritual strength even in their latter years; it does not diminish.

As we look at the life of Caleb, we see a faithful and devoted man who trusted God to fulfill His Promises when others allowed their fears to override their small faith. Even later, Caleb remained steadfast in his faith and did not waver one bit. And because of Caleb's unambiguous (without dispute) life as God's chosen one, He blessed Caleb for his faithfulness and patience, which should encourage us to believe in God in every detail of His Promises and provisions. Like Caleb, we should be prepared to follow God in every circumstance, patiently waiting for Him to fulfill His Promises and ready to act when the time is right.

When we think about the theme of this chapter, 'Godly Precision,' what comes to mind? For me, the first thing that comes to mind is God's creation. He created everything in the beginning with perfection, accuracy, and exactness. And in His original design of humans, we possess many of the same characteristics as a Holy God. Think about the power of that for a moment. However, the key to us glorifying and honoring Him with those exact characteristics lies in how we handle them daily.

Let's look at it this way. We often use precision and accuracy in the same way, but accuracy describes a particular measurement, in other words, how close it is to the truth, such as how close we are to the truth of God's word. But precision describes a measurement system, which is you and me. It measures how consistently we produce the same results, holiness or unholiness, in our lives. Never forget what we stated earlier, whichever reigns in us the most is what we will produce more of in our daily lives.

Just think: If God designed us with perfection at the beginning of creation, and when we go through the tests and trials of life, how close to that state of His original model of perfection are we going to be? In other words, how near or far off target are we to the truth of His commands? I am not saying we will ever be perfect, but if holiness is our precise benchmark in everyday life, think of the results that would glorify God if we put that into practice diligently! Unfortunately, due to one poor decision by humans in the Garden of Perfection, we have fallen short. But there's excellent news!

He knows that we all fall short of His standards (Rom 3:23). The beauty of God's grace, mercy, and love is immeasurable. He realizes that humans have failed, and that's why we have this sinful nature, but that's not an excuse for not trying. Once again, we're not talking about perfection, but a continuous improvement of godly progression with the sight of His holy precision in our lives. Always remember: Yahweh has provided us with every resource for living a godly life of precision. God's word reminds us in 2 Peter 1:3, "By his divine power, God has given us everything we need to live a godly life. We have received all of this by coming to know him, the one who called us to himself by means of his marvelous glory and excellence."

Remember what Paul tells us so eloquently in Phil 3:12-16,

> "I don't mean to say that I have already achieved these things or that I have already reached perfection. But I press on to possess that perfection for which Christ Jesus first possessed me. No, dear brothers and sisters, I have not achieved it, but I focus on this one thing: Forgetting the past and looking forward to what lies ahead, I press on to reach the end of the race and receive the heavenly prize for which God, through Christ Jesus, is calling us. Let all who are spiritually mature agree on these things. If you disagree on some point, I believe God will make it plain to you. But we must hold on to the progress we have already made."

In the power of this passage, Paul is telling us that our goal, just like his, is to know Jesus Christ, to be like Him, and to be all that our Lord had in mind for you and me as His faithful followers. I am fairly certain that many of us have good reason to forget our past because the ugliness of sin tarnishes it. If anyone could attest to this, it would be the great apostle Paul. And trust me, the enemy wants us to dwell on these past sins and make us feel we are not good enough to belong to Christ. He can lead us to second-guess our eternal life and security and disregard our sureness as God's children.

We all know that none of us is good (Rom 3:9–20), not one. However, we must never forget what Christ did for us on the cross and when He arose victoriously from the grave. That one event should give all Christians the powerful insight of hope that helps us let go of any shame or guilt from our past and move forward with a life of certainty. While the enemy wants to lead us down the path of imperfection and inaccuracy, God has a better path for you and me. The best way to let go of the past and press on toward that goal is to grow in the knowledge and wisdom of God's truth and know that, as His possessions, we are forgiven. He has removed those nasty sins as far as the East is from the West so that we can rest in our defined character as followers of Christ (Ps 103:12).

When we let go and move forward with God's precise accuracy, we are assured of His grace and do not engage in sinful acts. And in that closeness, through the power of His word and Spirit, we are careful, determined, and meticulous in our pursuit of rightness toward God's ways. If we pattern our Christian lives with this methodology, we will discover that we are more in line with God's exact purpose and goodwill in our lives. The key is that it takes due diligence, adhering to the truth of God's word, heeding the advice of the Holy Spirit, and continual spiritual growth, just like Caleb. The self-assurance that we now have—because of what He has done should motivate us more and more every day to carry on His Good News with perfection.

> 2 Tim 3:16–17, "All Scripture is inspired by God and is useful to teach us what is true and to make us realize what is wrong in our lives. It corrects us when we are wrong and teaches us to do what is right. God uses it to prepare and equip his people to do every good work."

Chapter Fifteen

'Godly Boldness'

> Josh 15:13–16, "The Lord commanded Joshua to assign some of Judah's territory to Caleb, son of Jephunneh. So, Caleb was given the town of Kiriath-arba (that is, Hebron), which had been named after Anak's ancestor. Caleb drove out the three groups of Anakites—the descendants of Sheshai, Ahiman, and Talmai, the sons of Anak." From there, he went to fight against the people living in the town of Debir, formerly known as Kiriath-sepher. Caleb said, "I will give my daughter Acsah in marriage to the one who attacks and captures Kiriath-sepher."

In Joshua chapters 15 through 19, we see the allotment of the Promised Land to the tribes of Israel. However, nestled within these chapters, we will examine some critical and vital attributes that Christians should possess. Why is it essential to exemplify Christlike attributes in our daily lives? It shows our development stages through the process of sanctification, but it also demonstrates Who we answer to, and that's Almighty God. It also illustrates that we've put on the new nature of Christ, ripped off the old ways, and nailed those old desires to the Cross. Our progression demonstrates our genuine position of faith, trust, confidence, obedience, and boldness, which are the key themes of this chapter.

The passage above has immense power because it showcases a person with such assertiveness that it can be applied to our own lives. Because of Caleb's zeal, boldness, and confidence in God's promises and provisions, he is used as a powerful example for us as genuine believers today. Remember, this is the same man (along with Joshua) who silenced the murmuring, fearful men of Israel by saying, "But Caleb tried to quiet the people as they stood before Moses. "Let's go at once to take the land," he said. "We can certainly conquer it!" (Numbers 13:30).

Caleb's firm stance in this powerful statement was that he followed the Lord wholeheartedly, not half-heartedly. Caleb believed in God's Promises to the Israelites with all his heart, soul, mind, and strength. He was a man of such spiritual ability because he did not focus on all the obstacles as the faithless men did. Instead, he believed that God would give them victory over the enemy.

We all know why the Israelites never possessed all the land God initially promised. The tribes of God's nation struggled with pushing out the enemies in their respective areas, and unfortunately, it was because they were so weak in their efforts that they even allowed the enemy to dwell with them. This is the opposite of God's plan, for He wanted these wicked people out of the presence of His children so they would not be tempted to follow their paganistic ways of life. Sadly, God's children did not obey God's commands.

They did not rely upon God's assistance in forcing the evil people out from amongst them, leading to an absence of God's blessings. And because of their negligence, they never possessed the entire boundaries of God's original Promised Land. But that is not the case with Caleb! God allowed this man of faithfulness to be in this storyline as an example for you and me today. He wants us to realize that when we are faithful, obedient, and trust in Him for all things, He will provide.

In this story, we see that Caleb was a man of bold deeds who encouraged others to do tremendous and courageous acts. He did this by offering his daughter in marriage to the man who was brave enough to conquer a city. Caleb's godly character, exemplified by courage, faith, gratitude, praise, obedience, trust in God's strength, and wholehearted devotion to God, inspired his daughter to emulate these traits. When a child of God possesses and exhibits the character of fearless and unafraid acts of godliness, they are confident, decisive, and high-spirited in Whom their assurance is. They don't move an inch in their self-reliance on the Lord, because it affects others around them in powerful ways, as it did with Caleb's daughter. What a powerful legacy and life-changing testimony that can be passed down for future generations!

Spiritual or biblical boldness is the courage to act or speak fearlessly despite real or apparent dangers. When a person acts boldly, they respond regardless of the risks, but it comes with godly discernment. And this gift, discernment, is crucial because it is the ability to make proper determinations, demonstrating God's guidance through His wisdom and insight. A discerning person will acknowledge the worth of God's Word because of their boldness to represent their Lord at all costs.

There is a strong bond between boldness and a discerning spirit, and the Bible offers numerous verses that encourage both boldness and discernment, guiding believers in making wise choices as they navigate life's challenges. Please read James 1:5, Proverbs 3:5-6, Philippians 1:9-10, Hebrews 5:14, and 1 John 4:1. We cannot forget that this divine characteristic, boldness, is one of the first that the Holy Spirit imparted when He came to indwell believers after Jesus ascended into Heaven. It is essential to recall that if a follower of Jesus Christ embodies every element of the Fruit of the Spirit, as outlined in Galatians 5:22-23 (love through self-control), spiritual boldness naturally flows out of them.

In his second epistle to the Corinthians, chapter 3, Paul reminds us that if the Old Covenant was so glorious, how much more glorious is the New Covenant? Our new, authentic, and real life in Jesus Christ should yield such confidence, assurance, and boldness in our lives that nothing can hold it back. We don't let the mortal man muzzle our words from speaking boastfully about all He's done, is doing, and will do for us as His own. When we hold back the Good News of Christ because of our fear of man, family, and friends, we don't possess Christlike boldness because we're more about being silent with man's version of political correctness.

In Acts 2, the followers of Christ had been hiding in fear of the Jewish authorities, praying and encouraging one another. Then the Holy Spirit came upon them, and those formerly terrified disciples became fearless preachers and spreaders of the Good News. A short time later, as the disciples faced persecution from the authorities, they prayed for boldness (Acts 4:29), and their prayer was answered. They were filled with the Holy Spirit and "spoke the word with boldness" (Acts 4:31). You see, this is important because God gives us boldness *when our objective is to glorify Him above all things.*

Spiritual boldness pursues the truth, works to destroy lies and error, and speaks of what is right regardless of how terrifying such action may be. However, their tone and approach will be one of gentleness, kindness, and words of grace and love. But worldly boldness, on the other hand, can become pushy or aggressive. It thrives on widespread approval and often ignores caution or sensitivity. We should not be bold in doing evil, accepting dares, or crossing boundaries to prove we can do things to attain favor in the eyes of others. That is more of our flesh at work than the Spirit.

Boldness without discernment can lead to foolish words and risky behavior. The book of Proverbs often connects rash boldness with folly. Proverbs 13:16 says, "Every prudent man acts with knowledge, but a fool flaunts his folly." Foolish people are so blind to their own error that they shamelessly brag about it. They boldly proclaim their erroneous viewpoints and are even more aggressive in implementing them. Consider this: "Human acts of the wrong type of boldness are fitting for a fool."

However, as followers of Christ, we should pray as Paul did that the Lord will grant us supernatural boldness to speak and live as He would have us do, with the guidance of the Holy Spirit. In this age of great deception and resistance to truth, we need boldness more than ever. Courage, coupled with love and humility (1 Corinthians 13:4–8; 1 Peter 5:6), is like a light in the darkness (Matthew 5:14). When we are convinced that our message is life-giving and eternal, we can speak with boldness, knowing that God will use it to impact our world (Isaiah 55:10–11).[1]

With that, are we genuinely bold in our stance for Jesus Christ in today's world? Is our position as Christians so firm in its belief that nothing can waver us from the Way, Truth, and Life? Is it rock-solid? Boldness isn't arrogance or cockiness but a biblical way Christians should behave. Nothing can harm or stand in our way if our confidence is in Jesus Christ. Let these quotes and verses below encourage us to find our boldness in Jesus and make a difference in a culture and society that acts in opposition to Christlike boldness.[2]

> "Uncertainty as to our relationship with God is one of the most enfeebling and dispiriting of things. It makes a man heartless. It takes the pith out of him. He cannot fight; he cannot run. He is easily dismayed and gives way. He can do nothing for God. But when we know that we are of God, we are vigorous, brave, and invincible. There is no more quickening truth than this of assurance." *Horatius Bonar*
>
> "Oh, how great peace and quietness would he possess who should cut off all vain anxiety and place all his confidence in God." *Thomas a Kempis*
>
> "Fight the good fight of faith, and God will give you spiritual mercies." *George Whitefield*
>
> "Faith, without trouble or fighting, is a suspicious faith; for true faith is a fighting, wrestling faith." *Ralph Erskine*
>
> "One of the special marks of the Holy Ghost in the Apostolic Church was the spirit of boldness." *A. B. Simpson*
>
> "A minister, without boldness, is like a smooth file, a knife without an edge, a sentinel that is afraid to let off his gun. If men will be bold in sin, ministers must be bold to reprove." *William Gurnall*

1. "What Does the Bible Say About Boldness?"
2. The following quotes are from Christian Quotes Site, "Twenty Powerful Quotes."

"The presence of hope in the invincible sovereignty of God drives out fear." *John Piper*

"His voice leads us not into timid discipleship but into bold witness." *Charles Stanley*

And Luke reminds us in Acts 14:3, "But the apostles stayed there a long time, preaching boldly about the grace of the Lord. And the Lord proved their message was true by giving them the power to do miraculous signs and wonders."

Here's the PowerPoint. How badly and sincerely do we want to live and speak more boldly for Jesus Christ? Do we want it enough to ask, seek, and knock *until* God answers us and implores us to take risks that will press out all our timidity and manmade fear? How much do we want to represent His Good News as His true ambassadors? Paul tells us powerfully in 2 Tim 1:7, "For God has not given us a spirit of fear and timidity, but of power, love, and self-discipline."

Here's our challenge of boldness for today, tomorrow, and the days to come, as expressed by the great apostle Paul, as recorded in Romans 1:16-17. When you read this passage, is the power of God's word channeling through our lives as His believers of boldness today? "For I am not ashamed of this Good News about Christ. It is the power of God at work, saving everyone who believes—the Jew first and also the Gentile. This Good News tells us how God makes us right in his sight. This is accomplished from start to finish by faith. As the Scriptures say, "It is through faith that a righteous person has life." Today, our genuine saving faith should portray and convey godly boldness in everything we say and do.

Chapter Sixteen

God*less* Fruit

Josh 16:1-10, "The allotment for the descendants of Joseph extended from the Jordan River near Jericho, east of the springs of Jericho, through the wilderness and into the hill country of Bethel. From Bethel (that is, Luz), it ran over to Ataroth in the territory of the Arkites. Then it descended westward to the territory of the Japhletites as far as Lower Beth-horon, then to Gezer, and over to the Mediterranean Sea. This was the homeland allocated to the families of Joseph's sons, Manasseh and Ephraim. The following territory was given to the clans of the tribe of Ephraim."

"The boundary of their homeland began at Ataroth-addar in the east. From there, it ran to Upper Beth-horon, then on to the Mediterranean Sea. From Micmethath on the north, the boundary curved eastward past Taanath-shiloh to the east of Janoah. From Janoah, it turned southward to Ataroth and Naarah, touched Jericho, and ended at the Jordan River. From Tappuah, the boundary extended westward, following the Kanah Ravine to the Mediterranean Sea. This is the homeland allocated to the clans of the tribe of Ephraim. In addition, some towns with their surrounding villages in the territory allocated to the half-tribe of Manasseh were set aside for the tribe of Ephraim. *However, they did not drive the Canaanites out of Gezer, so the people of Gezer live as slaves among the people of Ephraim to this day.*"

At the outset of this passage, we see the allotment of the land to Joseph's sons, Manasseh and Ephraim. In this chapter, we will look at the distribution of land to the Ephraimites. What is so interesting about this story is what's recorded at the end of the chapter. The Ephraimites desired the people of Gezer to be slaves for them, but did not attempt to force them out of the land as God requested. Think about this. They could have employed laborers among these people, but did not take the initiative to displace them from the land. And because they disobeyed God's original request, their paganistic traits tainted the ways of God's chosen ones for years and would have a domino effect for generations to come.

And here's the PowerPoint: The tribe of Ephraim certainly had the power to defeat them completely, mainly because Gezer was a city that Joshua had already conquered (Joshua 10:33 and Joshua 12:12). While this sort of compromise may seem innocent, it can also lead to the opening of more sinful acts. When the Israelites allowed pagan ways to dwell within their midst, they would eventually adopt and incorporate idolatry and immoral worship into their lives. And what happens over time is this: Chronic acts of sin will compound throughout the generations, where there is no trace of fruitfulness—unless someone severs the head of that six-headed beast![1]

As we will see in the case of the Israelites, they did not fully conquer the land God promised for two reasons. First, they wanted peace at any cost. Second, they wanted wealth. For the sake of *ease* and *money*, they disobeyed God and fell short of what He had in store for them, as we do today. What do I mean? The minds and hearts of today want more of their selfish desires, comfort zones, and worldly pleasures than the ways of God (like the Israelites and the Ephraimites). When this happens, we are not living fruitfully for our Lord, which leads us to be unproductive and useless (Once again, read the Parable of the Four Soils in Matthew chapter 13).

While Ephraim means "fruitful or productive," it is evident that their name would not bear the fruitfulness God planned. While these two tribes, Ephraim and Manasseh, received a substantial amount of land in the northern regions of Canaan, they eventually became two of the most powerful tribes in Israel. Especially during the time of the Judges, Ephraim is one of the strongest military tribes in the nation, but their godless lifestyle would lead to more fruitless behavior.

The tribe of Ephraim was chastised for idolatry (Hosea 4:17) and their partnership with wicked nations (Hosea 12:1). In time, they would be taken into captivity by the Assyrians in 722 BC when the northern kingdom of Israel was conquered. Even so, the Lord declared, "Is not Ephraim my dear son, the child in whom I delight? Though I often speak against him, I still

---

1. "Joshua 15, 16, 17. The Inheritance Judah, Ephraim and Western Manasseh."

Godless Fruit

remember him. Therefore, my heart yearns for him; I have great compassion for him" (Jeremiah 31:20).

For us today, even though we fall prey to the ways of a fruitless life at times (just like the tribe of Ephraim), the Heavenly Vine (our Lord) is ready to prune us in all His ways so we can produce a life of daily fruitfulness (John 15:1–17). We must never forget the purpose of pruning: God prunes us to remove those distractions and impurities so we can focus on the life He desires, and that's living a more fruitful life. Why? So we can spiritually grow and mature in ways like Christ. Always remember this key takeaway: God prunes us because He loves us and wants to shape us for His purpose, ensuring we can thrive spiritually for His glory.

I was reading an article in a well-known national column entitled "Fruit of a Godless Society," and saw some comments in the column from two of our Founding Fathers. Over two centuries ago, John Adams said: "We have no government armed with power capable of contending with human passions unbridled by morality and religion. Our Constitution was made only for moral and religious people. It is wholly inadequate to the government of any other." George Washington said, "Let us with caution indulge the supposition that morality can be maintained without religion. Religion and morality are the two great pillars of human happiness and indispensable to private and public felicity."

Sadly, we are no longer a nation of religious, moral, or virtuous values. People of strong religious convictions are often ridiculed and disdained as hypocrites or, at best, labeled dull-witted and backward. A man may think that eliminating God brings freedom, but as George Washington and John Adams warned and history corroborates, it only promotes unbridled passions, misery, and self-destruction. Keen observers of events should not be surprised. Why? Without fruitful living in our lives as a people and nation for our Holy Creator, there will be more acts of godlessness![2]

Since the beginning, God has always desired us to be fruitful and multiply. While many are single and have no children, God also intends us to be spiritually profitable. As followers of Jesus Christ, we all can have fruit-bearing lives, whether we have children or not. Indeed, we can be spiritually productive and multiply the citizens of the Kingdom of God when we obey Jesus' command and employ the Great Commission in our lives to "Go and make disciples of all nations" (Matthew 28:19).

Remember, as His devoted children, we're either living a life that is bearing fruit in ways that glorify God every day. Or we're living godless lives, which are 1) seedless—absent of the seed of Jesus Christ in our lives,

---

2. McKim. "Fruit of a Godless Society."

2) powerless—the Holy Spirit and word of God are not active in our lives, and 3) useless (we're spiritually immoral because we're internally empty). We cannot allow the darkness of this world and the enemy to deprive us of a fruitful life that our Heavenly Father desires. It is vital in our daily lives.

The Ephraimites struggled to learn of God's ways because, from the beginning, Ephraim turned away from God and did wicked things, as recorded in (Isaiah 28:1–3). But over time, we also find the tribe recognizing the need to repent and obey by following the prophet Oded's instructions (2 Chronicles 28:12). What a beautiful portrait, and it's this: When we enable the Holy Spirit to work out the Fruit of the Spirit in our lives, it separates us from the world and unto the One Whom we aim to please in our daily lives, bearing fruit that brings honor, praise, and glory to His Name and Kingdom! It's never too late to turn from a life of fruitlessness to one of more fruitfulness.

> 2 Pet 1:5–11," In view of all this, make every effort to respond to God's Promises. Supplement your faith with a generous provision of moral excellence, and moral excellence with knowledge, and knowledge with self-control, and self-control with patient endurance, and patient endurance with godliness, and godliness with brotherly affection, and brotherly affection with love for everyone."
>
> "The more you grow like this, the more productive and useful you will be in your knowledge of our Lord Jesus Christ. But those who fail to develop in this way are shortsighted or blind, forgetting that they have been cleansed from their old sins. So, dear brothers and sisters, work hard to prove that you really are among those God has called and chosen. Do these things, and you will never fall away. Then God will give you a grand entrance into the eternal Kingdom of our Lord and Savior Jesus Christ."

Chapter Seventeen

'Godly Assignment'

Josh 17:1-2, 12-18, "The next allotment of land was given to the half-tribe of Manasseh, the descendants of Joseph's older son. Makir, the firstborn son of Manasseh, was the father of Gilead. Because his descendants were experienced soldiers, the regions of Gilead and Bashan, located on the east side of the Jordan, had already been given to them. So, the allotment on the west side of the Jordan was for the remaining families within the clans of the tribe of Manasseh: Abiezer, Helek, Asriel, Shechem, Hepher, and Shemida. These clans represent the male descendants of Manasseh, son of Joseph."

"But the descendants of Manasseh were unable to occupy these towns because the Canaanites were determined to stay in that region. Later, however, when the Israelites became strong enough, they forced the Canaanites to work as slaves. But they did not drive them out of the land. The descendants of Joseph came to Joshua and asked, "Why have you given us only one portion of land as our homeland when the Lord has blessed us with so many people?"

"Joshua replied, "If there are so many of you, and if the hill country of Ephraim is not large enough for you, clear out land for yourselves in the forest where the Perizzites and Rephaites live." The descendants of Joseph responded, "It's true that the hill country is not large enough for us. But all the Canaanites in the lowlands have iron chariots, both those in Beth-shan and its surrounding settlements and those in the valley of Jezreel. They are too strong for us."

"Then Joshua said to the tribes of Ephraim and Manasseh, the descendants of Joseph, "Since you are so large and strong, you will be given more than one portion. The forests of the hill country will be yours as well. Clear as much of the land as you wish and take possession of its farthest corners. And you will drive out the Canaanites from the valleys, too, even though they are strong and have iron chariots."

As discussed earlier, Manasseh and Ephraim were large tribes; combined, they were greater than any other single tribe. However, they complained that they had not been allocated adequate land. You must love Joshua's words of wisdom. He tells them, "If you are a great people, then go and get the land for yourself; fully occupy what the LORD has given you."

These tribes had not yet completely taken possession of the mountain country within their allotted territory, as it would be hard and dangerous work. It was apparent that they did not want to make an effort to fulfill their duties to God. Manasseh and Ephraim seemed to be begging for more land but were afraid to drive out the wicked people in this pagan area. However, the great leader Joshua challenged them to prove their sincerity by clearing out the area God had allotted to them. They initially agreed—but failed to follow through on their godly assignment!

Did you notice the stark contrast of attitudes toward settling the Promised Land between Caleb and Joseph's sons (Manasseh and Ephraim)? Returning to chapter fifteen, we see Caleb accepted his lot graciously and moved forward to fulfill God's plan with zeal and boldness. What was the difference in their attitudes?

Caleb was confident that God would assist him in driving out the enemy, and he believed in his heart that God's provision and promise would stand true. Although Caleb's portion of land was nowhere near the size of Joseph's sons and as fertile and rich, he was thankful for that little amount God had given him. And in time, he would honor God and bless His Name by fulfilling God's request to push out the enemies.

However, Manasseh and Ephraim wanted more and the best of all the land. It's as if they expected it to be handed to them on a silver platter. In other words, they did not want to put in the effort. Instead of relying upon God's promises and going out and taking what He had given them, they complained about it. The same principle applies just as strongly to you and me today. If we desire more of something, we first should be humble, thankful, and content with God's blessings in our current state. We must pray and align our desires with God's purpose and plan. And in God's timing, if it's His will, He can open the door to more.

Please never forget this PowerPoint: If there is more work for us to do in fulfilling God's will, it is our assignment and responsibility to move

'Godly Assignment'

forward in honoring God with that task as His faithful servants. Why? Because it is part of His plan, and we should trust it! Example: Even with the Promised Land God had blessed the Israelites with, significant work remained. There were more battles to fight and territory to obtain in order to complete God's purpose for their lives.

Believers must realize that when God created us in His image, it was a gift to you and me for a reason, and we should be thankful for this life He has given us for the purpose of being His Living Sacrifice. We are all different in many ways, but we can bless and honor our Heavenly Father with faith as small as a mustard seed. He endowed us with a life that shares many of His divine characteristics, and that in itself is an honor and privilege that we should not take lightly.

No, we cannot measure up to the same standards as God. Still, He sent His Son, Jesus Christ, upon this earth as our example to follow to this very day. And He has given us His word and Spirit to show us His ways in living them out in our daily lives, such as Christlike love (agape), forgiveness, mercy, grace, service, worship, fellowship, praise, patience, kindness, righteousness, holiness, gentleness, goodness, and faithfulness. Please read 2 Peter 1.

Paul reminds us in chapter two of Philippians that we should have the same attitude as Jesus Christ daily. No matter where the Lord has positioned us, we can honor and bless Him right where we are. Our spiritual and godly assignment does not change just because our earthly assignment changes. Paul even tells us in his first epistle in the Corinthians that we must accept our lot in life, no matter how bad we think it is, and serve out our lives as His servants since we first became His children. The only thing that should have changed since we became followers of Jesus Christ is our maturity and sanctification, which is part of our spiritual growth stage. There should be more evidence of God's wisdom in our lives, allowing us to gain greater spiritual insight into His assigned plans that need to be fulfilled.

The entire letter of Philippians should be our roadmap for living out our godly assignment each day. This powerful letter to the Church of Philippi clearly shows us that Paul had a unique and beautiful relationship with this community of believers, the same kind of relationship we should have with God through Christ. Nestled in these powerful four chapters, we're challenged to 1) be firm students of the Gospel, hold to its truth and mature spiritually, 2) be His Citizens of Heaven on this earth, 3) exhibit joy as His servants in every area of our life (no matter the trials), 4) be cautious of evilness by living in His righteousness, 5) strive for unity through humility, 6) shine like bright lights for Christ, be imitators of Jesus, 7) believe with all your heart, soul and mind in the priceless gain of knowing Christ, 8) be gracious givers to the building of His Kingdom, 9) don't complain, argue, worry or be anxious about anything, but pray about everything. and 10) press on toward the eternal goal of Heaven. In other words, give it to Him, and through all the fires, be more Christlike in our everyday lives!

I love this article on John Piper's Desiring God site:

> "Your life is a *gift* and an *assignment* from God. This should infuse our life—its good and evil, its sweet and bitter, its health and affliction, its prosperity and poverty, its comfort and suffering—with an unfathomable dignity, purpose, and glory. You are not an accident. Neither are you a ruined potential, run off the rails because you were dealt a poor genetic hand of cards, suffered others' abuse, or made foolish and sinful choices, putting you beyond the hope of a useful calling in Jesus's kingdom."
>
> "No, you exist because God wanted you to exist. And you are *who* you are, *what* you are, *how* you are, *where* you are, and *when* you are because God made you (John 1:3). You were woven by the Creator in your mother's womb (Psalm 139:13). He called you to be his own (John 10:27; Roman 10:30), and assigned you a place to live (Acts 17:26). The greatest thing you can do with your life is to live to the hilt the adventurous assignment God has given you."[1]

Undoubtedly, many of us could make excuses about our current life circumstances and wish or hope for a life of peaches and cream. Most of us would love a life like walking in a blossoming strawberry field. However, to be more like Christ, we must endure suffering and persecution as He did. We will never go through as much as our Savior did—He went through more suffering in his last week of life on this earth than we all will go through in our entire lives.

But Christ knew He had the assignment to fulfill God's ultimate plan for you and me. It was not pleasurable in His flesh, full of more agony than you and I could ever fathom. But He had the power of God on His side. In his final days, He did not complain or murmur because, in it all, He knew His destiny was in the hands of His Father. And He completed His task with dignity, purpose, and meaning. It was finished! (Please read Isaiah 53.)

Christ was obliged to perform a task beyond my comprehension. By the authority of God, Jesus carried out His duty and Godly assignment for the will of His Father. His sole responsibility was unfathomable because it required a great deal of difficulty from a human perspective. But from God's perspective, it was the most important job or assignment of all time.

---

1. Bloom. "The Greatest Thing You Can Do with Your Life."

'Godly Assignment'

This one act saved our lives and gave us hope for today, tomorrow, and the future. Has your godly assignment of service given hope to that one person who may need it today? (1 Peter 3:18–22)

I believe the Lord is placing people in our life path on a weekly, if not daily, basis, where the Holy Spirit challenges us to reach out to them in our godly assignment for His glory. Trust me, many in this society and culture are aching, seeking, and searching for answers to fullness because there is a lot of emptiness and hopelessness in people's lives. In our zeal, confidence, and boldness, it is our duty and responsibility to share with them the Way, Truth, and Life according to the Bible. We are implored to use words of truth, grace, and love, not words that meet their fleshly comfort zone.

God is more concerned about how we carry out our daily jobs and assignments as His children on this earth. No matter the level of spiritual gifts we possess, whether one or many, He expects and commands you and me to voluntarily fulfill His daily, weekly, and lifetime plan and will. Why is this important? It demonstrates our complete obedience to His ways rather than man's. It shows our level of faith and loyalty to Him, which brings honor and glory to His Name.

> Eph 2:10, "For we are God's masterpiece. He has created us anew in Christ Jesus, so we can do the good things he planned for us long ago."
>
> 2 Cor 6:10, "Our hearts ache, but we always have joy. We are poor, but we give spiritual riches to others. We own nothing, and yet we have everything."

Chapter Eighteen

'Godly Assistance'

Josh 18:1-6, "Now that the land was under Israelite control, the entire community of Israel gathered at Shiloh and set up the Tabernacle. But there remained seven tribes who had not yet been allotted their grants of land. Then Joshua asked them, "How long are you going to wait before taking possession of the remaining land the Lord, the God of your ancestors, has given to you? Select three men from each tribe, and I will send them out to explore the land and map it out. They will then return to me with a written report of their proposed divisions of their new homeland. Let them divide the land into seven sections, excluding Judah's territory in the south and Joseph's territory in the north. And when you record the seven divisions of the land and bring them to me, I will cast sacred lots in the presence of the Lord our God to assign land to each tribe."

In this chapter, we could have easily written about the state of complacency or the path of least resistance among these seven tribes, as they were not adhering to God's plan to utilize what He had given them. As we see in this passage, the nation of Israel is in control of the land. By this time, the Canaanites in many places had become so weak that they were no longer a threat to the Israelites. However, these seven tribes still did not take the initiative when the opportunity presented itself to destroy the enemy. It was there and ready for the taking, and they still did not seize it when the time was right!

What was their problem, and why would they not want to possess their land? Why would Joshua need to nudge them to take their portion of the Promised Land? Probably because these were nomadic people who had

'Godly Assistance'

not lived in permanent dwellings for more than a generation, and they were afraid of something new, even if it was good. Perhaps they were reluctant to change and wanted to rely on these Canaanite people for their economic well-being. It could have been that they feared continued warfare and its detrimental effect on their tribe. Whatever the exact reason, the bottom line was neglect and disobedience. The bottom line is that they did not fulfill God's calling.[1]

Often in life, as mature believers and genuine followers of Jesus Christ, we must gently prod people to move them forward in their spiritual lives. This is vital because, in today's society and culture, too many people are becoming complacent or stuck in a spiritual rut and don't know how to rise above themselves and seize their blessed opportunities.

God did not create you and me to stay down and beaten to the point of helplessness, but to rise above the expectations of our earthly life and pursue the blessings He has in store for all of us. However, sometimes we need a spiritual boost to get our attention and press on in life. God wants to bless us because He takes pleasure in it. He even blesses us when we don't deserve it. However, it is essential to note that God blesses us when we obey Him and believe wholeheartedly in His ways. But He also blesses us when we're a witness to others because that blessing in our life can benefit others in glorious ways.

Remember, we have the power of God's word and the Holy Spirit as our Help and Guide. But sometimes, a solid and firm believer in Christ must step up and assist someone weaker in the faith because they need that spiritual steam of motivation! Joshua saw that these seven remaining tribes were not taking the necessary steps to possess their land of inheritance, so he had to nudge them.

In one of the most memorable passages in Isa 40:31, God's word reminds us, "Those who wait on the Lord will find new strength. They will fly high on wings like eagles. They will run and not grow weary. They will walk and not faint." No matter who you are, and you may think you're the strongest Christian in the world, there will come a time when we are loaded with heavy burdens and feel so weary that we spiritually faint.

But Almighty God has the power and ability to strengthen us because He is our Source for everything in life. We may feel lonely, hopeless, and crushed beyond all measure, but God can lift us up and renew our strength. However, as His children, we must come to the aid of someone who may be in a dire situation. Why? It strengthens our Christian life, elevates our

---

1. "Joshua 18,19. Inheritance of the Remaining Tribes."

testimony and cause for Christ, and demonstrates the Fruit of the Spirit in our lives. But most importantly, it honors and pleases our Heavenly Father!

Throughout Scripture, numerous verses challenge the mature Christian to assist those who are weaker in their faith. However, instead of helping or coming to the aid of another brother or sister in Christ, we often find ourselves being more judgmental, cynical, narrow-minded, critical, and selfish. When we allow the enemy to plant these barriers in our lives, they will always prevent us from assisting that one person in a situation that could be a matter of life or death. What is holding us back from helping or encouraging others?

This leads me to ponder: Are there some spiritual obstacles that may prevent Christians from assisting others? Perhaps it's a need for greater Christ-like humility, selflessness, and love. Could it be that we lack genuine care and passion for others because we are more focused on and concerned about what this level of assistance will bring into our lives? (Seriously, think about that.) Perhaps we hesitate to assist others because we fear it might involve a personal connection in that person's life. We shy away because that one person may possess a lot of emotional baggage, and we don't want to have any part of that in our daily lives.

Unfortunately, when we adopt a mindset and heart like this, there is no genuine, Christlike willingness or earnestness to assist others who may genuinely need help. It seems that some Christians don't want to incorporate the challenge of coming to the aid of others because it may cross their boundaries of physical, intellectual, social & cultural standards and racial attachments.

Sadly, it may even put them in a position to share their faith, forcing them to step out of their comfort zone. It's as if they are ashamed of the Gospel or have no intention of honoring God's word and command. Servants of Christ must understand this: "Real Christlike humility, selflessness, and love will take you from a fleshly comfort zone to the realm of His empowering Grace, once we completely surrender and submit our lives to Him. And when we do this, the spiritual blessings are unimaginable!"

Jesus reminds us in Matt 25:37–46 of these powerful words that should scare the spiritual jeepers-creepers out of us, "Then these righteous ones will reply, 'Lord, when did we ever see you hungry and feed you? Or thirsty and give you something to drink? Or a stranger and show you hospitality? Or naked and give you clothing? When did we ever see you sick or in prison and visit you?' "And the King will say, 'I tell you the truth, when you did it to one of the least of these, my brothers and sisters, you were doing it to me!'

"Then the King will turn to those on the left and say, 'Away with you, you cursed ones, into the eternal fire prepared for the devil and his demons.

'Godly Assistance'

For I was hungry, and you didn't feed me. I was thirsty, and you didn't give me a drink. I was a stranger, and you didn't invite me into your home. I was naked, and you didn't give me clothing. I was sick and in prison, and you didn't visit me.' "Then they will reply, 'Lord, when did we ever see you hungry or thirsty or a stranger or naked or sick or in prison, and not help you?' "And he will answer, 'I tell you the truth, when you refused to help the least of these my brothers and sisters, you were refusing to help me.' "And they will go away into eternal punishment, but the righteous will go into eternal life."

Nestled in this passage, we see Christ's challenge to our acts of mercy towards others. It does not depend on riches, our ability, or intellect, but these are Christlike acts that we voluntarily and freely give to others. When we respond in this way, it powerfully demonstrates that the work of the Holy Spirit is alive in us, and we're not holding back; it's as if it's second nature. This is not just a church thing; it's a personal involvement and engagement in the lives of others. It illustrates that we're willing to share the same blessings, grace, mercy, and love that God has abounded in our lives with others. And it's all for His glory and praise!

1 Thess 4:14, "Brothers and sisters, we urge you to warn those who are lazy. Encourage those who are timid. Take tender care of those who are weak. Be patient with everyone."

Always remember this idiom: "Sharing is Caring."

Chapter Nineteen

'Godly Honor'

Josh 19:49–51, "After all the land was divided among the tribes, the Israelites gave a piece of land to Joshua as his allocation. For the LORD had said, he could have any town he wanted. He chose Timnath-serah in the hill country of Ephraim. He rebuilt the town and made it his home. These are the territories that Eleazar the priest, Joshua son of Nun, and the tribal leaders allocated as grants of land to the tribes of Israel by casting sacred lots in the presence of the LORD at the entrance of the Tabernacle at Shiloh. So, the division of the land was completed."

This chapter will be lengthy, but it offers profound teachings that parallel many lessons derived from the allotment of the land of Canaan to the nation of Israel, and how these lessons can apply to our lives today. You see, the distribution of the promised land is a significant event in biblical history, particularly in the context of the Christian faith.

It is a fulfillment of God's promise to Abraham and his descendants, as recorded in the book of Genesis, which remains relevant today. This event is a pivotal moment in the Bible, exemplifying the establishment of the nation of Israel and the beginning of their covenantal relationship with God. By the time we reach the end of this chapter, we will have seen compelling comparisons that are relevant to us today.

In this chapter, we see where the remaining tribes received their inheritance of the Promised Land. Now, all of God's children within the nation have been allocated their respective land. What will they do next? Will they honor God by fulfilling His requests and demands, or operate their blessings from God in their own way? Would they become so complacent and content in their current state of affairs that they would forget what God desired and required of them, by taking the rest of the land He had given them, which could be passed down to their future generations?

As noted, the distribution of the land was a significant point for the nation of Israel because it would determine whether God's chosen people would trust and obey His guiding principles or not (just like us today). But just as important, it would signify that His children were honoring God's holy bond with Him, which is enormous! You see, the distribution of land is of immense importance. How?

It symbolizes God's covenant with His chosen people, their inheritance, and their relationship with God, as well as with one another. The land was a gift (just like faith to you and me today). Each tribe was given a specific portion, reflecting their role and history within the nation and how they would handle their godly responsibilities. This distribution also underscores the idea of fairness and the process of Yahweh's divine order, ensuring that each tribe received their rightful share according to God Almighty, not man.

Many would ask: Why didn't God unite all the nations within the land? Let's look at some of the reasons why God outlined their land proportionately by tribe. However, as we examine some of these points below, we can all discern an underlying message in these truths that applies to our lives as Christians today. These are some profound parallels that could be life-applicable and honoring to our Heavenly Father when we incorporate these PowerPoints into our daily lives.

1. God established boundaries within each tribe to develop "personal ownership of God's blessings." It would require absolute devotion to God's ways within their own community while promoting accountability, loyalty, and unity. If obedient, their wholehearted commitment to God's commands would foster their spiritual maturity, which would in turn honor Yahweh.

    a. Each of God's children (you and I) has unique, personal, and blessed gifts and talents as followers of Christ. When we enforce them for God's glory, they show our dedication and loyalty to our Holy Creator, and this level of commitment fosters unity within the body of Christ (Read Ephesians 4). This is critical because when we employ our God-given gifts daily, it depicts our personal relationship with God through Jesus Christ, and this powerfully portrays Who truly owns us. Remember what God's word tells us in Luke 16:10. When we are responsible for little, He will give us more. "If you are faithful in little things, you will be faithful in large ones. But you won't be honest with greater responsibilities if you are dishonest in little things." This is important in our spiritual growth stage because when we utilize our gifts to their fullest for His Kingdom, it honors our Lord and God! (Please read Romans 12:6, 1 Corinthians 12:4–11, 1 Timothy 4:14, and 1 Pet 4:10–11).

2. Each tribe developed its own culture, so distributing the land accordingly would prevent conflicts within the entire nation; it was a means of establishing stable control in their lives. So, God separated them to create a state of normalcy and prevent internal conflicts, division, civil wars, and oppression. Can you imagine the disputes and fights amongst the tribes for the best land available if they were all together? Undoubtedly, God knew what He was doing, and it was for their good. He desired each of His tribes to focus on their portion of His blessings, be content and faithful, and be accountable children of God.

   a. As God's children and followers of Jesus Christ, it is imperative that we develop a community of steadfast believers within our sphere, encompassing Christlike unity and love. We need to be cautious in mingling with the world's unbelieving ways, which can create a great divide between the Lord and us (like the Israelites did). Always remember that we cannot serve two masters (Matt. 6:24), and we're either serving the flesh or the Spirit (Galatians 5 and Romans 8). *Never forget this: When we mix with the wrong groups and blend in with their lifestyle that is spiritually unhealthy, we dishonor our Lord!*

3. The boundaries in the land of Canaan fulfilled the promised inheritance of each tribe, going back to the days of Abraham, Isaac, and Jacob as recorded in Genesis. God told Abraham that he would be the father of many nations. The key takeaway is this: It validates and solidifies the power of God's promises, provisions, faithfulness to His people, and the truths of His word—yesterday, today, and the future. When God's nation witnessed His promises coming to reality before their very eyes, it should have enticed them to be more faithful and obedient to all His ways.

   a. When God's word and promises come to fruition in our lives, it should encourage and motivate us to follow our Lord and God with more commitment for today and the future! The truths of

'Godly Honor'

His word should give us great boldness and confidence in our Promised Hope for the future— (Isa 40:31, Deut 31:8, Isa 43:2, 2 Cor 1:3-4, 2 Cor 3:7-18). Remember: Living out our Living Hope (Christ) and genuine saving faith enveloped in our love for the Lord pleases and honors God our Father!

4. These established boundaries were set forth to promote obedience to God. Yahweh required that, after He had given them their inheritance, they should fulfill His request and commands by forcing out the enemies and all acts of evil within their territory. Their obedience or lack thereof would be the tell-tale sign of their devout ways as His entrusted children.

   a. Today and the rest of our days on this earth, God desires His children to bless and honor Him by obeying the truths of His word! Jesus Christ reminds us in John 14:15, "If you love Me, keep my commandments." Obeying our Lord according to His holy word, guided by His Spirit, springs forth a life of holiness and righteousness that honors Him! When we rid ourselves of those old ways of unholiness, it illustrates our steadfast devotion to our Heavenly Father!

5. The distribution of the Promised Land by tribe denotes that God can show favor to His children, based on His *sovereign choosing* (Ps 5:12, Prov 3:4, and Rom 9:18). It depicts that He will bless them, in His perfect timing and according to His purpose and plan. But through these blessings, Yahweh expected His children to bless Him through their faithfulness and obedience.

   a. As God's chosen ones today, when our Heavenly Father shows His favor on us and blesses us even with those little things in life, we should reciprocate (return) that blessing to Him with praise and thanksgiving (like a sweet aroma of sincere gratitude before His throne). We must count all the blessings He's showered upon our lives, no matter the size (big or small). We should remember that God also expects us to bless others because it honors our Lord when we bless others through the blessings He has bestowed upon us (Philippians 2, Matt. 5:16, Phil. 2:3-4, 2 Cor. 9:8-11, Prov. 11:25, 1 Pet. 3:9). This is important because it demonstrates our genuine faith, obedience, and love for Him and others.

6. The land was distributed fairly *because God allotted it, which demonstrates that He has complete authority and control in all that He does.*

But in doing this, God shows us, as His children, that when we do things fairly (in His eyes), we can eliminate envy and jealousy when we lean upon His guiding principles. *Can you imagine the levels of envy and jealousy running rampant within the nations of Israel when one obtained more territory than the other?*

    a. We all know that envy is one of those detestable sins in the eyes of God (Prov 6:16–19). Envy and jealousy are unpleasant emotions that can be harmful to our mental and spiritual health. When we envy others, we focus on what we lack rather than what we have, which can lead to feelings of inadequacy and ultimately consume our lives with selfish desires. When this happens, it will prevent us from being content with the blessings God has placed in our current lives. These two unspiritual detriments can also create tension and conflict in our personal relationships, which can lead to hatred, covetousness, and a distance from God's purpose and plan. Remember: *Righteous actions will spring forth when the heart is right with God* (Matt 15:19; 1 Pet 1:22). We must never forget that our human behavior should always align with God's divine nature and characteristics, as well as His ultimate plan.

7. It minimized their travel and enabled them to focus on the needs of their own people and the care of their respective lands.

    a. So often, when we have too much on our plates, we can lose sight of God's will and drift away from His plan. Our thoughts and hearts can easily get distorted when we're too caught up in the busyness of life and not focused on God's business of taking care of ourselves and others for His glory—(Col chapter 3).

8. God expected the nation of Israel to choose and follow His plans and be His channel of holiness to the other nations. He did not want them to get caught up in their own selfish desires, so Yahweh established numerous guidelines of holiness for His children, enabling them to set their hearts and minds on His ways. He did this because He knew that there was a lot of prevailing evil amongst them and He wanted their undivided attention toward His guiding ways. Undoubtedly, God did everything possible to prevent the Israelites from complete rebellion and disobedience so they could fulfill His plan of possessing their blessed inheritance. However, despite all their shortcomings, God was not done with His people. He planned to bring his children back into His presence by giving them the land of Canaan

'Godly Honor'

(please read Hosea 11). However, it ultimately comes down to their choice to trust and obey His ways *or not*.

- a. Even today, humans rebel against God and turn away from the blessed life He has in store for them. Sadly, man chooses a life that embraces death and his own definition of good and evil. Instead of choosing the blessings and prosperity of God's inheritance of eternal life (through Christ), they allow sin to dominate their lives, leading to curses and disaster (Please read Deuteronomy 30). He gives us all a choice to follow Him or not right now, today. You see, the land of Canaan is a symbol of God's provision, rest, and blessing for His chosen nation. For us today, this is a foreshadowing of our ultimate inheritance of Heaven and the spiritual rest and everlasting peace that can only be found in Jesus Christ.

9. The Almighty One commanded each tribe to manage the people within their community by this critical guide: "God as their King, not man." If they obeyed God's commands, there would be unity and respect within their own group of people. However, if each tribe strayed away from God's regulations, chaos, confusion, and disorder would indeed exist. The PowerPoint is this: As noted earlier, if Israel remained holy within their own community of people, honoring God's commands, they would have a better chance of living in a state of godly unity. And make no mistake: If God were being honored to the fullest in one tribe or nation, that news would eventually spread to the other nations, which could surely have an impact on honoring Yahweh abroad.

    - a. In our modern-day government, there is apparent friction and division among people. The reason for this disorder is a failure to honor God's commands and means of holiness. With this lack of honor and respect for God's word, we see the escalation of evil and the state of a reprobate mind. This will lead many to an absolute eviction and separation from the presence of God—(Rom 6:23, Gal 5:19–21, Jas 4:17). When there is no foundation of honoring God and all His ways, there will never be an abundance of His blessings, spiritual discipline, godly structure, peace, and unity. If we want to experience blessings from God, sustain a spiritually disciplined and structured life, and live in His peace and harmony, it's simple: Allow Jesus Christ to be the Lord of your life, for this honors God! Also read Acts 17:26–28.

10. The new Promised Land was a symbol of God's presence amongst them. This new land would be a place where God's company, closeness, and blessings would be felt. It would be a place: a) Where the Israelites could worship and serve their God alone. b) Teach all the wondrous things they had witnessed by the hand of God that could be passed down to future generations. c) There would be relief from their wandering years, and now they could enjoy God's provisions and refuge of peace, comfort, and joy. d) Where God's truth and the fulfillment of His covenant could be experienced and shared with other nations. e) It would serve as a means of protection from oppression. If His children would trust and obey Yahweh, He would protect them from the idolatry and oppression prevalent in the surrounding nations. f) And lastly, it would be that place where they can show wholehearted loyalty to the Almighty through their faith, trust, and obedience in all His ways!

    a. Think about the profound points above that parallel our lives today, as we prepare for our Promised Land! Right now, do you know that God wants to dwell with you and me through the power of His Word and Spirit, so He can continue to stay connected with us. And when we are in His presence, He can counsel, comfort, correct, and communicate with us so that He can reassure us of our blessed future? He wants to provide for us, protect us from all evil, and preserve us for that glorious day! He desires for us to experience His peace, joy, and comfort in this life. He wants us to worship and fellowship with Him, and serve Him in our everyday lives with a genuine, humble, and selfless heart. However, this all hinges upon our faith in His Son, Jesus Christ, which will depict our complete trust and obedience in all His ways.

11. The distribution of the land was also a means of establishing a holy nation that would identify God's chosen ones as being His light of holiness to the other nations. As His children, Yahweh wanted them to demonstrate their real relationship with the one true God and a life of His righteousness. But just as important, God's choice of Israel was a means of ushering in a new society that would represent God's greatness and goodness that could be passed down from one generation to another.

    a. Christians are called to be the light of the world in a society and culture that is darkened by sin. It is our high calling today, as followers of Christ and His chosen royal priesthood (1 Peter 2:9), to guide a world that has lost its way. This calling from our Lord and God extends to us, which requires us to live out our genuine saving faith by both doing good deeds and exposing the darkness of deception and half-truths. The light of Jesus Christ brings forth truth and hope, drawing people closer to Him and away from the errors of man and this world (Matt 5:14–16). As Christians, we have the privilege and responsibility to share this Light, leading others out of the darkness and toward the "light of life."

12. The bottom line is this: In His distribution of the land proportionally, it was 'God's will.' The will of God is His blueprint and master plan for His creation, encompassing all things under His sovereign control. In all His divine power, He will deploy His purpose and plan over nations and individuals that will ultimately characterize His will. In other words, as noted earlier, "Our God does whatever pleases Him." In all His doings, God Almighty is the Initiator in executing a grand plan involving events that make up human history. He has laid the course of events for His purpose and plan, and in the end, He will be glorified and honored.

   a. God's will for you and me is to accept Christ as the Savior and Lord of our lives, striving for righteousness and holiness. When we do this wholeheartedly, we honor God in every area of our lives. He wants us to be joyful and thankful, regardless of our life circumstances. Like the Israelites, He wants to walk with us, stay in His presence, surrender and submit to His purpose and plan, pay attention to Scripture, apply it to our lives, and obey His Word. As His children, He wants us to heed the guidance of the Holy Spirit and exemplify Christlikeness daily.

While some of these may sound repetitive to you, they touch on key points in various ways. If you look at some of these areas, you'll find they're life-applicable to our current lives. Doing so will demonstrate our genuine pursuit of God's holiness while honoring our Lord in all our daily activities. Setting aside self and striving for His godly characteristics exemplifies a humble, faithful, obedient, trusted, and loving servant. And if God's children are pursuing His divine Holiness, they will show Honor to Him in all areas of their lives. It will surely depict an attitude of undeniable Christlike Humility!

I love how this chapter ends with Joshua, the great, faithful, and humble leader, receiving his portion of the land, not first, but last. He never went to God and asked for his portion of the land first because of his role as a leader. He knew Yahweh's plan and purpose for His children and wanted to serve God's will first and foremost, which honored his Lord. Joshua embodied selflessness and humility to the fullest. He was more concerned about God's plan first and then caring for His children.

This kind of godly service and concern for others paints Joshua as a remarkable portrait of Jesus Christ. When a servant is faithful to God, striving for His holiness, and honoring Him in all they say and do, they show absolute reverence and respect for Almighty Yahweh. This type of person signifies a loving follower of God who is devoted to His interests. Our Creator desires us to possess the same kind of heart David did, and that's a person after God's own heart!

Honor means to *demonstrate high respect or great esteem for someone. By honoring another, you are saying you see great value in them and what they offer.* So, if you put this description into its proper theological perspective, when we disobey God's word and grieve the Holy Spirit, we show no value to the One Who created you and me for a purpose and plan. Remember, we do not praise God as Christians out of a sense of duty or to gain His favor. Instead, it expresses our authentic recognition, respect, and gratitude towards the One who loved us when we were sinners and His enemy.

To honor God means, first and foremost. In other words, we recognize Him as the highest authority in Heaven and on Earth. He is the One who created the universe, from the largest planet to the tiniest grain of sand, and no person, power, spirit, or force can contend with His greatness and might. We can honor God with our time, prayers, actions, tithes, offerings, thoughts and attitudes, hearts, words, service, worship, thanksgiving, and praise, as well as our bodies. The bottom line is that it should be our entire life. (Rom chapter 12).

And yes, we can honor God in our homes as parents, in our neighborhoods, workplaces, churches, schools, on the streets, in our marriages, and our fellowship with other believers, as well as in our respect for authority and leaders in the church and government. When it comes to our schools, churches, and government, it is essential to honor them *when their actions align with the truths of Scripture.*

We honor God by obeying our parents and helping the elderly, the poor, and the needy. In everything we do in words and deeds, we can glorify our Heavenly Father. But most importantly, we cannot honor God if we're not honoring Christ as the Lord of our lives. This is crucial because when we honor Jesus, we obey God's word and are faithful and true to Him. Look at this way: When we model the One (Christ) in our daily lives, through the guidance of His Spirit and word, it will surely honor our Holy Creator.

'Godly Honor'

Why is godly honor so important? Because this glorifies, exalts, and magnifies God our Father above all things. One of the many truths of the Kingdom of God is that if we honor God, He will honor us. If we dare to disrespect Him, we will also be treated as the least in His kingdom. Who would flirt with the threshold of dishonoring or defaming our Lord and God? Never forget what Christ tells us in Matt 10: 32–33, "Everyone who acknowledges me publicly here on earth, I will also acknowledge before my Father in heaven. But everyone who denies me here on earth, I will also deny before my Father in heaven."

We are stepping onto dangerous ground *when we dare not claim* His prescriptive acts of holiness in our daily lives. We cannot forget what the great apostle Paul tells us in 2 Timothy 1:9: "We were saved and called to live a holy life." And the author of Hebrews also reminds us in Hebrews 12:14, "Work at living in peace with everyone, and work at living a holy life, for those who are not holy will not see the Lord." Living a life of holiness honors God by reflecting His most divine characteristics and values in every aspect of life. When we live by this standard, it demonstrates the presence of God in our lives. And this is precisely what God expected of His children thousands of years ago when they entered their Promised Land.

Once again, we're talking about perfection, but a life that reflects a continuous flow of godliness, which in turn honors God. With that, the initiative and proper steps rest with you and me today, for our choice to honor Him will rely upon His entrusted ones. Think about this PowerPoint: *Our response to God determines His response to us*. Ponder these powerful passages below and ensure you honor God and our Lord first in every part of your lives!

1 Sam 2:30, "Therefore, the Lord, the God of Israel, says: I promised that your branch of the tribe of Levi would always be my priests. *But I will honor those who honor me, and I will despise those who think lightly of me*."

John 12:26 says, "Anyone who wants to serve me must follow me because my servants must be where I am. *And the Father will honor anyone who serves me.*"

1 Pet 2:15–17, "It is God's will that your honorable lives should silence those ignorant people who make foolish accusations against you. For you are free, yet you are God's slaves, so don't use your freedom as an excuse to do evil. Respect everyone, and love the family of believers. Fear God, and respect the king."

Chapter Twenty

'Godly Seeker'

Josh 20:1-3, "The Lord said to Joshua, "Now tell the Israelites to designate the cities of refuge, as I instructed Moses. Anyone who kills another person accidentally and unintentionally can run to one of these cities; they will be places of refuge from relatives seeking revenge for the person who was killed. Upon reaching one of these cities, the one who caused the death will appear before the elders at the city gate and present his case. They must allow him to enter the city and give him a place to live among them. If the relatives of the victim come to avenge the killing, the leaders must not release the slayer to them, for he killed the other person unintentionally and without previous hostility. But the slayer must stay in that city and be tried by the local assembly, which will render a judgment. And he must continue to live in that city until the death of the high priest who was in office at the time of the accident. After that, he is free to return to his own home in the town from which he fled."

Israel is a new nation in a new land, so it would need a new means of governing the people. God set the precedent earlier with Moses on how this new government should be set up and operated. The key was this: It had to align with God's design and purpose. If it functioned any other way, outside of God's commissioned plan, calamity, disorder, and malfunction would surely rise.

God wanted the Israelites to implement a specific responsibility once they entered the new Promised Land, and it was to designate certain cities as "cities of refuge." They were to be scattered throughout the new land with the primary purpose of preventing injustice, especially in the case of revenge. God assigned his exceptional leaders, the Levites, to be in charge

'Godly Seeker'

of these cities, as they were the most responsible tribe among the others in the nation. God knew that the Levites, as His appointed leaders, would follow the details of His principles of justice and fairness amongst the people. But here was the key: These cities of refuge were for people who committed unintentional murder. They were to protect someone in the case of manslaughter instead of murder.

God needed to assign the right leaders to represent His guiding principles. The Levites, as God's priests in the nation, had experience dealing with God's children. Over time, the nation came to trust the Levites as its advisors. Undoubtedly, they would be the most suitable and impartial judges because they looked out for the best interests of God's commands and regulations, not man. Their presence and godly counsel amongst the people might even restrain the stormy passions of the "avenger of blood." You see, the Levites served as mediators between the Israelites and God. As such, they would have been gifted by Yahweh to calmly mediate between the attacker and the victim's family, ensuring no further bloodshed would occur.[1]

This was important because such a person needed protection against the "avenger of blood." You may ask, who is an avenger of blood? The Avenger of Blood is typically the nearest male relative of a person who has been unlawfully killed. This individual, often referred to as the "go'el," has the responsibility to ensure justice is served for the shedding of innocent blood, which may include avenging the murder by slaying the murderer if found outside a city of refuge. But it's important to note that while the person who unintentionally killed someone, God was passionate about ensuring that murderers were punished in ancient Israel. Why? Because God said in Numbers 35: 31–34 that unpunished murderers defiled the land.

God's word says in this passage, "Also, you must never accept a ransom payment for the life of someone judged guilty of murder and subject to execution; murderers must always be put to death. And never accept a ransom payment from someone who has fled to a city of refuge, allowing a slayer to return to his property before the death of the high priest. This will ensure that the land where you live will not be polluted, for murder pollutes the land. And no sacrifice except the execution of the murderer can purify the land from murder. You must not defile the land where you live, for I live there myself. I am the Lord, who lives among the people of Israel."

It is important to note that God laid out a plan to assist those who committed acts of killing unintentionally. However, intentional acts of murder were never accepted in the eyes of God because they tainted the

---

1. "What were the Cities of Refuge in the Old Testament?"

land with evil. So, when someone needed God's assistance, fleeing from an avenger of blood and *seeking a city of refuge*, he told his case to the elders at the city gates. After explaining the case, the fleeing person could expect to find protection within the walls of the city of refuge, provided they remained there and lived in the town to enjoy that protection.

To be protected against the avenger of blood, the slayer had to remain within that city until the proper authorities fully heard his case and until the death of the standing high priest. After being declared innocent of murder by the appropriate authorities and after the death of the standing high priest, the slayer could return to his home and be protected against the wrath of the avenger of blood.[2] Seeking a city of refuge indicates protection from retribution, where individuals would be granted justice and a fair trial. These cities of refuge symbolize God's mercy and grace for anyone who seeks His protection!

What a beautiful portrait these cities paint for you and me in what we possess in Jesus Christ, in whom sinners find shelter from the destroyer (Satan) of our souls. Just as a person could seek refuge in the cities set up for that purpose, we flee to Christ for shelter (Hebrews 6:18). We run to Christ to escape the condemnation of the law, the wrath of God, and from eternity in hell, for only Christ provides refuge from these things.

Seeking Jesus Christ is where we can find our place of comfort and safety, embrace His protection and provision, find strength in Him, and trust in God's sovereignty. Just as the cities were open to all who fled to them for safety, Christ provides you and me security to all who come to Him for refuge from sin and its eternal punishment. However, it does require two significant steps: repentance for your sins and faith in Christ (Please read Romans 10: 8–13).

Today, do we, as Christians, really see the value of seeking our Refuge in life? After all, He is the only One Who can provide us with eternal security from the extensive dangers around us. In our most profound times of distress, there is a place where we can go for complete spiritual protection and rest. This is vital because the trials, temptations, and storms of life that confront us daily can easily entangle us emotionally, mentally, and spiritually, causing us to stray from God's protection, provision, and promises.

Undoubtedly, every believer has struggled beyond all measures at one point in life. With the rise of wickedness and corruption all around us, we need a spiritual outlet where we can run to and escape the evil that has become so prevalent in this society and culture. Make no mistake, in our

---

2. Joshua 20. "The Cities of Refuge."

lowest despairs and disheartenments, we all need a path in life where we can escape, break free, and find the retreat and peace of our Lord.

We need to remember what Jesus tells us in Matt 11:28–30, "Come to me, all of you who are weary and carry heavy burdens, and I will give you rest." In Matt 6:33, "Seek the Kingdom of God above all else, and live righteously, and he will give you everything you need." This verse invites you and me to live with a sense of purpose, trust in our Lord's guidance, and walk in obedience to His will. By seeking the kingdom of God, our needs will be met and our souls will find true satisfaction and contentment. But regrettably, many are so enwrapped in the busyness of life that they so easily forget there is One Who is always there, ready to help the most willing and humble person.

With that, you could say that we could easily define five groups of people in today's society. Sadly, just like the Parable of the Four Soils, it seems that only one is seeking God and the Lord with all their hearts, minds, souls, and strength. Here's the breakdown:

1. The genuine believers who constantly seek God for help, refuge, and strength. They are devout in their faith, trust, love, and obedience, and embody humility and the elements of the Fruit of the Spirit (Gal 5:22–23). They know that God and Christ, our Lord, and the Holy Spirit is their Primary Source for all things!

2. Regrettably, there are those believers who are stagnant and don't move with the Lord or seek Him because they are stuck in their comfort zone of the flesh and consumed with their worldly desires. The main problem with stagnant Christians is that they are full of self-pride and possess no spiritual intentions. Until they let go of self and the things of this world, they will never move from the flesh and seek God! Why? Because they want to taste more of the world than God's goodness. Bad mistake! *John 15:4 reminds us that a branch cannot bear fruit without the Lord!*

3. Unfortunately, some people seek God on a need-to-know basis or *when they need Him the most*. It's based more on their terms and personal agenda rather than God's divine timetable.

    a. They are half-hearted seekers (part-timers) and not wholehearted in their pursuit of God's guiding ways. Many would call them lukewarm believers. In other words, they are *not all in* for the Lord. *Luke 16:11–12 tells us that if a person is not faithful in little, they will not be faithful in much!*

4. Sadly, some don't know how to seek a God of Refuge. They want to run to Him, but seem confused about the right direction to take in connecting with Him. This is because they are immature in their faith, trust, and obedience, and are not growing biblically. *They are more spiritually blind than clear-sighted by the ways of God!*

    a. The key issue here is that these individuals often become easily overwhelmed by the numerous obstacles in their daily lives and struggle to cope with them. The only way to overcome this is by continually seeking God through prayer and searching for answers in His Holy Word, guided by the Holy Spirit. *Jesus tells us in Luke 6:46-49 that people claim to call Him Lord but don't do what He says. He reminds us in this powerful passage that we must build our foundation of Christianity on the truths of the Bible, not just bits and pieces.*

5. Lastly, and tragically, some run from God. They don't seek His help and even want His guidance or presence in their lives.

    a. These people are lost and full of darkness and possess no light of the Truth. They are consumed with the world's way of "living life" their own way.

In Psalm chapter 10:1-6, the psalmist reminds us, "O Lord, why do you stand so far away? Why do you hide when I am in trouble? The wicked arrogantly hunt down the poor. Let them be caught in the evil they plan for others. For they brag about their evil desires; they praise the greedy and curse the Lord. *The wicked are too proud to seek God.* They seem to think that God is dead. Yet, they succeed in everything they do. They do not see your punishment awaiting them. They sneer at all their enemies. They think, "Nothing bad will ever happen to us! We will be free of trouble forever!"

Never forget this key takeaway: As firm believers in Christ alone, when we seek God's counseling and guidance for all things in life and yearn to dwell in His presence, our eternal life is secured through His Son. Yes, it's easy to fix our hearts and minds on the wrong things in life. That is why God wants us to continually seek Him through His word and rest in His *Blessed Assurances*, for He will provide and protect us as His children. When we do this, we will all discover that our Heavenly Father and Lord will always be there for us. However!

God never promised us that our lives on this earth would be smooth sailing. Yes, we will face fear, loneliness, anger, grief, loss, sadness, rejection, depression, or any other emotion or circumstance that can pull us away from God's plans. However, when we seek God first, we remain focused on His eternal purposes. When we find ourselves too caught up in the emotions of worldly things and not Godly things, the bottom-line issue is our Trust in God.

This is going to be a gut punch for many of us. When we don't trust in God's Promises, Protection, and Provisions, we can lose hope, peace, joy, and comfort in His word. It can damage our faith, obedience, and genuine love. It can create an ill spirit that is detrimental in many ways because we're not sincere, godly seekers who are not grounded students of His holy word. All scriptures help us to diagnose the rights and wrongs in life. His word counsels us with the guidance of His Spirit to all truths that enable us to see things through God's eyes, not man's. (2 Tim 3:16–17)

The significant obstacle to seeking the Lord first and foremost is pride. "In the *pride* of his face, the wicked does *not seek* him," as we saw in Psalm 10:4. Therefore, humility is essential to seeking the Lord. The great promise to those who seek the Lord is that He will be found. This is key because the power of seeking and finding God lies in a quest that can lead to a deeper faith, trust, love, obedience, peace, joy, and purpose in our lives.

God's word assures us that He is not far from us and that we can take steps to deepen our relationship with Him if we're willing to listen and understand His ways. We can cultivate this relationship through prayer, worship, and reading His word, but most importantly, putting it into practice. Never forget that our Loving, Merciful, and Gracious God and Lord is always near, waiting for us to reach out and engage with Him.

God's word reminds us in 1 Chronicles 28:9, "For the Lord sees every heart and knows every plan and thought. If you seek him, you will find him. But if you forsake him, he will reject you forever." And here's a great promise for you and me today: When we draw near Him and find Him, there is a great reward for those who rest in His eternal protection, which is in Jesus Christ. And when we have Him, we have everything we need in life, and we don't need anything from this world. Therefore, "Seek the Lord and his strength so you can dwell in his presence continually*!*"[3]

One of the most memorable passages in the Bible is in Psalm 46. The psalmist reminds us that God is our refuge and strength, always ready to help in times of trouble, and we do not need to fear. Because He is an ever-present help in trouble, those who belong to Him can commit their way to Him, take rest, and possess His peace, comfort, and joy.

Even if the world ends, a godly seeker of God's grace, love, and faith in Jesus Christ is safe from harm (Please read Romans 8:31–39)! God is

---

3. Piper. "What Does it Mean to Seek the Lord?"

reassuring you and me today, and it's this: a) 'Be still and know that I am your God (Ps 46:10)', b) 'Trust Me in all things (Prov 3:5-6)', c) 'Believe in My word and promises (2 Cor 1:20)', d) 'If you love Me, then Obey My Word (John 14:15)', e) Seek Me for all things in life 9Jer 29:13).' Isaiah 55:6 reminds us, Seek the Lord while you can find him. Call on him now while he is near." Time is of the essence for everyone today before it's too late!

Look at the table below, which clearly contrasts a godly seeker versus a seeker of this world or man. Conduct a genuine examination and determine where your heart truly lies today. Is it more in the ways of God or this world?

Worldly Seeker	Godly Seeker
Seeks the approval of man.	Desires the approval of God.
Their goal in life is more materialistic and power.	Seekers of God aim to grow spiritually, not worldly.
Wants more of the world or man's knowledge.	Yearns for more of God's wisdom.
More focused on temporal things.	Fixed on the eternal matter: Faith, Hope, & Love.
Develops more ways of man and the world.	Developing more of the Fruit of the Spirit.
They believe they can accomplish things on their own.	Yields to the Power of God for all things.
Possesses pride, selfishness, and a lack of repentance.	Displays a humble, remorseful, and repentant heart.
When going through trials, they are complacent.	Evidence of godly endurance and perseverance.
There are no traces of Bible application & obedience.	Portrays a pattern of Biblical living and Christlikeness.
A weak life of service, prayer, fellowship & worship.	Exhibits a life of wholehearted loyalty to God!

When we seek God first in our lives, it clearly shows that we're responding to God because we rely upon His guidance and teachings. You see, seeking God is a form of responding to Him, which demonstrates a desire to know and connect with Him in every part of our daily lives. Once again, as a reminder, we can do this through prayer, fellowship, worship, reading His Word, and, most importantly, applying it. It signifies a shift from a passive to an active relationship with God, where one actively pursues Him in all aspects of life.

Remember what we said earlier, how we respond to God is how He will respond to us. What do I mean? Example: If we seek repentance for

'Godly Seeker'

our sins, God is faithful to forgive our sins as far as the east is from the west (Ps 103:12). If we trust Him, He will direct our steps (Ps 37:23-25). If we obey Him, we can experience His peace and blessings (Deut 28:1-2). If we are faithful to God in all things, He provides us with a deep sense of His security and assurance (Phil 4:6-7).

Just think, when we respond to God in the manner He desires, it determines that we have a dynamic relationship with our Divine Creator and Father. Our response to God can lead to restoration and a renewed relationship with our Lord. Seeking God's guidance and wisdom through prayer, as highlighted in James 1:5, is a response that can lead to God's provision and protection.

Look at it this way: When our response to God is weak and not genuine, we're missing out on His empowering grace. And when we don't rely upon His grace, it opens the door to our life's portal being vulnerable to the enemy's attacks. When we don't respond to God with all our hearts, minds, souls, and strength, it not only shows that we're not seeking Him first, but we're also ignoring Him, which can lead to dire consequences.

Throughout the Bible, His Holy Word reminds us that those who ignore or turn away from God will eventually face judgment and loss of His favor. And not only that, but it will also lead to restlessness and a sense of unfulfillment with no clear purpose in life. As I ponder these dangers, why would anyone not want to seek the abundant life He has in store for us? Never forget this: God's word constantly reminds us that God's actions and blessings are influenced by our actions and responses, particularly in matters of our faith, trust, and obedience.

Always remember that seeking God first, above all things, illustrates our complete devotion, faithfulness, trust, and obedience to God's way in our lives. In our high pursuit of God, we will discover spiritual strength, moral guidance, and a deeper relationship with our Heavenly Father and Creator. It is not just a privilege, but it's our responsibility as His children to place Him first in every area of our lives. It's worth the effort for His glory!

Matt 6:33-34, "Seek the Kingdom of God above all else, and live righteously, and he will give you everything you need. "So don't worry about tomorrow, for tomorrow will bring its own worries. Today's trouble is enough for today."

Ps 14:2, "The Lord looks down from heaven on the entire human race; he looks to see if anyone is truly wise, if anyone seeks God."

Chapter Twenty-One

'Godly Rest'

Josh 21:1-3, 43-45, "Then the leaders of the tribe of Levi came to consult with Eleazar the priest, Joshua son of Nun, and the leaders of the other tribes of Israel. They came to them at Shiloh in the land of Canaan and said, "The Lord commanded Moses to give us towns to live in and pasturelands for our livestock." So, by the command of the Lord, the people of Israel gave the Levites the following towns and pasturelands out of their own grants of land."

"So the Lord gave to Israel all the land he had sworn to give their ancestors, and they took possession of it and settled there. *And the Lord gave them rest on every side, just as he had solemnly promised their ancestors. None of their enemies could stand against them, for the Lord helped them conquer all their enemies. Not a single one of all the good promises the Lord had given to the family of Israel was left unfulfilled; everything he had spoken came true."*

In the beginning passages, we see God's provision for His priesthood, the Levites. The tribe of Levi was not allocated any portion of the Promised Land because God declared that He would be their inheritance (Joshua 13:14, 33). Can you imagine our Lord coming to you and me asking this priceless question: "Do you want me as your inheritance, or all of the riches of a certain land?" Take your pick! Any right-minded and spiritually mature believer would say, "Give me more of you, Lord, and less of this world." Why? Because in Him, we are guaranteed rest for today, tomorrow, and the future. But in the things of this world, we are not guaranteed anything but headaches and heartaches!

Since the Levites possessed no land, they had to find alternative accommodations. So, with this declaration, God expected each of the other tribes to allot cities within their respective land to His royal priesthood. This was vital because God wanted the Levites to be "distributed" throughout the land of Israel (among all the tribes). You see, God never intended the tribe of Levi to be a separate nation, because He wanted every tribe to have a priestly and holy influence, as well as His divine presence among them. He wanted the other tribes to have His royal ambassadors and representatives living among them to remind them of God's guiding principles and will.

In the same sense, Christians (being priests, 1 Peter 2:5 and 2:9) are to be "dispensed" throughout the world and society, fulfilling the Great Commission (Matt 28:19-20). This does not mean we have to be assigned missionaries in another land. However, as followers of Jesus Christ, we are responsible for utilizing our God-given gifts as His representatives in our homes, neighborhoods, workplaces, schools, on the streets, churches, communities, states, and around the world. That is our high calling today, tomorrow, and in the days ahead.

But I love the humility and heart of this passage in Chapter 21 because the priests received their allotment of towns, not first, only after the thirteen tribes received their portions. The Levites received their allotment of towns last because they were not allocated their own territorial land when the Israelites entered the Promised Land. Why? This arrangement was designed to ensure that the Levites could fulfill their role as priests and religious leaders throughout the nation without needing their own land to oversee it. Their primary responsibility as God's chosen servants was looking out for the best interests of others within the tribes!

As we've seen throughout the Old Testament, the Priests were appointed to serve others, not to be served. The Levites were unique in that they did not inherit land but received God Himself as their inheritance, highlighting their special status in the eyes of God. It was all due to their absolute loyalty and dedication to Yahweh, as seen in the story of the golden calf in Exodus 32, where they stood by Moses against idolatry. Undoubtedly, there is something priestly and holy about letting others go first. You see, being "about others" is essential to the Body of Christ today because it embodies humility, selflessness, and wholehearted devotion to the Lord. Why is this critical?

Selfishness and pride can ruin a church and community. But when we put others first, we are putting God first in everything, just like the Levite Priests did thousands of years ago. This is important in the churches today because godly unity is crucial among the body when they act in accordance with the Bible, guided by the Holy Spirit (please read Ephesians 4). Why?

Because it can thwart jealousy, pride, envy, prejudice, division, and self-centeredness—*and establish a place full of His rest and peace.*

Paul reminds us powerfully in Philippians 2:3-5, "Don't be selfish; don't try to impress others. Be humble, thinking of others as better than yourselves. Don't look out only for your own interests, but take an interest in others, too. You must have the same attitude that Christ Jesus had." Jesus Christ gave up His rights as a man with humility and a willingness to obey God and serve others. This type of attitude is so important because when we inherently possess the same mind and heart as Christ, it brings an overwhelming state of peace in our lives.

You see, serving others is a powerful sense of spiritual rest. How? It engages us in acts of service that can lead to profound spiritual satisfaction and rejuvenation, as it allows individuals to connect with the needs of others, but most importantly, stay connected with their Lord and God. This is so important because serving others is a way to find peace and tranquility, rooted in our faith and trust in God's promises. It can reduce stress and elevate our sense of purpose for God's glory. But just as important, it fosters unity within the body because it embodies godly compassion.

But you must love the summation of this chapter in Joshua 21 because if this profound passage does not comfort you and reaffirm the truths of God's promises in His word, I don't know what will. The binding tie at the end of this chapter tells us that Yahweh, Almighty God, was faithful in fulfilling every promise He had given His children. *Nothing was left undone; everything He committed to His children about the Promised Land was completed. They now had rest on every side of life! Think about those compelling words from our God, "rest on every side of life!"*

In giving them the land of Canaan, God had promised to go before them and defeat all their enemies so that they could live securely (Deuteronomy 12:9-10). All that was required of God's new generation was to trust in Him and His promises fully. However, they refused to obey Him 100%, as we've seen. Instead, they murmured against Him like that first generation did for years. To be compared to that first generation should be a caution sign for anyone. Why?

Because they even yearned to return to their bondage under the Egyptians (Exodus 16:3; 17:1-7; Numbers 20:3-13). And we know how that story ended for the unbelieving generation: "They could never enter the 'rest of God' because they did not trust and obey Him wholeheartedly." Seriously, think about this! How can we enter the unbelievable rest of God when we want to continue our sinful ways and remain in bondage to the enemy? 1 John 3:6 and Romans 6:1-19 remind us that *true rest in God* is characterized by a life that reflects His character and is free from the bondage of sin. If we're still in bondage, it is because we're not living out our genuine saving faith where trust and obedience should be active!

God solemnly said the Israelites who disobeyed Him would never enter His rest (Hebrews 3:11)—because of their disobedience. God gave them so many chances by warning them of their defiant ways. Even after witnessing all His acts of mercy, grace, and love, they still rebelled against Him. Unfortunately, they would be excluded from the Promised Land (Hebrews 3:16–19). However, eventually, the next generation placed their faith in God and believed in His provisions and promises. They would follow Joshua's leadership, and some forty years later, they entered into God's rest, the land of Canaan (Joshua 3:14–17).[1]

Yes, some of God's promises took years, but in His timing, they were meant to establish His children's faith and obedience to Him and all His ways. But nestled in this passage, we not only see that God is always faithful to His word, but just as importantly, we see that God operates according to His timetable, not ours. This is so critical for us to understand because patience is one component we "fail" to possess often in this life.

God was utterly faithful regarding the land He Promised, but God's children were not because they still failed to possess all the land "by not obeying all His commands." He wanted them to push out the enemy and remain faithful to Him as their King. It was not because God had not made adequate provision for His children; it was because Israel had failed to follow the LORD fully and wholeheartedly.

And even for us today, God has been entirely faithful to you and me, even though we may not realize it at that moment. He has made provisions for our continual victories over those little battles that we willingly and humbly surrender to Him. He has given us great things, but what do we possess that honors Him in return? Do we have absolute trust and belief in all His promises and provisions? Do we take ownership in absolute obedience to His every command, demonstrating our genuine saving faith and love? Never forget this: When we are not possessors of the godly attributes that show our daily commitment to Him, *we will lose rest in the promises of His truths*. Our attributes should be: Trust, God-fearing, holiness, righteousness, humility, repentance, dependence, boldness, diligence, and every element of the Fruit of the Spirit (Galatians 5:22–23).

So, how do we stop trusting ourselves and doing things our own way? How do we place our complete trust in God and all His promises? How can we possess that same rest on every side of life, like we saw at the end of this chapter in Joshua 21? In our times of conflict and hardship, I am pretty sure

---

1. "How Can We Enter into God's Rest?"

that we all yearn to experience His rest amidst life's turmoil, which seems to come from every angle. And the answers lie in the heart of His promises in Scripture, and so many are layered throughout the Book of Psalms.

However, it begins with us seeking God first in all things, as we discussed in the previous chapter. You see, we enter into God's rest by first understanding our total inability to enter God's rest on our own, but having trust in Him alone. When we seek God with a wholehearted reliance on Him and possess a repentant and humble heart, everything changes. Next, we enter His rest through our total faith in Christ's sacrifice and complete obedience to God and His will (Hebrews 3:18-19). Unlike the Israelites, whose unbelief prevented them from entering the Promised Land, we are called to enter God's rest by faith in His Son, Jesus Christ—a faith that is a gift from Him by grace (Ephesians 2:8-9).

God's rest is so important because, through the power of His word and Spirit, we can experience a comforting peace and joy in the hope for what is to come. This spiritual rest enables us to revive a life that God desires daily. With all the prevailing ways of godliness today, what Christian would not want to aspire to this scriptural prescription? Once again, Jesus reminds us in Matt 11:28-30 that His yoke is easy, and His burden is light when we surrender it all to Him through humble submission.

When you feel like your life is in chaos internally, with a lot of spiritual labor and weight that is creating strain, stress, and tension, let go of yourself and give it to God. Our Lord wants you and me to possess an overflow of His abundant rest so we can let go of the mass internal and external pressures in our lives. We cannot live a life with a renewed mind, heart, soul, and spirit if we're toting too much of our self-baggage. The rest of God can bridge a life of hopelessness and helplessness to His side of grace, mercy, and love that is full of Living Hope. Find everyday rest from all life's worries, anxieties, and trials in Jesus Christ, as Paul did in Romans 7! Here are some powerful points below to assure us of a rest that we can all take comfort in today!

- "In the light of the Cross, is it not true that the enemy has no right to dwell in our land of God's presence?"
- "Is it not true that Satan's claim to your life was taken from him at Calvary?"
- "Is it not true that sin has no right to a foothold in the life of the child of God?"
- "Is it not true that Satan has no power in the presence of the Omnipresence, Omnipotence, and Omniscient One?"

- "Is it not true that Jesus Christ is pledged to destroy the enemy utterly by His blood and His resurrection, once we give our lives to Him?"
- "Is it not true that in the indwelling power of the Holy Spirit, there is strength for every temptation, grace for every trial, and power to overcome every difficulty?" (Alan Redpath)[2]
- All of these guarantees and promises are found in the truths of God's Word for our state of peace, comfort, and rest in Him!

The author reminds us in Heb 4:6–11," So God's rest is there for people to enter, but those who first heard this good news failed to enter because they disobeyed God. So, God set another time to enter his rest, which is today. God announced this through David much later in the words already quoted: "Today when you hear his voice, don't harden your hearts." Remember, there is power in the rest of God, and it's this: From the creation of humans in Genesis to the teachings of Jesus, rest is portrayed as a divine principle that's essential for human well-being and growth. When our hearts, souls, and minds are in His resting arms, it demonstrates that we're giving Him our all, with every fiber of our spiritual strength!

---

2. Joshua 21. "Cities Appointed for the Levites."

Chapter Twenty-Two

'Godly Understanding'

Josh 22:1-6, 9-10-12, 15-16, 21-27, "Then Joshua called together the tribes of Reuben, Gad, and the half-tribe of Manasseh. He told them, "You have done as Moses, the servant of the LORD, commanded you, and you have obeyed every order I have given you. During all this time, you have not deserted the other tribes. You have been careful to obey the commands of the LORD your God right up to the present day."

"And now the Lord your God has given the other tribes rest, as he promised them. So go back home to the land that Moses, the servant of the Lord, gave you as your possession on the east side of the Jordan River. But be very careful to obey all the commands and the instructions that Moses gave to you. Love the Lord your God, walk in all his ways, obey his commands, hold firmly to him, and serve him with all your heart and all your soul." So, Joshua blessed them and sent them away, and they went home.

"So, the men of Reuben, Gad, and the half-tribe of Manasseh left the rest of Israel at Shiloh in the land of Canaan. They started the journey back to their own land of Gilead, the territory that belonged to them according to the Lord's command through Moses. But while they were still in Canaan, and when they came to a place called Geliloth near the Jordan River, the men of Reuben, Gad, and the half-tribe of Manasseh stopped to build a large and imposing altar."

"The rest of Israel heard that the people of Reuben, Gad, and the half-tribe of Manasseh had built an altar at Geliloth at the edge of the land of Canaan, on the west side of the Jordan River. So, the whole community of Israel gathered at Shiloh and prepared to go to war against them." "When they arrived in the land of Gilead, they said to the tribes of Reuben, Gad, and the half-tribe of Manasseh, "The whole community of the Lord demands to know why you are betraying the God of Israel. How could you turn away from the Lord and build an altar for yourselves in rebellion against him?"

"Then the people of Reuben, Gad, and the half-tribe of Manasseh answered the heads of the clans of Israel: "The Lord, the Mighty One, is God! The Lord, the Mighty One, is God! He knows the truth, and may Israel know it, too! We have not built the altar in treacherous rebellion against the Lord. If we have done so, do not spare our lives this day. If we have built an altar for ourselves to turn away from the Lord or to offer burnt offerings or grain offerings or peace offerings, may the Lord himself punish us."

"The truth is, we have built this altar because we fear that in the future your descendants will say to ours, 'What right do you have to worship the Lord, the God of Israel? The Lord has placed the Jordan River as a barrier between our people and you, people of Reuben and Gad. You have no claim to the Lord.' So, your descendants may prevent our descendants from worshiping the Lord."

"So, we decided to build the altar, not for burnt offerings or sacrifices, but as a memorial. It will remind our descendants and your descendants that we, too, have the right to worship the Lord at his sanctuary with our burnt offerings, sacrifices, and peace offerings. Then your descendants will not be able to say to ours, 'You have no claim to the Lord.'

What a powerful storyline in this passage that depicts the importance of understanding the big picture before we jump to our fleshly conclusion and perceive things through our own eyes. In this profound chapter, we see where the tribes of Reuben, Gad, and the half-tribe of Manasseh were commended for helping the other tribes conquer land on the west side. But what we'll see more than anything is this: "When there is no clarity and clear communication, misunderstandings can take precedence and create possible dissension."

At this point in the story, the relationship between the Eastern and Western tribes is very good. Example: They have supported each other, witnessed God's victory and blessings on His people, and the land was divided in mutual consensus; there is now peace and mutual trust amongst the nation. The western tribes were aware that the tribes of Reuben, Gad, and the half-tribe of Manasseh had already been allocated land in the east before the conquest of the Promised Land commenced. So, at this stage, they are all on the same page as God's children.

If we look back at Numbers 32:1, it reveals one reason these two-and-a-half tribes wanted the land east of the Jordan: "The Reubenites and Gadites, who had vast herds and flocks, saw that the lands of Jazer and Gilead were suitable and seen as a prime area for raising livestock." At first, Moses opposed the idea of some tribes staying east of the Jordan. Why? Because he thought these tribes attempted to avoid helping their fellow Israelites in the military campaign to subdue the enemy in their conquest of the land for the entire nation. However, these tribes responded with a pledge to help their fellow people.[1]

So, before they could settle in their land on the east side, they had to promise to help the other tribes conquer the land on the west. Man, you talk about faithful commitment, obedience, patience, and due diligence; we will see these godly components come to life in this chapter. They were already given a portion of God's Promised Land and could have quickly neglected their fellow brothers and sisters, but they had a God-given duty to help others, which would fulfill God's ultimate plan.

When the tribes of Reuben, Gad, and the half-tribe of Manasseh reached Geliloth near the Jordan River, they wanted to build a massive and impressive altar. This was significant because of its size and the meaning of an altar, which is a designated place for sacrifice, worship, commemoration, and a reminder of God's promises and provisions. However, the bigger picture is that this altar had meaning and purpose, both now and in the future.

The intent and desire of these two and ½ tribes were to build a Godly memorial that would remind future descendants that they, too, have the right to worship the "Lord Almighty as one." And the altar was given the name "Witness." Although the eastern tribes were separated from their fellow brethren by geography, they wanted to show their spiritual solidarity by building this site to commemorate their unity with the One True God.

However, the western tribes learned of the altar that the tribes of Reuben, Gad, and the half-tribe of Manasseh were constructing. They thought they were building a pagan god, not one in honor of Almighty God. They were so upset that they reacted out of the flesh and conspired to wage war against some of their own people. Why did they react so quickly? They feared that the wrath of God would be upon them for their idolatry (as seen at Baal Peor, Num 22:17, or when Achan sinned, as recorded in Joshua chapter 7). So, they feared God's judgment, which would weaken Israel and ultimately lead to defeat, loss of blessings, and disunity within the nation.

But if we look at the entire context of this message, what could have been done by both sides to prevent the flesh from reacting out of haste? First, if the tribes of the East and West were in such unity, you would think the tribes of Reuben, Gad, and the half-tribe of Manasseh would have proactively conveyed to the rest of the nation their intent and motive. But

---

1. "Why Did Reuben, Gad, and the Half-Tribe of Manasseh want to live on the East of the Jordan?"

also, on the flip side, the nations from the West, before accusing the Eastern tribes of idolatry, should have asked why they built this altar.

When we understand the whole story better (from both sides), we can prevent ourselves from reacting out of instinct to a specific matter. That's why gathering all the facts first is essential, which can help us respond to circumstances in a more Christlike manner. One of the worst ways to become entangled in falsehoods is when we don't have all the facts first. Remember, a fleshly presumption can lead to an off-target assumption or belief. When we "selfishly" presume, judge, or speculate on a situation, it often carries an underlying tone of arrogance, egotism, and disrespect, which can lead to division and discord. Why? Because we think we have all the answers and don't seek God's counsel and guidance for a better biblical and spiritual understanding.

The Merriam-Webster definition of understanding is clear comprehension, mental grasp, and the capacity to apprehend general relations of things. It's the power to make experienced and intelligible decisions by applying concepts. It's a mutual agreement, not formally entered into, but to some degree binding on each side. It's a friendly or harmonious relationship, an agreement of opinion or feeling, and an adjustment of differences.

God reminds us in Amos 3:3, "Can two people walk together without agreeing on the direction?" This is particularly important in our relationship with the Lord, as understanding is often linked to moral character in the Bible. Godly understanding is the ability to discern right from wrong while possessing a more accurate perceptive spiritual insight through the guidance of God's Word and Spirit. And just as compelling, understanding is seen as a gift from God (Dan 2:21).

Here is the key to understanding in the Bible. Without it, we cannot attain God's knowledge and wisdom behind His purpose and plan. Biblical and spiritual understanding comes from the Holy Spirit, and it can transform our finite thought process about what we need to understand in life. When we delve into the depths of His holy word, guided by the Spirit, we can tap into God's wisdom and gain a more precise understanding of God's work in our personal lives. This is vital because, so often in life, we need to grasp a deeper understanding and knowing of God's working plan in our lives rather than relying solely on our own understanding.

The word "know" (meaning to realize and understand) relates to God. In other words, for us to know God is not to know about Him in an impersonal manner but rather to enter into his saving works by faith. Micah 6:5 tells us that the Lord did everything He could to teach us about His faithfulness. To know God is not to struggle philosophically with His eternal essence but to recognize and accept His claims as a Sovereign and Holy God.

Is this important? Yes, because it demonstrates our obedience and absolute faith in the truths of His word![2]

There is no basis for proper knowledge that does not come from the power of God's Spirit and His word (Heb 4:12-13). And this is key: A spirit of revelation is in sync with spiritual understanding; they go hand in hand. Why? Because they are wired with God, drawing from His fountain of wisdom and knowledge. Don't you love it when God reveals something to you that gives you a better understanding of what He's doing and maybe why He's doing it? Those powerful and precious moments can serve as our testimonies of God's power!

Look at Job's story—he did not understand why God subjected him to intense trials and tests, and he lost his worldly possessions. And then there's Jonah, who did not understand why God wanted to send him to a wicked city to evangelize to them, but little did he know that the most remarkable revival recorded in history would occur. I am sure Noah wondered if God's plan was the best, especially considering the time it took to build the Ark. What patience! And I am confident that Noah did not comprehend what rain was when it started to pour down from the Heavens for forty days and forty nights.

Did Jacob have to trick his father, Isaac, to fulfill God's plan? We often do not know what God is doing in our lives to execute a plan for His glory. The crucial truth is we don't need to know what God is doing now to follow him in faith. God has his reasons for concealing his purposes. Sometimes, it concerns His timing, as it did for Peter. And many of us can relate to the powerful testimony Paul laid out for us in Romans chapter 7. He did not understand the battle within his mind, but over time, he came to realize that the answer lay in Jesus Christ. So often in life, we must genuinely examine our spiritual lives and see if Christ is truly present (2 Cor 13:5).

Look at the story of Abraham, who praised God beneath the stars—even though he didn't understand how he'd ever become the father of nations. David praised God in the wilderness, even though he didn't know why he was running for his life instead of sitting on the throne. The Israelites praised God with a mighty shout—even though they didn't understand Jericho's wall would fall without a fight. Moses questioned God multiple times because he did not understand how an Almighty God could use someone with so many inadequacies.[3]

Even the mother and father of Jesus Christ did not fully understand what was happening when they were told they would bear a Son who would

---

2. "Baker's Evangelical Dictionary of Biblical Knowledge of Know."
3. Bloom. "You Don't Need to Understand Now."

'Godly Understanding'

become the Savior of the world. And the disciples of Jesus Christ never understood everything Jesus was trying to teach them while He was on this earth. These stories of people who could not grasp God's purpose and plan are blueprints for our teachings. The list of those who did not understand God's will, but relied upon Him, is countless. But in time, because of what God revealed to them and through their trust, faith, and obedience, the list of God's servants fulfilled His acts that laid the course of our biblical history.

For us today, and even then, one central reason for the distance between humans and God is that we spend more time questioning Him or even rejecting, doubting, or getting angry about certain events that are part of His plan. However, we must, on the other hand, surrender and submit ourselves wholly to His will, and obey and believe in His guidance because His way is always the right way. We must understand and recognize the gap between our human weaknesses and the strength of our Almighty God.

Only when we come to a better understanding of the power of prayer, God's word, the Holy Spirit, worship, fellowship, praise, thankfulness, repentance, forgiveness, our God-given gifts, serving, giving, and the Fruit of the Spirit, will we see Christ more at the center of our lives. When we apply the Truths of the Bible with the guidance of His Spirit, we will better cling to His Sovereign grace, mercy, and love, and know it is always for our good (Romans chapter 8). Today's most important thing to understand is this: "Know how badly we need the Lord for everything in our daily lives."

Perhaps that's why Ecclesiastes 11:5 reminds us: "Just as you cannot understand the path of the wind or the mystery of a tiny baby growing in its mother's womb, so you cannot understand the activity of God, who does all things." God sees more than we can see—He knows more than we know—and works in ways beyond our comprehension (Isa 55:8–11).

And if we agree to follow Him wholeheartedly, we will understand what He's doing. And trust me, when we're in that closeness with God, there will be those times when we'll stop dead in our tracks because we're experiencing His unfathomable wonders. And in the power of those awe-striking moments, we will better recognize and understand our Sovereign God and seize to fulfill His purpose.

Many Christians question God mainly because they don't understand "why He's doing what He's doing." That's because they've been taken out of their earthly comfort zone. He rattles our spiritual cage to get us out of the flesh and into the Spirit so that we can align with His plan. In our finite minds, we cannot fully rationalize His purpose, and this lack of understanding can create a distance between people and God because they lack a spiritual understanding. Whether it is the loss of a close one, personal struggles, or trials and intense tests, they cannot grasp a Sovereign God when they try to figure it out on their own. But Isaiah 55 tells us why.

If we would only remember what God requires of us, as noted so eloquently in Deuteronomy 10:12-13, we would come to grips with and better understand God's will in our lives. He requires us to fear Him (reverence and respect), to walk with Him in obedience, to love Him with all our hearts, souls, minds, and strength, to abide by His commands, and to serve Him with a faithful and loving heart. We must be willing to set ourselves aside and be humble in our service to Him while exalting His Holy Name. This is what pleases the Lord, which in turn glorifies Him. He must be the nucleus of our everyday life, regardless of the storms and persecution that come our way.

In Jesus' final days, he is preparing His disciples for what is to come and their future expectations. They did not fully grasp all the things Christ, their Lord, was doing and saying. But in time, they would—when the Holy Spirit came upon them. Jesus replied, "You don't understand now what I am doing, but someday you will." And as we see in the book of Acts, when the Holy Spirit came upon them, they understood their purpose and deployed their Christian actions throughout the lands. It was a domino effect that has occurred throughout history around the world.

The fundamental principle lies in this: when we heed the guidance of His Spirit and His Word, it keeps us at the center of the Lord's will and plans and equips us for the final days ahead (2 Timothy 3:1-5). When we recognize our true calling in life, based on God's divine purpose and plan, and allow the power of God's word and Spirit to guide our lives, we will positively impact this society and culture like never before. Remember, to know is to possess facts, information, or awareness of something or someone, such as the Bible and God. And when we have divine knowledge of God, we understand His nature, character, and identity.

This process of growing our knowledge and understanding of God will require you and me to engage and interact with God on three different levels: 1) Intellectually (2 Pet 3:18), Experiential (experience Who He is, Ps 34:4, 2 Tim 3:15-17), and 3) Spiritual (John 4:23-24). We cannot grow in knowledge and understanding of God if we leave our minds and hearts out of the process. Neither can we, indeed, be in awe of who God is until we experience His presence. These steps are vital to gaining a deeper understanding of God's wisdom, enabling us to discern life more consciously from His perspective rather than our own. This is a lifelong process; it does not happen overnight. It takes dedication and a willingness from the heart, soul, and mind, with all our strength![4]

Isa 55:8–9, "My thoughts are nothing like your thoughts," says the Lord. "And my ways are far beyond anything you could imagine. For just as the heavens are higher than the earth, so my ways are higher than your ways and my thoughts higher than your thoughts." Never forget what our Lord tells us in John 20:29, "Blessed are those who believe without seeing Me."

---

4. Haynes. "How Can We Grow in the Knowledge and Understanding of God?"

Chapter Twenty-Three

'Godly Fight'

Josh 23:1–16, "The years passed, and the Lord had given the people of Israel rest from all their enemies. Joshua, who was now very old, called together all the elders, leaders, judges, and officers of Israel. He said to them, "I am now a very old man. You have seen everything the Lord your God has done for you during my lifetime. The Lord your God has fought for you against your enemies. I have allotted to you as your homeland all the land of the nations yet unconquered, as well as the land of those we have already conquered—from the Jordan River to the Mediterranean Sea in the west. This land will be yours, for the Lord your God will himself drive out all the people living there now. You will take possession of their land, just as the Lord your God promised you."

"So be very careful to follow everything Moses wrote in the Book of Instruction. Do not deviate from it, turning either to the right or to the left. Make sure you do not associate with the other people still remaining in the land. Do not even mention the names of their gods, much less swear by them or serve them or worship them. Rather, cling tightly to the Lord your God as you have done until now. "For the Lord has driven out great and powerful nations for you, and no one has yet been able to defeat you. Each one of you will put to flight a thousand of the enemy, for the Lord your God fights for you, just as he has promised. So be very careful to love the Lord your God."

"But if you turn away from him and cling to the customs of the survivors of these nations remaining among you, and if you intermarry with them, then know for certain that the Lord your God will no longer drive them out of your land. Instead, they will be a snare and a trap to you, a whip for your backs and thorny brambles in your eyes, and you will vanish from this good land the Lord your God has given you."

"Soon, I will die, going the way of everything on earth. Deep in your hearts, you know that every promise of the Lord your God has come true. Not a single one has failed! But as surely as the Lord your God has given you the good things he promised, he will also bring disaster on you if you disobey him. He will completely destroy you from this good land he has given you. If you break the covenant of the Lord your God by worshiping and serving other gods, his anger will burn against you, and you will quickly vanish from the good land he has given you."

In Joshua's message to all the leaders of the nation of Israel, he delivers his farewell address. But as we can see in his message, as God's humble and faithful leader, he glorifies God above all things. It would have been easy for Joshua to focus on everything he accomplished as a military leader, given its undoubtedly impressive nature in human eyes. But Joshua knows Who was before, beside, and behind him every step of the way. And that is why he is far more interested in glorifying God than talking about himself. Even close to his death, Joshua's God would be exalted.

Under Joshua's leadership, the army of Israel broke the back of the Canaanite military. Now, as noted so many times earlier, it remains up to each tribe to fully possess what God has given them, which means they must be prepared to fight for what God has promised them. And in the same way, for us today, God has given every believer a Promised inheritance. We have been blessed beyond measure with every spiritual blessing in Christ (Ephesians 1:3), and God has a definite part for us to play in coming to possess that inheritance. It's this: We must endure and persevere through constant fights on this side of Heaven. But just like Joshua, it is critical that we know Who is fighting for us, and with us, each step of the way (Neh 4:20, Josh 1:9, Rom 8:31–33).

Even though Joshua is dying, he will give the nation of Israel words of encouragement, but also with godly instructions. He knows the weak spots of his people and how easily they can slip into a life opposite to God's way if they are not careful. In his message, he conveys profound words and directions to the leaders to pass on to God's people. Joshua tells Israel not to even mention these false gods of the Canaanites. Instead of learning about them, they should hold fast to the LORD their God and His teachings.

The author in Hebrews reminds us in 10:23–24, "Let us hold tightly without wavering to the hope we affirm, for God can be trusted to keep his promise. Let us think of ways to motivate one another to acts of love and good works." I cannot count the times when Christians would get so far down the funnel of learning about other false beliefs that their thought process gets distorted, and they lose focus on the core principles of God's teaching.

Yes, it is wise to be aware of the falsehoods surrounding us today and their false doctrines, but the master key is knowing the fundamental truths of our genuine saving faith in the One True God and our Savior. Please never forget this takeaway: We can quickly lose focus on His good works in our lives, becoming His 'Onward Christian Soldiers' if we dabble too much in other beliefs.

We have heard the old adage, "Keep your friends close, but your enemies even closer," but this is precisely what Christians *are not* to do. By and large, the typical Christian is not called to become an expert in the cults or heresy of this evil world, but to become an expert in Jesus Christ. He wants us to hold fast to Him and be prepared to defend our faith as sound and grounded students of the Word. "The key is abiding in Him so He can abide in us and reveal His truths." Apart from that formula, we are doomed, and off course! The proof lies in this: When the nation of Israel obeyed God's commands, they saw evidence of God doing great things, fulfilling all His provisions. They saw one victory after another, undeniable blessings in their lives, and a unity in the nation. Remember, none of us can accomplish His good works if we're not in that closeness of obedience and conformity to the ways of the Lord (Read Romans chapter 12).

And here's the key! When we continually live in God's faith, love, and grace, we will see trust and obedience take center stage in our lives. However, if we're too entangled in the ways of this world and man, we will never be a godly influence in other people's lives. All because we are heavily dominated by the ungodly things of today that have deterred our path of righteousness. Remember what the passage in Joshua 23 states above: "Do not deviate from it, turning either to the right or to the left. Make sure you do not associate with the other people still remaining in the land." What does this mean?

When our God tells us, "Do not deviate from it, turning either to the right or to the left," it emphasizes the importance of adhering strictly to God's commands and guidelines only. If we don't adhere to God's plan wholeheartedly, we will eventually stray from the path of righteousness, which can lead to failure, misfortune, and a lack of His blessings (just as the Israelites of that one generation). And here's the key takeaway: We must be careful in following other gods or deviating from the laws and commandments of God, or we will get snared by the enemy!

With that, don't we realize we're in a spiritual warfare, right now? Unfortunately, so-called Christians of today are blinded by this fact! How? A startling statistic from the Barna Group from a few years back stated that

'Godly Fight'

most American *Christians do not believe that Satan or the Holy Spirit exists.* And the root of this misinterpretation is this: *Americans are struggling to make sense of their faith!* [1] And without a firm stance in the true faith, there will never be a level of trust and obedience in a Higher Power! It is evident that the spiritual enemy has hoodwinked (misguided) people into not believing or trusting in the One Power that can help us overcome our battles in life. What do I mean?

Today, we're seeing an "innocent Canaanite" all around us. If we don't quickly separate ourselves from these types of temptations, they can become a spiritual torturous thorn and snare in our lives. These ungodly influences never advertise themselves as instruments of affliction; they present themselves as wonderful things. But we're in trouble if we don't see past these things spiritually and biblically. And when there is an absence of God's wisdom and a discerning spirit, we can never accurately assess the difference between right and wrong fights.

I love this quote by Alan Redpath, a well-known British evangelist, pastor, and author. "How often we see that the temptation we have pampered, encouraged, and indulged in has become a scourge and a thorn in our side. The compromising Christian is not a happy man. Let the enemy remain in a Christian life; let him have one foothold, and he soon becomes a scourge." (Redpath)[2]

He also made this profound statement that correlates with the storyline in this passage: "The Christian life doesn't get easier as one gets older." In other words, we're constantly in one fight after another on this Side of Heaven. Never forget what Paul tells us in Galatians 5: Only two forces are fighting against each other, and they cannot co-exist. We're talking about the flesh and the Spirit. And make no mistake about this: One of these forces is controlling our lives more than the other. Do you know which force is controlling you more in everyday life?

The Bible mentions fighting in several contexts, including the fighting of a soldier against an enemy army (Josh 8:1–11; 1 Sam 14:52; 17:19). Then there's the fighting that occurs between people because of an argument or other conflicts (2 Cor 7:5). And as noted above, there's the fighting of the Christian's soul against spiritual forces of evil (Eph 6:12; Jude 1:3), the fighting that occurs between angels and demons (Rev 12:7), and the fighting of a person trying to overcome his own sinful tendencies (2 Tim 4:7; 1 Tim 6:12). Depending on the situation, fighting can be noble and good—or sinful, but fighting is not wrong in itself. The key is, however,

---

1. Barna Group. "Most American Do Not Believe that Satan or Holy Spirit Exists,"
2. Joshua 23. "Joshua's Farewell Address."

Who is leading your battles in life. Is it one of righteousness or evil? Is it one for your personal gains or for God's glory? Is it for your claim to fame or for God's Kingdom?

With this said, fighting in the Bible can be physical or spiritual. Either way, the conflict is intended to establish dominance over the opposition. That opposition can be a human army, Satan, or sin. However, fighting is often a sign of sin in our lives. James gets to the heart of the problem in James 4:1: "What causes fights and quarrels among you? Don't they come from your desires that battle within you?" And this is often overlooked in Christian lives today because they are more consumed by the ways of man and this world, rather than God's word and the promptings of the Holy Spirit.

Christians are called to fight physically when necessary. There is nothing wrong with fighting to protect the innocent or defend one's home, family, or country. For example, a Christian soldier is required to fight for his military commanders. Soldiers are mentioned throughout the Gospels, and Jesus never treats them as sinful or wrong in carrying out their duties, nor does He command them to leave the service. John the Baptist tells them to be fair and honorable (Luke 3:14). In the Bible, several soldiers are also described as devout and faithful men (Acts 10:7; Matt 8:5–13). At the core is this: The "true intent and desire" of Who they are serving and truly fighting for.

Undoubtedly, the most important fight for all Christians today is a spiritual one. And the great news is that God provides us with the armor (Eph 6:10–17). The spiritual war is waged against sin, against erroneous doctrines and practices that corrupt the church, and against the old sinful nature within us. A believer's life is likened to that of a fighting man (2 Tim 2:1–4; Philemon 1:2). According to the Bible, if the opposition is evil and the cause is good, there is nothing wrong with fighting.[3] But make sure that our acts are guided by more of His righteousness and holiness than lawlessness.

Remember, the key to our small victories in all our battles in life is our obedience to God's word. We must rely upon the guidance of the Holy Spirit and believe beyond a shadow of a doubt that He's always there to help our cause, especially if our motives align with God's plan. We must abide in Him so He can abide in us—never partnering with the ways of the enemy, as Joshua reiterated to the Israelites.

This is essential, and it's this: We must continue our march in God's love and grace in today's society and culture, separating ourselves from the

---

3. "What Does the Bible Say About Fighting?"

'Godly Fight'

ungodly influences that can taint our lives. Because when we get too involved with the darkness of this world, we're taking up a worthless fight that will emotionally and spiritually drain us and drift us away from His Truths!

Regrettably, we often pick the wrong fights in everyday life, progressively applying unnecessary energy and strategies in our Christian Walk that lead nowhere because they are not spiritually productive. Our ineffective and unproductive time has created more frustration than God's peace, joy, comfort, and self-control. The main reason for those poor decisions is that we're more in tune with our flesh than with His Spirit (Galatians 5:17). Many believers want to fight against "man's flesh and blood" rather than the principalities of darkness. Don't we realize these forces are fundamental and out to divide and destroy every follower of Christ?

Almost all of us have found ourselves in a situation where we're fighting to resolve a particular issue, but everything we've done has made things worse and is beyond our control. We found ourselves in the position of more damage control rather than in the position of Christ. The book of Ephesians is a beautiful roadmap to our path in fighting the right battle on this side of Heaven. And that is 1) having spiritual wisdom as Christians, 2) possessing a oneness in Jesus Christ, 3) yielding to His word and Spirit for power, and strength, 4) enabling unity and peace in the body, 5) living in His constant light, 6) putting on the spiritual armor of God and 7) praying for His guidance. Now you're ready for the right battle!

What a striking parallel between Joshua and Paul. As the appointed humble, obedient, and faithful leader, Joshua fought the good fight for God and His children to the bitter end. And just like Paul, the great apostle of Christ in the New Testament, fought the good fight to the end as the Lord's humble, obedient, and faithful servant. What can we learn from these two great spiritual warriors?

Joshua reminded his fellow people to obey God's commands and avoid evil before he died. And just like the apostle Paul, he tells us in 2 Tim 4:7 that he had fought the good fight and finished his race for the Lord, but the key was this. Through all the intense trials and tests, he kept the faith. When Paul states, "I have fought the good fight," it is significant for believers today because it serves as a stark reminder that the Christian life is a struggle against evil, both within ourselves and in the world (John 15:9; Romans 8:7; James 4:4).

Paul's life and ministry give us a powerful example of modeling Christ today. Earlier in this same epistle, Paul reminded Timothy to "endure hardship as a good soldier of Jesus Christ" (2 Tim 2:3). Paul knew that his death was near (verse 6), but he had no regrets. After Jesus took control of his life (Acts 9:15–16), he lived life to the fullest, fulfilling all that Jesus had charged and empowered him to do (Eph 3:6; 2 Tim 4:17). He had a remarkable sense of fulfillment and contentment with his life in Christ because he was in the right fight for his Lord (Phil 4:11–13; 1 Tim 6:6–8).

There was nothing the world could offer this great man of the Lord that would surpass all his gains of service and fight for the cause of Christ. God's word reminds us in 2 Tim 2:3–5, "Endure suffering along with me, as a good soldier of Christ Jesus. Soldiers don't get tied up in the affairs of civilian life, for then they cannot please the officer who enlisted them. And athletes cannot win the prize unless they follow the rules."

Way too often in life, we see people willing to sacrifice their personal lives for an earthly cause they are passionate about. They will even endure scorn from others because of their devotion to it with all their heart. However, our attitudes shift when it comes to serving the cause of Christ. What do I mean? People seem unwilling to endure as much for the Lord as they do for the ways of man. If believers are reluctant to endure hardship for our Lord, they will accomplish little, if anything. They will give up as soon as something hard is required of them.

Always remember the power of Jesus' words in Matthew 16:24–26: 'Then Jesus said to his disciples, "If any of you wants to be my follower, you must give up your own way, take up your cross, and follow me." "If you try to hang on to your life, you will lose it. But if you give up your life for my sake, you will save it. And what do you benefit if you gain the whole world but lose your own soul? Is anything worth more than your soul?"

As believers today, we can have no greater sense of fulfillment than to know, as Paul and Joshua did, that we have fully accomplished all that the Lord has called us to do (Matt 25:21). May we "fight the good fight" and be watchful in all things, endure afflictions, do the work of an evangelist, fulfill ministry as His faithful servants for the cause of Christ. (2 Tim 4:5). It is priceless and worth the cause. [4]

---

4. "What Did Paul Mean When He Said He Fought the Good Fight?"

Chapter Twenty-Four

'Godly Pledge'

Josh 24:13-17, "When you crossed the Jordan River and came to Jericho, the men of Jericho fought against you, as did the Amorites, the Perizzites, the Canaanites, the Hittites, the Girgashites, the Hivites, and the Jebusites. But I gave you victory over them. And I sent terror ahead of you to drive out the two kings of the Amorites. It was not your swords or bows that brought you victory."

"I gave you land you had not worked on, and I gave you towns you did not build—the towns where you are now living. I gave you vineyards and olive groves for food, though you did not plant them. "So, fear the Lord and serve him wholeheartedly. Put away forever the idols your ancestors worshiped when they lived beyond the Euphrates River and in Egypt. Serve the Lord alone. *But if you refuse to serve the Lord, then choose today whom you will serve.* Would you prefer the gods your ancestors served beyond the Euphrates? Or will it be the gods of the Amorites in whose land you now live?"

"But as for me and my family, we will serve the Lord." The people replied, "We would never abandon the Lord and serve other gods. For the Lord our God is the one who rescued us and our ancestors from slavery in the land of Egypt. He performed mighty miracles before our very eyes. As we traveled through the wilderness among our enemies, he preserved us. "

In these passages, we see how the faithful and obedient servant and leader, Joshua, refreshed the nation of Israel with all the victories God had won on their behalf. This powerful set of scriptures should remind us, even today, "What an Awesome God we serve!" The great leader of God conveyed these powerful words to them: "It was not your swords or bows that brought you victory." It was God Himself. What a striking parallel to the last chapter, "Godly Fight."

Joshua wanted the nation of Israel to know and remember that everything they now possessed was not of their own making, but through the Almighty One! However, with all these blessings and provisions, Yahweh expected one thing in return: "To fear the Lord and serve Him wholeheartedly." He wanted their total commitment and pledge of service and loyalty to Him alone, and this would require God's children to have complete trust and obedience in all His ways as they prepared to settle in their new land.

As we reach the end of this beautiful book, we see at the beginning of this last chapter that Joshua is giving the Israelites a comprehensive overview of the history of everything God has done for them over time. So often today, we must be still and reflect on all God has done for us in our life's journey. We usually forget all the battles He has fought for us against our foes and all the victories (big and small) He has brought into our lives.

This is a crucial stage in our lesson as we conclude this magnificent book on Joshua's life as the faithful leader of Yahweh and the subsequent massive steps God's children took. With that, we need to take a moment to reflect on this profound statement: "For us to give our 100% commitment to the Lord, we must be still in His Sovereign presence, because without a healthy spiritual rest, we will not give Him our complete pledge of allegiance." Why? Because we're too fixed on the things of this earth and not Him! And this is imperative, as we will see later.

Undeniably, God used Joshua in multiple ways. In this dramatic and powerful last gathering of Israel (before Joshua's passing), the great leader spoke as an inspired messenger of God, like a prophet. Through Joshua, God wanted to remind His children that their descendants before Abraham worshipped other gods. However, in God's grace and mercy, He chose Abraham to become the father of many nations and start things anew.

Abraham was chosen because he was a faithful man to God alone (Heb 11:8–19). He started packing as soon as he understood what God was saying to him in Genesis chapter 12. He did not question God and was not hesitant; he instantaneously gathered his personal belongings and his wife and went on his way to a future land with God's guidance. He was loyal to Yahweh, would pledge his faithfulness and obedience to Him, and trust His guidance in this quest to a new land.

But it's also worth noting a powerful truth when God chose Abraham, the father of the Jewish people and the first Jew, and it was this: Abraham was not born a Jew. He grew up in a pagan home, and his relatives were heavily involved with idolatry. What a profound illustration that shows us God can take the worst of any family circumstance, regardless of how badly

'Godly Pledge'

our relatives act, and do great things when He chooses one for His glory. Look at the worst of all sinners (Paul, 1 Tim 1:15-16). If you don't think God can do miraculous things in people regardless of their ugly past, think again. However, just like Abraham and even Joshua, He wants our devout commitment to Him alone.

God chose Abraham to make him a blessing, first to the nation that would come from him—the Israelites—and ultimately to all the people of the earth. However, we must not forget that this blessing was also intended to prepare the way for the Messiah, our Lord and Savior, Jesus Christ. God promised that in Abraham's offspring, all the nations of the earth would be blessed (Gen 22:1-18). The reference to Abraham's "offspring" in this passage is to Jesus Christ, through whom all the people of the world would be blessed with the opportunity for eternal life. In other words, if you accept and follow Christ by faith and trust and obey Him, you are Abraham's offspring and an heir according to the promise of God.

Paul explains this in Gal 3:16-18: "God gave the promises to Abraham and his child. And notice that the Scripture doesn't say 'to his children,' as if it meant many descendants. Rather, it says 'to his child'—and that, of course, means Christ. This is what I am trying to say: God's agreement with Abraham could not be canceled 430 years later when God gave the law to Moses. God would be breaking His promise. For if the inheritance could be received by keeping the law, then it would not be the result of accepting God's promise. But God graciously gave it to Abraham as a promise."

But also, just as important, God chose Abraham to reveal His faith as an example for us. The author in Hebrews 11:8-10 reminds us, "It was by faith that Abraham obeyed when God called him to leave home and go to another land that God would give him as his inheritance. He went without knowing where he was going. And even when he reached the land God promised him, he lived there by faith—for he was like a foreigner, living in tents. And so did Isaac and Jacob, who inherited the same promise. Abraham was confidently looking forward to a city with eternal foundations, a city designed and built by God." [1]

This is important for us today because we are challenged to follow Abraham's pattern of faithful obedience when we are called to leave our worldly pursuits and the comforts of everyday life. Before God challenged Israel, He reminded them of His faithfulness, and His goodness was evident from the beginning of His dealings with Abraham and his descendants, as we saw in the earlier passages. You see, God showed His favor on Abraham by crediting him with righteousness by faith. And despite his own failings,

---

1. "Why Did God Choose Abraham?"

Abraham was declared righteous because of his faith in God. God chose Abraham because of his willingness to trust and obey Him so that He could establish a people for Himself in the new Promised Land. What a high calling!

Today, when we've genuinely tasted the Goodness of God and His favor, do we draw near to Him and maintain a consistent pattern of godly standards in our daily lives, or do we become too caught up in our own world and forget His blessings and high calling? I hope it's not the latter! Always remember this: When we're consistently meditating and focused on His goodness, when He speaks to us, we pack up and *faithfully follow Him*, as Abraham did. It should be our daily aspiration to forgo all the things of this world and pledge our all to Him in this life's journey—every step of the way—all for His glory! This is all because we believe and trust our God and Lord to lead our lives in the way He desires.

As we've seen throughout this remarkable journey, God's faithfulness to His word and promises is linked to the goodness and lovingkindness that He has provided in our lives. How do we respond to these undeniable blessings when He shows His favor upon us with such significant enrichment? Above all things, God loves for us to demonstrate our faith (Heb 11:6).

As we've discussed many times, our faith involves trusting in God's character before we see how He will work things out. He has given us His Word and Spirit, and His Promises still stand today and tomorrow. You see, our trust and faithfulness should grow as we see His words fulfilled in our lives. Just as our confidence in others grows through daily interaction, our trust in God grows in the same way.[2]

Throughout the Bible, God has laid out Promises that should give us a sense of security, assuring us that He will always protect and provide for His children. He will never forsake us, and He will be our Ever-Present need in times of trouble (Psalm 46). He reminds us throughout His words that He will teach, guide, and help us in our times of need. There is nothing that will prevent Him from coming to the aid of His children, but always remember it's in His perfect timing.

Ultimately, He wants the best for us and desires to see Christlikeness in our everyday life on this Side of Heaven. And if we know that He wants the best for us (spiritually), we should give Him the same in return. As His chosen ones, for such a time as today, our Heavenly Father expects you and me to commit to Him this: And that's showing His path of righteousness, holiness, and truths to our heirs so they may pass it down to others. With that, I found myself pondering.

---

2. "How Can I Learn to Trust in the Faithfulness of God?"

'Godly Pledge'

Do we ever reflect on our pledge and promise to our Holy Creator, which should be our daily vow and commitment to our Lord (Ecclesiastes 5:4)? After all, a promise is a commitment by someone to do something, which requires action. So, we know that a promise is a word, *but actions speak louder than words.* Just as God began with Abraham in fulfilling His promises throughout the Bible, so can we start with our words of wholehearted commitment to God in our daily lives. Committing our all to God means entrusting Him with complete authority over our lives. It relies on us trusting in the One we pledge to with all we have, and there is no wavering along the way.

Many people get caught up in the passage that we should never make a promise or oath; our words should be either 'yes' or 'no.' The proper application of Jesus' principle of "let your yes be yes" is that Christians must be truthful in all circumstances, especially in their daily dedication to the Lord. Many people use this passage as a scapegoat, which shows a lack of accountability. It's as if they don't want to be held accountable to a higher calling.

But make no mistake: God expects all His children, just like the Israelites, to commit wholeheartedly to serve Him faithfully and obediently every day. When we shy away from our total commitment to Him, we're part-time believers, not full-time. And if you think about it, is there such a thing as part-time believers in His Kingdom? These are harsh and straightforward words, but we must understand the importance and severity of dedicating ourselves entirely to Him.

This led me to ponder our Pledge to the U.S. Flag: Do we know the history of our nation's Pledge of Allegiance and its importance over time? Years ago, millions of U.S. children returned to school nationwide in August and early September. For most, their mornings begin with them standing, hand over their hearts, and reciting the Pledge of Allegiance to the U.S. flag. *The precedence is established first thing in the morning, before class begins,* when they recite this pledge. There was a priority of allegiance to something with a cause and purpose. *Consider this in a spiritual context. When we rise in the morning, do we demonstrate our complete loyalty to the Lord through prayer and a focus on His Word? Do we set the spiritual and biblical precedent of our daily lives when we commit our all to the Lord before we start our day?*

For many generations today, we recall standing in that classroom and reciting the Pledge of Allegiance to the U.S. flag. Do you remember placing your hand over your heart? Did it mean anything? Did we genuinely grasp the very words coming from our lips? Were we going with the traditional flow of things, or did we mean it with all our hearts, minds, and souls? Were we faithfully committed to being honorable, trusting, and moral citizens of our country?

In 1942, as part of the progression of the Pledge of Allegiance, President Franklin D. Roosevelt signed a "Flag Code" law that Congress had passed. It established rules for displaying and caring for the flag, including the Pledge of Allegiance. But just as important, a 1954 law added 'under God' to the Pledge, making affirmation of religious belief an official element of patriotism and a part of the nation's religiosity.

Reciting the Pledge thus became a *daily religious exercise* in schools. On June 14, 1954, President Dwight Eisenhower signed a bill to insert the phrase "under God" into the U.S. Pledge of Allegiance, which children recited every morning in school. Previously, the pledge—initially written in 1892—had contained no reference to religion.

However, adding "under God" to the Pledge was for the nation to affirm the distinctive and defining characteristics of the American way of life, demonstrated by their undeniable belief in God. The incentive and push to add "under God" to the pledge gained momentum during the second Red Scare, a period when U.S. politicians were keen to assert the moral superiority of U.S. capitalism over Soviet communism, which many conservatives regarded as "godless."

Conversely, what many people once thought was godless has now taken precedence in the hearts of humans today. What do I mean? So many people and leaders in today's culture want to remove God from every aspect of our institutions and personal lives! It's like they want to erase the very fabric of our allegiance to God from every heart, mind, spirit, and soul. What has happened to people's commitment and loyalty to God over the years?

If you think about it, when we pledge our allegiance to the flag, it's akin to someone making a vow in a court of law. At that moment, before the judge and court, they are committed to telling the whole truth and nothing but the truth, 'so help me God.' Their hands are placed over the religious book of their choice, and in most cases, that is the Bible and the Holy Scriptures. Are people even aware of what they are committing to when they place their hands on the Holy Words of God?

It is evident that our words of commitment to the loyalty of our Creator and His commands have vanished like a vapor in the wind. Speaking of our own country, He has enriched this nation for over 250 years, but we fail to acknowledge Him for the most minute things in life. We have taken these blessings and His amazing grace for granted. There seems to be no ownership or accountability for taking up His cross and following Him to

'Godly Pledge'

the hill, which should wave our allegiance to the One who paid it all for us, then and now.

We moan and groan over those who kneel during the national anthem and don't pledge their allegiance to this country for the blood of those who sacrificed their lives for the very freedom we possess. We wonder why these people dishonor our nation with their words and deeds (or lack thereof). There are various reasons why people are no longer loyal to the United States; they feel that the country does not represent the ideals of "liberty and justice for all," as stated in its own words. They also disassociate themselves from loyalty to this country due to our leaders. But make no mistake about this: Millions show no allegiance to our country and God because they do not possess the godly faith to be honorable servants of the Lord!

However, there is another movement that declares, "The Pledge Is Pure Indoctrination." It is out to destroy and remove the very core of our allegiance to an Almighty God. They feel so strongly about this movement that they even want to remove "One Nation Under God." Just as we can tell the difference between those who are passionate (or not) about their country and its historical foundation, laws, and principles, so can we also distinguish between those who are loyal to Christ.

Yes, we should judge them by the fruit they bear, and if there is no fruitfulness, then there is no desire in their hearts to pledge loyalty to the One who paid it all for their freedom. These are piercing words! But if we are not loyal to the One Who shed His blood on the cross for our eternal freedom, we have no reason to pass guilt. We love to point fingers at others for their lack of accountability, but we forget that the finger goes both ways (Read Romans 2). Christians should always strive to take the higher road in pursuing their supernatural calling for the good of our Lord. *Always ensure your spiritual house is in order biblically before casting stones.*

Our daily Godly Pledge should read like this. "My Heavenly Father, I pledge to you on this day that I will love and honor your words and commands with all my heart, mind, soul, and strength, and make every effort to exemplify the model of Your Son, Jesus Christ. I promise that if I am convicted of wrongdoing by the power of the Spirit, I will acknowledge that guilt and plead for repentance. I commit myself to the hope and faith in the One who paid the price for all my sins and provided me with eternal freedom. I trust and believe in your guiding ways today, tomorrow, and in the future, no matter the obstacles that may come my way. I vow to you on this day that I will take every step in applying the truth of your Holy Scriptures to my life and exhibit the Fruit of the Spirit in all that I say and do for your glory, honor, and praise, so help me God!"

When we pledge to our Heavenly Father and wholeheartedly commit to Him alone, Jesus is our Sole Authority, Guiding Light, and Unswerving Compass. Committing to Christ means being fruitful and devoted servants to His calling and purpose in our lives. Our daily proposition and saying as loyal believers should be concise and girded in this: "For me to live is Christ."

The great Apostle Paul reminds us in Phil 1:20–22, "For I fully expect and hope that I *will never be ashamed, but that I will continue to be bold for Christ*, as I have been in the past. And I trust that my life will bring honor to Christ, whether I live or die. For to me, living means living for Christ, and dying is even better. But if I live, I can do more fruitful work for Christ."

In our life's journey, our daily pledge should be to commit all our hearts, souls, and minds, with all our spiritual strength, to the One Who has made promises of fulfilling truths. They cannot be broken because our Heavenly Father keeps His word to the very end of our lives on this earth and thereafter.

If we don't make a daily commitment to our Lord and give Him our best, is it because Christians are ashamed of their faith (Rom 1:16) in the One Who has already laid the path for those who want to cross over from this side of immoral and untruths—to His side of everlasting truth? Yes, there is a lot of pain, suffering, trials, and intense tests that we must endure and persevere through on this Side of Eternity.

But in the end, all these times of torment will pass once we decide to follow the One to that day of eternal glorification. Can you even imagine how glorious that day will be when we finally cross into His very presence? Remember this: Our daily pledge to glorify, honor, and praise God and our Lord in all that we say and do clearly indicates that our faith, trust, and obedience are in all His ways—*for there is no other way!* No matter what, keep the Lord close so you are more able and empowered to commit your all to Him, where you can trust and obey the Lord, and keep your vow to Him as a good and faithful servant.

Ps 37:5, "Commit everything you do to the Lord. Trust him, and he will help you."

Jon 2:9, "But I will offer sacrifices to you with songs of praise, and I will fulfill all my vows. For my salvation comes from the Lord alone."

In Summary

"They Finally Made It!"

The book of Joshua records the culmination of Israel's journey to the Promised Land, where we see God finally fulfilling His Promise to give the land of Canaan to Jacob's descendants. In this journey, we see a beautiful illustration where Joshua portrays the Lord as their general, who would lead His people to victory in conquering their future land. However, it would still require their absolute trust and obedience to God's ways. So often, we've seen that God's children needed to rely entirely on His promises, no matter the trials they would confront. We also see that despite Israel's failings, God would keep His commitments and provide for them to the end.

This remarkable book profoundly shows us God's faithfulness to His covenant with the Israelites, bringing them into the land He promised Abraham over 400 years earlier. This book highlights the importance of serving the Lord with trust and obedience, both before and after God fulfills His promises to His children.

And here's a key takeaway for the Israelites, then, and for you and me today: We must always be mindful and thankful to serve the Lord with gratitude because of all the promises He has fulfilled in our everyday lives. And no matter the trials that may blind us to those wonderful blessings, please never forget that we have ultimate victory through our absolute trust and faith in the Lord!

And here's our proof! Because of God's faithfulness, the Israelites finally crossed into the Promised Land. When they crossed the Jordan River, led by Joshua, the waters miraculously parted, allowing them to pass through on dry ground, marking their entry into the prosperous land. After a generation of faithless and disobedient Israelites wandered aimlessly in the wilderness and would eventually die there, the next generation of God's children would enter the Land that God had promised His nation.

Through all the trials, God's people have finally made it. It took a lot of patience, endurance, and perseverance to see God's promise finally come to fruition. Would this generation of believers continue to be strong, courageous, and obedient, setting an example for the generations to follow? Would they share with the succeeding eras how God keeps His promises to the very end, no matter the storms that come?

As we've seen throughout this journey, one of the greatest fulfillments of God's promises in the Old Testament is in the book of Joshua. It shows His children that the faithfulness and validity of His promises, as laid out in His words, will come to pass. It proves that His word is true and infallible, for God is not a liar, and regardless of the circumstances, He will bring His purpose and plan to reality. And now, in God's perfect timing, He will finally bridge the gap for His chosen ones—the nation of Israel—from their wandering years in the wilderness, full of so much brokenness, to a Promised Land flowing with all of God's richness.

This land would restore intimacy with God and promote human flourishing, guided by the ways of Almighty God. The Bible tells us that this beautiful land, full of Yahweh's abundant riches, would provide the Israelites with security, identity, purpose, and life. It was a place where God's name would be made great, glorified, honored, and praised. You see, this Promised Land was to bring God's children to a state of unity, once and for all.

And think that the same promise of a future land of His fullness and unity awaits anyone ready to accept by faith His Son, our Lord Jesus Christ (Acts 4:12, Romans 10:9). Anyone who makes this decision and is willing to follow Him with complete trust and obedience has the undeniable opportunity to be secure for the rest of their life. Yes, you and I have the privilege of choosing to be identified as one of God's chosen, if we are wholeheartedly committed to Him and all His ways.

As noted earlier, and as a reminder, for the Israelites to enjoy this land of restoration, they would be required to listen to Yahweh, obey His teachings and laws, follow through on each one with 100% compliance, and ensure that God's greatness and goodness were shared with future generations. The Israelites' faith and trust in God's ways would be their defining point if the land God gave them were taken 100%. However, as we're all aware, they failed in many ways because they did not possess all the land they were promised. It was clear that they did not rely on God wholeheartedly. They lacked faith, trust, and obedience in His ways to inherit all the land. And the recording of this shortfall in the nation of Israel serves as an example for us today.

"They Finally Made It!"

As we summarize this unbelievable journey, we must examine the steps God's children needed to take to reach His side of richness and fullness. When we look back at the "brokenness" of that generation of Israelites in the wilderness, we see repeated displays of doubt, disobedience, and lack of faith in God while wandering through the desert after leaving Egypt. They too often complained about their circumstances, questioning God's leadership and rebelling against Moses, despite witnessing numerous miracles from their exodus to all of God's provision for them.

Their disbelief in all of God's promises would essentially lead to their inability to fully trust God in the face of hardship. And this lack of trust would lead to a state of physical, mental, and spiritual brokenness. At this stage of their crushed spirits, it is clear that their disobedience led to their wandering stage, as they chose to defy God's guiding principles. And this waywardness would eventually lead them to drift away from Yahweh, senselessly going in the opposite direction of God's path. With that loss of guidance, it was evident that they had no godly ambitions or point of direction from God, which led to their spiritual sense of being lost and unsure of the way forward.

You see, disobedience leads to "wandering" because when someone disobeys rules or instructions, they often end up lost, aimless, or without a clear direction or path forward. For the Israelites, and even for us today, disobeying God's words can lead to a sense of being lost or unsure of where to turn. And when God's children were feeling deeply hurt and emotionally broken, they had nothing to fill their void because they refused to go in the manner God desired.

As discussed so often, instead of turning to God and trusting in His guidance, they turned to idolatry. They continually rebelled against His regulations, resulting in their profound unbelief in God's promises. If they had only listened to God despite their shortcomings, they would have experienced His clarity and purpose, developing a closer relationship with Him that would have led them to the Promised Land. Why is this important for us today?

When faced with challenging circumstances, the Israelites' story serves as a cautionary tale, highlighting the dangers of doubt, a lack of faith, and misplaced trust when we focus too much on the uncertainties in life. Additionally, it highlights the importance of obedience. You see, their struggles in the wilderness reflect the human tendency to question God's plan and not submit to His will, which ultimately led to their most challenging stage of life.

Simply put, God wanted their 100% dependence on Him and Him alone. If they had relied on Him wholeheartedly, they could have journeyed from the wilderness to the Promised Land. Today, we must ensure that we do not possess the same attitude as the first generation of Israelites (as mentioned so often in this journey), especially if we want to be on God's side in eternity. We cannot afford to be in a state of complacency in our Christian Walk because if we are, then we're not trusting God's guiding ways.

Today, as followers of Jesus Christ, we can ascertain many powerful insights from this invaluable book that will help us stay connected with our Lord and ensure we're on His path to our destined land. We've learned the lesson of trusting our Lord, and the importance of obeying and relying on Him through all our trials in life. We've seen the magnitude of seeking God's counsel, and our challenge to cling to the Lord through all our battles.

We've discovered the value of choosing the ways of our Lord versus the ways of man and this world. We also realized that with the Lord on our side, we can be strong and courageous through all our spiritual warfare. After all, who can be against us (Romans 8:31)? Undoubtedly, we know that God is merciful and, in the end, will always be faithful to His promises. Through it all, God does amazing things even though we may not see them at the beginning.

By now, we can see the importance of planning and preparation as we formulate and piece together our spiritual efforts to go to war against our #1 enemy. Example: Remember earlier in the book, we saw how God helped Joshua implement and enforce the divide-and-conquer strategy? We learned how Joshua would prepare the armies of God's children to attack the smaller cities and groups of Canaanites separately, which prevented the enemy from forming a strong coalition against Israel.

In doing so, Joshua could focus on one target at a time, then capitalize on their weaknesses, maximizing his chances of success. Isn't this how we should combat Satan by focusing on one key area at a time where we're the most vulnerable, so we can maximize all our efforts in defeating him? This is vital! Why?

You see, this same strategy (divide and conquer) is how our #1 enemy (Satan) attacks us. He has employed this tactic on all his demons and principalities to separate God's children from our Heavenly Father's purpose and long-term plan (please read Mark 3:23–27, Luke 11:17–22). That is why, as firm believers and dedicated followers of Christ, we must put on the Whole Armor of God daily (Ephesians 6:10–20). That is why we must incorporate this set of passages into our spiritual lives, so we can counter his deceptive ways without compromising our trust and faith in the Lord.

Just think of the strong parallel of this deceptive ploy (divide and conquer) we confront today against our worst foe. He targets that one weak area in our lives, which can soon escalate into larger issues if not addressed

"They Finally Made It!"

biblically and spiritually. And if not handled in a godly manner, it will not only affect us but could have long-lasting detriments on others close to us.

Our enemy wants to maximize his forces in that one area of our life that we may not have surrendered and submitted to the Holy One, which will have a domino effect of casualties in our personal lives (Please read Rev 12:9–10). And when the enemy gets a stronghold in our lives, it will surely affect our levels of trust and obedience in the Lord (Please read Ephesians 4:27–29).

In other words, our faith and trust could be in danger if we don't lean upon the Lord's wisdom, knowledge, and guidance daily. That is why Christ's ways should continually grow in our lives, thoroughly preparing us for our ongoing battles against our enemy in today's society and culture. Never forget this: *There should be stages of elevated maturity in the wisdom and knowledge of our Lord, our constant faith and trust in the Lord, with improved areas of obedience to all His ways.*

We cannot allow negativity, pride, anger, hatred, discord, or any sin to take root in our lives and cause division within the body of Christ, because if it does, we are giving a stronghold to the enemy, and in time, he will defeat us. We must clothe ourselves with all the ways of Christ in our daily lives (Colossians 3) and consistently wear the Whole Armor of God so that we can go to battle with absolute trust and confidence in all His ways.

Remember what God wanted His nation of Israel to portray earlier in the book? To prove their identity as His chosen ones, He wanted them to *be the example of His divine deliverance from their bondage and to be the carriers of God's revelation for future eras.* You see, trusting and obeying God exemplifies us as His bearers of Christ by reflecting His lovingkindness and care in all our words and deeds. Just as the Israelites thousands of years ago, today, you and I are called to be the image bearers of God's revelation and redemptive plan, which means we are designed to mirror His goodness, love, and Christlikeness. Please make no mistake: This is essential for living out our genuine saving faith. Obviously, the first generation did not live up to these standards and expectations set forth by Yahweh.

With that, here's a short comparison test for us today vs. the Israelites. Regardless of the levels of suffering that we may be enduring at this very moment in our lives, does the unbelieving world and the weaker in faith identify you and me as God's true chosen ones *who portray His divine deliverance from whatever oppression or bondage we're dealing with*? In other words, they see more of Christ's freedom in us than in the chains of the enemy. Another way to put this: Are we glorifying God more through all our challenges in this life than defaming or degrading His Holy Name? Are we living up to His standards and expectations by trusting and obeying Him for the good of others, but mainly for God's glory?

But also, does the world view you and me, as today's Christians, as genuine bearers of God's revelation of a redemptive plan (through Jesus Christ) that will lead to a glorious ending? Do others within our proximity see a level of supernatural trust and obedience to a Higher Power that is second to none, all because of our faith? How much of an impact and influence does our trust and faith in our Lord have on others around us? Are we genuinely progressing to our future Promised Land in a manner that God desires, but also leading others down this same path?

Daily, we must put ourselves to the actual test (biblically and spiritually, 2 Cor 13:5)! After our test, this should be evident! The Lord is our commander and leader in everyday life, where we are serving Him wholeheartedly in His long-term plan. Today, Christians are called to serve God, trust in the truths of His promises, and be led by the Holy Spirit, with Jesus as their Lord and Savior of their lives. And this cannot happen if we do not surrender and submit to God's commands, which is essential for Christian growth and maturity, where the world sees a level of trust and obedience that impacts others. Please never forget this: If we disobey and do not comply with His plans, we will be in jeopardy of being punished.

As we come to an end, always remember these three things: 1) Our lives on this Side of Heaven are full of tests, trials, and tribulations to help us grow and become more like His Son, our Savior, Jesus Christ (please read James 1). 2) Our lives on this earth are a temporary assignment, but while we're here, we're to be Citizens of Heaven on Earth, paving our way, and for others, as Kingdom Builders (please read Philippians 1:20–30). 3) We should trust and obey God through every phase of our lives until the very end of our life journey (please read Isaiah 26:4), when we finally see our Lord and Savior in our new residence. What a day that will be!

But please always remember: If we struggle with trust in our Lord, we must go back and self-examine our Christian Walk to ensure we're on His righteous path of holiness and not falling to the ways of this world. If we don't, there's a danger to come, like that one generation of Israelites. Entrusted followers of Christ should know that distrust in our Heavenly Father and Lord and all His promises is a condition that can profoundly affect an individual's spiritual, mental, and emotional well-being.

And if it is not addressed biblically, it can hinder our faith, obedience, hope, relationships within our community of believers, and the peace that God desires for all His people. It can surely prevent us from the victory God has in store for us if we don't surrender and submit to Him our all. Please never forget this as we come to the end of this journey: Our lack of trust and faith in the Almighty One in every area of our lives could prevent someone from making it from this side to His side of eternity. As we will see, it's vitally important!

'The Danger of Distrust'

Almost four thousand years ago, generations of God's chosen ones were held in bondage for over 400 years, enduring harsh slavery and unfathomably oppressive conditions. The evil leaders of Egypt forced them to toil in turmoil for centuries, which undoubtedly led them not to believe wholeheartedly in an Almighty and Sovereign God because they saw no hope in being saved. There is no doubt that their lack of trust was due to the fear of the unknown, plus all the intense emotional, physical, and spiritual pain they were experiencing. But most importantly, the missing link for the Israelites was not staying faithfully connected with God throughout these years of torment.

It was apparent that many of the Israelites turned their backs on God because their rebellion was characterized by their initial resistance to Moses's leadership and their struggle to trust in God's deliverance. What would it take for God's children to have complete trust and faith in Him? I am pretty certain that the patience of God's children grew increasingly thin as each day and year passed, when they felt God was not responding to their cries, which led them to lose complete faith and trust in Yahweh.

Did thousands of Israelites, if not millions, doubt God's ability to deliver them? If they believed in God with all their hearts, souls, and minds before going to Egypt, what happened to their trust and faith in God, especially during those most intense years of being in bondage by the enemy? Many today ask this question: "Why did God allow His nation of people to be held in captivity for so many years?" As mentioned earlier, Yahweh wanted to develop Israel's national identity as His chosen people. But also the oppression and suffering that God's children endured would give us a historical line of God's divine deliverance and plan of victory in the end. This act of God would strengthen their sense of national purpose as carriers of God's revelation.

'The Danger of Distrust'

Even though one generation failed, God expected the next generation to be His bearers and messengers of His divine redemptive plan. One key takeaway from this book is that "God will be glorified when His children (including you and me) allow Him to control their destiny!" You see, the promise of God's redemption plan for humanity has been our source of hope for countless generations, which is through His Son, Jesus Christ. And He expects us to bear this revelation for all our future eras. It will come down to our absolute trust and obedience in all of God's ways, which will measure the depths of our genuine saving faith!

It's essential to note that the covenant between God and Abram (Abraham) lays the groundwork for the nation of Israel's distinctive role in God's long-term plan. And Deuteronomy 32:8-9 reminds us that God's plan is precise, purposeful, and centered on His promises to Israel. But the beauty of this magnificent plan is that Gentiles have been grafted into this great promise. And that alone should give us all hope and motivate us increasingly each day to trust God in all areas of our lives!

God's redemptive plan, as outlined through the nation of Israel, is presented in Romans 11. Despite Israel's unbelief, they remain the chosen people, and God's love for them endures even to this day. However, please remember, as we've seen so often throughout this journey, when we test God's patience and continually rebel without trusting and obeying His guiding principles, there will be consequences (as seen in the example of the first generation).

Sadly, the repeated complaints of that one generation highlight their lack of confidence and desire to move forward with God, for they had the audacity of wanting to return to Egypt, the place where they were enslaved in horrific bondage. Many of us look back at this tragic story of God's nation and see that they did not fully participate in God's plan, which was spiritually unproductive and would eventually lead to their demise.

Even for us today, we need to be cautious and not copy the behaviors and attitudes of that one generation of Israelites. If we do, we will be adrift from God's plan wholeheartedly. One thing is sure: We must fully participate in God's long-term plan in order for us to be fruitfully productive, or we will open the door to the enemy's plan in our lives, which is completely the opposite of God's will.

Evidently, the enemy's work planted seeds of doubt in the hearts and minds of that one generation of Israelites, leading them to test God's patience because they did not wholeheartedly believe in Yahweh's future plan. And we all know how that story ended for the first generation of God's children from the exodus: 'Their distrust, disloyalty, and disbelief led to their utter destruction.'

Trusting God to the Promised Land

Could the next era be more faithful to God by trusting and obeying all His ways? As discussed earlier, due to God's immense grace, mercy, and love, a new generation will be given an unbelievable opportunity to move to a land of great promise, where they can be united with their Ever-Loving God. Our Gracious God is definitely a God of second chances. *But with that chance comes a choice to change for His glory!*

Make no mistake about this: There is no more grave danger than distrusting God. How? When a believer chooses not to trust God, they will experience spiritual stagnation and complacency. They will constantly struggle with doubt, anxiety, fear, worry, self-pride, and disobedience, and this is exactly where Satan wants us. When a person is in that spiritual state of brokenness, the enemy's works have undermined that person's faith because he does not want us to be part of God's long-term plan. It leads us not to obey the foundation of God's message because we lack confidence in His guidance.

And when this happens, it becomes clear that they are not seeking help from the source, where one can find strength in God's word, guided by the Holy Spirit. Once again, distrusting God can lead people to a sense of being lost and confused, which can distance anyone from the presence of our Holy Creator! It becomes a domino effect of all types of dangerous detriment! It is essential to understand that when we lack trust and faith in God and our Lord, it will lead us not to produce fruit, which is demonstrating spiritual growth and good works.

You see, while the root of our salvation is by God's grace through faith (Ephesians 2:8–9), the fruit of our salvation will be evident in the selfless and humble works we perform for God's glory (James 2:14–26). We don't do them because of a personal obligation or chore; it's supernatural, and over time, it becomes like second nature. In other words, we do it for God, not us! Look at it this way: When Christ abides in us and we in Him (John 15), we bear fruit. When we produce the by-products of the Fruit of the Spirit (Galatians 5:22–23) these qualities are seen as evidence of the Holy Spirit's work in a believer's life, which is tied to their trust in and relationship with God.

Even look at the powerful passage in Jeremiah 17:7–8, where we see the great prophet's words, "But blessed are those who trust in the Lord and have made the Lord their hope and confidence. They are like trees planted along a riverbank, with roots that reach deep into the water. Such trees are not bothered by the heat or worried by long months of drought. Their leaves stay green, and they never stop producing fruit."

Here, we see that this emphasizes our connection with trust in God, so we're more spiritually stable, resilient, and continuously fruitful. This is

'The Danger of Distrust'

so important because, as we will see, distrusting God is a sign of lacking genuine faith, which can hinder or prevent the production of spiritual fruit. Please never forget this as we progress: Without the bearing of fruit, there will never be an outward manifestation of a transformed life lived in alignment with God's will.

Once again, since the fall of man, we've been surrounded by brokenness because of man's desire to choose a life that God did not intend. So, our battle in this journey—that we call life— continues each day with one obstacle to overcome after another that can easily damage our faith and trust in the Almighty One. And when this happens, we must seek the presence of God through prayer, fellowship with the Lord, and a strong community of believers, daily worship of praise and thanksgiving to God, reading, meditating, and the application of His word into our lives, and yielding to the power of His Spirit for counseling, comfort, and guidance.

Yes, unfortunately, we will face difficult times while we're here on this earth, and many will lose their desire to move forward, and others will lose passion for seeking their purpose and plan for God's glory. This happens when we wander too far away from His presence and miss the signals and invitations like a burning bush. He's calling us back to Him because He knows we are spiritually weary and heavy with constant burdens, which are preventing many of us from a life with purpose and meaning.

We cannot forget (once again) what Jesus' half-brother tells us in his first epistle, Jas 1:2-8, "Dear brothers and sisters, when troubles of any kind come your way, consider it an opportunity for great joy. For you know that when your faith is tested, your endurance has a chance to grow. So let it grow, for when your endurance is fully developed, you will be perfect and complete, needing nothing. If you need wisdom, ask our generous God, and he will give it to you. He will not rebuke you for asking. But when you ask him, be sure that your faith is in God alone. Do not waver, for a person with divided loyalty is as unsettled as a wave of the sea that is blown and tossed by the wind. Such people should not expect to receive anything from the Lord. Their loyalty is divided between God and the world, and they are unstable in everything they do." *We cannot afford to be spiritually unstable, lukewarm, and non-productive in a society and culture that is definitely more fruitless than fruitful.*

Dr. Neil Anderson, a best-selling Christian author and evangelist, made this profound discovery in his book 'Daily in Christ.' "Nobody loses control to Satan overnight; it's a gradual process of deception and yielding to his subtle influence. It is my observation that no more than 15 percent of the evangelical Christian community is entirely free of Satan›s bondage. These people consistently live a Spirit-filled life and bear fruit."

When I read this influential report, it made me ponder: *What about the other 85 percent?* It is apparent as I read more into this article that the majority of "proclaimed" Christians are struggling *'fruitlessly'* at one of at least three levels of spiritual conflict, which is their constant battle with the flesh, the world, and the enemy.

Christians, we cannot allow the desires of the world, the enemy's tactics, and the lust of the flesh, eyes, and the pride of life to rule our lives (1 John chapter 2). It seems apparent that many Christians do not know how to overcome the ongoing spiritual warfare in their daily lives. It's as if they don't know how to get from this world of darkness to the spiritual realm of the Lord's Light by living out their saving faith through their trust and obedience in the Lord.

Dr. Neil Anderson's process of "true repentance and faith" in God, which leads to fruitfulness, estimates that only 15% of Evangelical Christians in the United States are entirely free and, therefore, able to be spiritually fruitful. However, this also means there is a potential for spiritual fruitfulness for the other 85%. Unfortunately, many Christians struggle to address their deepest life woes, to dedicate themselves fully to the Lord, to cultivate greater fruitfulness in their daily lives, and to embark on a path that leads to the promises God has in store for His children. [1]

While there will be many who would say that 15% is a very high number and even the strongest saint can never escape the bondage of Satan, and we're not entirely free from our adversary, we must remember that our sanctification process is not a static and unchanging state—but a growing, lifelong, continually forming one that will overcome many of the enemy's tactics. It is helpful to be reminded of John 8:31–36, which concludes with the statement that "if the Son makes you free, you shall be free indeed." What does this mean, you may ask? All the sin, shame, and guilt have been dealt with when Jesus sets us free because of what He did on the cross. You and I no longer have to carry that burden of humiliation that leads us to a state of brokenness. Why?

Because we are forgiven and genuinely free (spiritually) indeed. When believers understand the depths of that promise and the truth of what Christ has freed them from, it sets the stage for them to live in what Christ has freed them to—a Promised Land of no more hurting and pain. As we grow, with the power of His indwelling Spirit in us, we not only bear fruit but also produce more and more fruit in our Christian lives (John chapter 15).

As we progress as His chosen ones, we're not focused on the fruits that fall from the tree and rot on the ground; we allow our Vine (Christ through

---

1. Anderson. Neil. "The results of brokenness."

'The Danger of Distrust'

His Spirit) to prune us and make our fruit good and grow even better. What we will see over time is a weeding out of all those unrighteous areas of our lives that prevent us from living a life of victory in Christ.

However, the ultimate danger is when a person never accepts Christ by faith because they have decided not to believe and trust the truths of God's word that could save them (Please read 2 Timothy 3). And that one poor decision leads to eternal death. Unfortunately, so many of the unbelievers in the world look at so-called Christians and see that our faith is not genuine. This leads me to ask: Are we exemplifying the genuine faith that saved us to a new life in Christ that is illuminating to everyone around us? Please read Colossians 3.

Have you ever heard the statement, "fake faith is distrust?" This statement suggests that when faith is insincere or not genuine, it can be a source of distrust. This is because a lack of authenticity in faith can erode people's trust in their spiritual beliefs, and most importantly, in our God and Lord. When someone is not genuinely living out their saving faith, they may develop a sense of internal self-deception (too easily deceived), leading to a lack of trust in godly values in our daily lives.

However, just as important, when we fall into this weak area of trust, it leads us to refrain from acting on our spiritual convictions. If not addressed, this can manifest in individuals failing to live out their faith, which can negatively impact their spiritual well-being. Over time, some may question the genuine reality of that person's faith and trust in God when they observe hypocrisy or a lack of authenticity in their life, *especially when they claim to be believers*. This is not the entrusting believer that God desires in you and me! Why?

This can lead the world of unbelievers, as well as the weaker in faith, to question our spiritual beliefs, for we're inconsistent in our walk of faith, trust, and obedience, *being the so-called followers of Christ*. This is a severe danger zone because we can then be labeled as a pharisaic person. Look at it this way: A Pharisaic attitude refers to a person who outwardly appears righteous but inwardly lacks true faith, humility, or love. Jesus strongly condemned this in the Gospels, especially in Matthew 23, where He called the Pharisees *whitewashed tombs*—beautiful on the outside but full of decay inside (Matthew 23:27)

In essence, the phrase "fake faith is distrust" highlights the potential for a lack of real faith that can have a rippling effect of disastrous outcomes. It can damage a person's self-image, relationships, and belief system. After all, we were created in God's image, where we have the undeniable honor, privilege, and opportunity to display many of His divine characteristics, not those that are sanctimonious, hypocritical, holier-than-thou, insincere, deceiving, phony, pietistical, two-faced, and self-righteous.

When one doesn't trust God, it can be challenging to maintain a positive outlook and hope for the future, especially during difficult times. Once again, it can lead to making decisions based on fear and a lack of faith rather than seeking God's guidance and wisdom. Trusting God means being open to the possibilities and opportunities He may present, while distrust can lead to missing out on blessings and growth, and even cause us to doubt God's love and care for us.

Doubting God's love and care can create a sense of distance and disconnection from Him. Just think: Distrusting God can foster a negative and unspiritual mindset, *where one sees only the challenges and difficulties in life rather than focusing on God's goodness, faithfulness, and all the things that are worthy of His praise (Philippians 4:8). And it's all due to us not surrendering to self and not submitting to the Power of our Heavenly Father!*

Once again, when we fail to surrender and submit to the Almighty One, some of our personal beliefs, opinions, and man-made theories will clash with God's teachings, leading to internal conflict. As genuine believers in Christ, in a world of mistruths, we must continually examine our faith and ensure that Jesus Christ is at the center (2 Cor 13:5). We will soon see that we must seek His wisdom and knowledge and uphold our Trust Factor like never before (Read Proverbs chapter 3). When we fervently and diligently pray, yield to His guiding ways, and continually yearn for His word and Spirit, we will discover our weaknesses, seek His empowering strength, and be on the right path of God's plan.

Let's delve more deeply: "Real faith" refers to a genuine belief and trust that manifests in pure actions, resulting in a transformed life that honors and glorifies God. It is constantly and perpetually active, and it continues to demonstrate, through genuine deeds, that surely pleases God. On the contrary, once again, "fake faith" refers to a superficial profession of belief that lacks genuine commitment to the principles of the real faith, resulting in no real change in a person's behavior. It is merely verbal and lacks tangible results, a point often underscored by the saying, "Faith without works is dead," as James, Jesus' half-brother, reminds us in his epistle, as noted earlier for our daily reminder.

Undoubtedly, genuine saving faith should motivate people to live in a way pleasing to God daily. It means that we believe in and trust His existence and creation, and that He rewards those who seek Him above all else. Faith believes in and trusts God through all the circumstances of life. It is expressed through complete love and obedience and is bold, not timid (2 Tim 1:7). This type of faith is confidence in the God of the Bible, whose

'The Danger of Distrust'

presence and power flow through those who have chosen to believe and trust in Him and His Son in this life and the new one to come.

You see, real faith recognizes that God sent His Son to the cross to reconcile us to our Heavenly Father, and this type of faith pleases Him. It is a solid belief in the Almighty One and that He can and will do what he says. This leads us to trust in our Holy Father and Creator, and we put that belief into practice, which leads to the progression of our sanctification process. Always remember this: 'Faith is that gift from God that grows over time.' And our trust is the act of putting our faith into practice; it is a willful choice that grows out of our absolute faith and obedience to all His ways.

So, here's our challenge for today: We must surrender to 'self' and submit ourselves humbly to God's empowering grace. If not, we will have constant fights in our hearts, minds, and spirits. That is why we must incorporate an intense and fervent life of prayer, and not only read His holy Word, *but also apply the truths of His Scriptures in our lives.* It's imperative that we foster and nurture genuine fellowship and worship with our Lord each day, embodying Christlikeness. If we don't live by these standards of God, we will fail in the areas of absolute trust and obedience.

As we've seen throughout the story of Joshua and in God's word, without complete belief and trust in God's guiding principles, *we will never have faithful obedience in our lives.* Please never forget that faithful obedience is a significant and central theme in the Christian faith because it reflects a believer's commitment to follow God's commands and live according to His will.

In other words, if we lack in our trust and faith in all of God's ways, we will not only struggle to obey His word, but we will not yield to His Spirit's guidance, and this will open our life portal to the one thing the enemy wants us to do—and that's you and me doubting God's plan in our lives! As growing Christians today, we should all know by now that doubting God in any way, shape, or form is the opposite of His will in our lives!

To gain a more robust perspective, a Barna Group survey conducted a few years ago, entitled "Two-thirds of Christians Face Doubt," revealed several key takeaways. But the one that stood out to me was this: When going through times of spiritual doubt due to intense trials and tribulations, where did you find help or answers? The response from Christians was staggering to my eyes because the survey revealed that less than 30% go to the primary source for all the right answers, which is God's word. How can this be? I wanted to learn more about this particularly disheartening statistic. [2]

---

2. Barna Group. "Two-Thirds of Christians Face Doubt."

As I pondered and researched, I observed that it is clear today that too many distractions and disturbances in our spiritual lives lead us to deviate from God's intended message and plan for our lives. In my first book, God Values Our Daily Steps, I highlighted a key point from a survey conducted by the American Bible Society a few years ago, which stated that only 9% of Christians read the Bible daily. To take this further, many theologians, scholars, and researchers say that less than half of these apply God's word to their daily lives.

Folks: We're talking about less than 5% of proclaimed followers who read God's word daily *are the only ones* yielding productive and fruitful lives (Once again, read the Parable of the Four Soils in Matthew, chapter 13). But here's the other gut-wrenching takeaway: 'The other 95% of Christians do not trust in the application of God's word in their lives. It is obvious that the majority of Christians are falling into the group of the 2nd and 3rd soils in Matthew 13. And if that does not riddle (pierce) your heart, mind, soul, and spirit, I don't know what will!

Here's a call-out to Christ's followers Today: "Don't we realize that when we apply God's word and seek His counsel, it can help us to gain more insight into God's purpose and plan in our lives. It helps us to progress spiritually in His wisdom, where we can have more trust in our Lord and obedience to His guiding principles." If you seriously think about it, we cannot move forward productively and fruitfully in our Christian Walk without daily compliance with the guidance of God's Word. If that first generation of Israelites is our example for today, we can clearly see that they did not listen to and adhere to God's message and plan, which led to their destruction.

Today, people walk the aisles and dedicate their lives to the Lord, professing their faith through baptism and even signing up as volunteers to serve in various capacities. Millions weekly want to rededicate their lives to the Lord because they have trusted more in the ways of man and the world than in their Savior. However, and sadly, too often, people profess faith in Jesus as their Lord, but it is merely a profession without genuine faith (please reread James 2:14–26). How is this being an actual true representative of our Lord and King when we're not living out our absolute trust, faith, and obedience to Him alone?

We don't want to be critical and judgmental, BUT there must be signs of constant spiritual change, weeding out areas of unrighteousness, continual biblical growth, and accountability within the community of believers for us to effectively spread the valid message of the Gospel to the world. This leads me to ask: As Christ-followers, is the fruitfulness of our faith reflected in our daily trust and obedience? We must challenge ourselves: Does the world view you and me as faithful and fruitful followers of Christ, or have they labeled us unfruitful because we live by more of the ways of this world and humanity? Never forget what our Lord and Savior, Jesus Christ, says: We will know them by their fruit (Matthew 7:16–23)!

If you read this passage in Matthew 7, the statement "You will know them by their fruit" teaches that one can discern faithful followers of Jesus from false prophets by observing their actions and the outcomes of their behavior. In the Bible, "fruit" refers to the results of a person's life and character, indicating that their good actions and moral integrity will reflect their true faith, while evil actions will reveal falsehood. In other words, *do followers of Christ represent more of God's truths than the falsehoods of man?*

Essentially, it means that an individual's conduct and manner on a daily scale reveal the real measure of that person's heart's genuine desire and motive (Read Matthew 9:14, 15:9, and Jeremiah 17:5–10). This leads me to an alarming issue: Are Christians today living more as part-time producers (lukewarm) for their Lord, or are they truly committed to every detail of God's word? And we all know how our Lord feels about lukewarm believers, *those who straddle the fence and teeter-totter back and forth between the Lord and the world.* If you fall into the category of a lukewarm believer, never forget what our Lord says: He will spew them out of His mouth (Rev 3:16)!

Yes, once again, we will all stumble from time to time because we all fall short of God's glorious standard (Rom 3:23) and we all go through seasons of bearing little fruit (1 John 1:8). However, 1 John 3:4–10 makes it clear that those who genuinely know God and desire to please and honor Him in their everyday life *will not continue a lifestyle of bearing bad fruit and portraying a life cycle of complications.* We have been transformed, and the fruit of our lives should be evidence of that transformation (2 Cor 5:17).

The great minor prophet Hosea offers us some powerful words in Hosea 8:7: "The phrase 'sowing the wind, reaping the whirlwind' is a vivid metaphor used to describe the consequences of Israel's unfaithfulness and idolatry." In this set of passages, we can even see that the succeeding generations failed to maintain absolute trust and obedience in the ways of Yahweh. What will it take for God's children to finally get it? If we're honest in our spiritual examination today, we can all ask ourselves this very question as well. What do I mean? *It seems that we fall way too much in our spiritual lives because we're stumbling into the ways of man, this world, and the enemy. Sounds just like the Israelites!*

Throughout this journey, we've seen many valuable teachings for genuine followers of Christ. We have also learned some priceless lessons from the first and second generations of Israelites. Today, do we ever reflect on our level of trust and faith in our Holy Father? Do we think about the consequences if we are not loyal to God and trust Him in every part of our lives?

Seriously consider these PowerPoints: As discussed earlier and as our daily reminder, when we don't trust our Lord in every step of our Christian Walk, we're simply taking all our life circumstances into our own hands. When we do this, we tend *to prioritize our problems over our relationship with God*. Remember: Not trusting and believing in God with all our hearts, souls, and minds will lead to disobedience and rebellion.

That is why we must continually grow and spiritually mature in God's wisdom, holiness, and righteousness, which we should constantly seek first above all things. Always remember: The power of God's wisdom leads us to trust Christ as the Lord of our lives. And this trust enables us to yield to His wisdom and walk the righteous and good paths described in Proverbs.

And this encourages our trust and reliance on Him for strength and guidance, through His Word and Spirit, no matter what the enemy hurls our way. This leads me to ask: With the power of God's wisdom that can help us on this Side of Eternity, have you asked for this most precious gift from God, as James tells us in James 1? Because it can surely keep us steadfast on God's path until our grand entry one day soon!

Next Steps

'Trust God's Wisdom!'

When the floodgates of distrusting our Holy Creator try to overtake our lives, we need to bank on the Wisdom of God! There is undoubtedly no greater comfort in our daily lives than when we rely upon the wisdom of our Heavenly Father. Why? When we seek divine guidance and understanding from God, rather than relying on human insight and our own perspective, it means we're depending and resting upon His wisdom, where we find peace, hope, and clarity in making tough decisions. This is vital because when we trust in the wisdom of our Creator, we accept and believe in the truths of His promises and live by His divine characteristics that will lead to a stronger relationship with God and our Lord. And this is so needed in our everyday lives! Why, you may ask.

We all know that in today's times of uncertainties, worries, fears, and burdens that can consume our lives, it is pretty evident that things happen to us that do not make sense in our own eyes. Yet, in all His infinite ways, unlike us, God sees all, knows all, and has a good plan in the end (Please read Isaiah 55 and Romans 8:28). You see, the wiser ones who have a close-knit relationship with God trust Him in all of life's misfortunes even when He does not make sense to them. What is so different about the wiser and more mature ones in their Christian Walk versus those who lack in this key area of growth? Here it is:

They seek truth in the Holy Scriptures and live by them daily. They acknowledge God's sovereignty, faithfulness, goodness, lovingkindness, grace, mercy, and trustworthiness, which leads them to surrender to self and submit their all to the will of the Lord. They develop patience and perseverance through the power of prayer. You see more of the Fruit of the Spirit in their daily lives than in the ways of the world. They take the enlightening words of God as their primary source of information, which helps them to learn more and grow in His knowledge. It's as if they want to consume the word of God like Ezekiel did in chapter 3 of his book.

"The voice said to me, "Son of man, eat what I am giving you—eat this scroll! Then go and give its message to the people of Israel." So I opened my mouth, and he fed me the scroll. "Fill your stomach with this," he said. And when I ate it, it tasted as sweet as honey in my mouth." The power of God's word (Heb 4:12–13) and all His wisdom is sweet to those who have a burning desire for it, but bitter to those who are not fully committed to our Almighty One. If you're a genuine follower of Jesus Christ, do you aspire to grow more and more in all His ways? Here are more assets you can possess through the wisdom of God.

By the power of the Holy Spirit, the wiser ones ascertain discernment where they can dissect between things that are spiritually right versus those that are not. Once again, they don't just read and study the Bible, but they apply the depths of His word into their lives. You see more obedience to the ways of God than rebellious acts. In other words, there is more righteousness in their active lives than in the unrighteous ways of man and this world because they possess a repentant heart.

We cannot forget this profound passage from the Apostle Paul in Colossians 3:16–17, "Let the message about Christ, in all its richness, fill your lives. Teach and counsel each other with all the wisdom he gives. Sing psalms and hymns and spiritual songs to God with thankful hearts. And whatever you do or say, do it as a representative of the Lord Jesus, giving thanks through him to God the Father."

When faithful followers of Christ live by these words, this is all due to their heeding the guidance of the Holy Spirit, which leads to a wholehearted commitment to God. These steps, taken by the righteous and wise, help them to build confidence and enthusiasm in living a life like the character of Christ. And this enables them to cultivate a deeper, more unwavering trust in all of God's ways.

When followers of Christ trust in God's wisdom, they are more consistent in their words and actions because their lives are grounded in the power of God's holy word and His Spirit. They will display more humility in their lives, embracing joy and peace, forgiveness and mercy, thankfulness and praise, as well as words of grace and love. They will also offer selfless service, accompanied by a willingness to listen and seek godly advice, so they can continue to grow. They are truly building blocks of godly generations for the Kingdom of God! Do these divine traits describe you as a Christ-follower today?

'Trust God's Wisdom!'

As we conclude this long journey, as faithful Christians, we should now understand that when we believe in and trust the process designed by our Holy Creator in our personal lives, we are more likely to remain dedicated to His long-term objectives. How? Because we will apply ourselves with all our hearts, minds, souls, and strength consistently for God's glory. Over time, we learn from our mistakes and view those temporary setbacks as part of God's working process. This enables us to gain understanding and adopt an approach of wisdom and discernment (through the power of the Holy Spirit) without becoming discouraged or disheartened.

As we grow and mature, we respond more than react to life's circumstances. This is important because reacting is an impulsive (spontaneous) and compulsive (uncontrollable) behavior that occurs in situations with potential consequences that can not only affect us individually but also have a possible ripple effect on others. In contrast, responding is more thoughtful because it involves reflecting on the problem and considering your options before taking action. When Christians take this latter approach, it is primarily due to one key fact: 'They are persuaded by the power of God's Wisdom in their lives through His Word and His Spirit.'

And when this occurs, as mentioned earlier, they are more apt to trust God's divine intervention and guidance. This is definitely a life lesson the first generation of Israelites needed. You see, growing in God's wisdom is vital because without it, God's insight and understanding are absent, as well as His knowledge and the gift of discernment. Without His wisdom, we lack guidance, faith, hope, and love, leading us to be more disobedient to all His ways. If we're not seeking and growing in the wisdom of God, we're more likely too focused on the wisdom of man and this world.

Never forget this: God's word consistently teaches us that reliance on worldly wisdom is fraught with danger, leading to spiritual blindness and a separation from God's purpose and plan. Believers are called to seek and trust in the wisdom that comes from above, which is pure, peace-loving, and aligned with God's will. Think about this: The wisdom of God was missing in the Israelites' hearts, minds, and souls thousands of years ago. And we do not want to fall into that same pit. To validate this point, look at the power of God's word in Deut 32:28–29 below:

"But Israel is a senseless nation; the people are foolish, without understanding. Oh, that they were wise and could understand this! Oh, that they might know their fate!" This set of passages is a powerful section of the Song of Moses, a lament over Israel's future unfaithfulness. It paints a vivid picture of their disobedience, folly, and the consequences they will face, ultimately highlighting God's justice and the bitter fruit of their choices, which were opposite to God's desire and plan. This emphasizes the nation of

God's children's lack of wisdom and discernment, a critical aspect missing from their lives that led to their rebellion against God.

Undoubtedly, Israel was a nation void of God's counsel, with no understanding among them to stay on Yahweh's course of plan to receive enriched blessings. Yes, in time, they inherited the Promised Land, but as we've seen throughout this journey, they still lacked faith, trust, and obedience in taking all the land God had given them. What a missed opportunity of blessings, all because they did not heed God's instructions. Israel's lack of wisdom, guidance, and belief at this point serves as a prophetic warning and a reflection on Israel's spiritual state; a state of spirituality that we must avoid at all costs!

As mentioned earlier, and often, when we lack God's wisdom, we struggle with complete trust and faith in all His ways. Just think: These two master components, trust and faith, applied to God's children thousands of years ago, just as they do today. When we lack in these two areas, we struggle with complete compliance with God's ways, opening the floodgates to the enemy's ways. Please remember this: When we spiritually fail and encounter shortcomings in our lives, the enemy seeks to undermine our genuine connection and relationship with our Lord. The enemy knows that doubt can challenge our trust and faith barometers when things are not going right.

While doubt can challenge our faith, it also holds the potential to strengthen and deepen our relationship with God. When we turn to our Living Source, which is God's Word, genuine believers and followers of Christ are encouraged to navigate doubt with honesty and trust in God's faithfulness. It will surely help us overcome and continue down God's path! Our trust in God comes down to you and me making the choice that God's way is the only way that can sustain us through it all. And when we have this type of mindset and heart, it is mainly due to our growth in God's wisdom.

And think, when we try to use our own wisdom and control our lives in our own limited power, we become more discontented, lack joy, comfort, and peace, and even experience increased anxiety and worries. And it does not stop there. We begin to develop a critical and cynical spirit, a hardness of heart, and spiritual blindness that leads to a departure from God's presence. And when we continue to defy and rebel against our Heavenly Father's wisdom, it will eventually lead to God's wrath. Once again, think about that first generation of Israelites. Their demise was due to disobedience and not believing in God's most divine ways, which was surely a lack of God's wisdom in their lives.

Why is this important, you may ask? We all must undergo the fine-tuning phases of our sanctification process, where we are refined, reshaped, and renewed, especially when we endure intense trials and tribulations that affect our trust and faith. You see, these times of spiritual renewal will enhance our Christian Walk, deepen our relationship with God, and strengthen our trust and faith, which can indeed affect others in our life journey. This legacy demonstrates that we have always trusted in the Wisdom of God, a gift that we can lean upon and learn from Him constantly.

As noted earlier, always keep this in mind. When going through times of distrust, discouragement, disheartenment, and distress, we all need that one component that will help us understand the depths of God's work in our lives: *His wisdom*. Let's not forget what Jesus' half-brother James tells us in James 1: "If you need wisdom, ask our generous God, and He will give it to you." He will not rebuke you for asking. But when you ask him, be sure your faith is in God alone. Do not waver, for a person with divided loyalty is as unsettled as a wave of the sea that is blown and tossed by the wind. Such people should not expect to receive anything from the Lord. Their loyalty is divided between God and the world, and they are unstable in everything they do."

We can even refer to the wisest man in the Bible, Solomon, as our example in 1 Kings 3. In this profound chapter, we see God appearing to this great king in a dream and asking him what he wanted. Almighty God said, ' Ask, and I will give it to you. ' Solomon could have asked for anything, but he chose wisdom. Why? Solomon asked God for wisdom because, as a young king, he recognized his lack of experience and the immense responsibility of leading God's people, understanding that wisdom was crucial for just and effective governance. Solomon knew that God's wisdom was the foundation of trust in God's guiding ways!

And over time, this is the same king who would say in 1 Kgs 8:56, "Praise the Lord who has given rest to his people Israel, just as he promised. Not one word has failed of all the wonderful Promises he gave through his servant Moses.' Solomon came to realize, after receiving more of God's wisdom, that there is more to life to come. As he grew closer to God through that depth of understanding, his trust and faith in God's ways reached new heights, for he came to understand that God's way was the only way. Read the book of Ecclesiastes, written by Solomon, and we will see that without God's leading, there is no point to life, with no purpose or direction.

Looking at Solomon's one request, this makes me wonder: If God asked His true believers today, what is the one component we need in life in order to sustain and maintain that close walk with Him until our Day of Glory? Yes, we need God's grace, for it is by this precious gift through faith in Christ that we obtain salvation! But with all the internal and external battles against the unspiritual waves of this society and culture today, we indeed need God's wisdom, because with it we ascertain His knowledge, understanding, and discernment, which can lead to spiritual growth and a deeper relationship with God.

I see God's grace and wisdom as two sides of the same coin. Both attributes are essential for living a life that reflects God's character and purpose. As noted throughout the book, grace is when God gives you what you don't deserve, and wisdom is when God provides His true children the understanding to make the best choices in life.

You see, God's wisdom involves understanding and acting according to His will, which helps us to trust Him more because we rely on His guidance more each passing day. God's wisdom is not just knowledge but a deeper understanding and application of His truth into our lives, which helps us discern what is good from what is evil and what is true from what is false. By seeking and acting on God's wisdom, we learn to trust His character and His ability to lead us. His wisdom enables us to view situations from an eternal perspective, fostering greater faith and confidence in His plan.

Throughout my years of service in the ministry, I firmly believe that God's wisdom is a vital component and gift that is lacking in the lives of many Christians. Why? Even for followers of Christ today, millions struggle with doubt and a lack of trust, and can't discern right from wrong in everyday life. These are clear indicators that a Christian is deficient in God's wisdom. The evidence is found in the passage of Jesus' half-brother, James, that we read above. When they waffle in their stance as a believer and follower of Christ, they are not steadfast in their faith and trust because they lack wisdom. Sounds so much like the Israelites…what a profound parallel!

You may ask. How can I determine if I lack God's wisdom, which can help me develop trust and faith in His plan to move forward with our Lord and Savior? Here it is: As stated earlier and often throughout the book, when we face our intense battles and struggles in life, we must be grounded in the sound truths of God's Word, where we receive it, accept it, apply it, and obey it, guided by the Holy Spirit. We must focus on His Scriptures throughout each day and gain a deeper understanding of our weakest areas in life, where the enemy constantly attacks us. We must implement biblical principles and hold ourselves accountable in our daily lives as Christians.

Additionally, we should be part of a strong community of believers where we can absorb more of God's wisdom from others. God's word provides us with guidance on how believers can embody God's wisdom in their actions, decisions, and interactions with others, which can be passed on to others for God's glory. Throughout the scriptures, the Bible encourages us to listen to wiser people and learn from them. We are to encourage and edify others, building them up in the Body of Christ. Please read the following passages and live by these words from God: Proverbs 1:5, 27:17, 2 Timothy 2:2, and 1 Thessalonians 5:11.

And this is important because when we lack support from the Word of God, His Holy Spirit, and the Body of Christ, we will face relentless battles with the enemy, where we may fall prey to trusting and obeying our Lord and King in everyday life. You see, trusting in the wisdom of God is that powerful attribute that keeps us anchored in all His protection. How? When we rely on God's wisdom, we know that His love for us will be our safeguard from harm and will guide us through life's most challenging moments!

Please understand that the wisdom of God is a gift, and we cannot obtain this most precious quality unless we seek God first above all things. We must pray and ask Him generously for it with a humble and pure heart. When given, we must live by it faithfully, where we become wise and live in God's wisdom. It's imperative that we listen, learn, and practice what God teaches us through His Word, so that our minds are renewed and we gain more of our Heavenly Father's insight. Undoubtedly, the wisdom of God is one of the most important gifts we can receive from our Creator. Why?

From the river of God's grace, His wisdom springs forth godly knowledge, spiritual discernment, enabling us to live a godly life with an eternal focus. It helps us to grow spiritually, utilize our gifts, and gain His insight as we navigate the storms of life. It enables us to stay more in His presence, making it less likely for us to stray away. It helps us find real meaning and purpose in our lives through service to our Lord. As we grow closer in this area, we discover and experience more of his spiritual blessings in our lives, which lift our spirits to great heights that can be shared with others.

And when we possess this most essential trait of holiness, through His Spirit, we are empowered to trust and obey our Lord and God more and more each day because we believe in the truths of His promises. We are more able to live a godly life of holiness and righteousness. This is why we are told in 2 Peter 3:18 that we must grow in grace and knowledge of our Lord Jesus Christ, which can only happen if we have the knowledge of the Scriptures by reading them, where we can obtain that powerful source of peace, security, and hope. And this is all from the Wisdom of God!

As we discussed earlier, we must be cautious about how we live in a world of untruths, distortions, and godlessness. The great apostle Paul even reminds us in Ephesians 5:15–17, "So be careful how you live. Don't live like fools, but like those who are wise. Make the most of every opportunity in these evil days. Don't act thoughtlessly but understand what the Lord wants you to do."

'So do not do as the unwise but as the wise, making the most of every spiritual opportunity for His glory, because the days are evil.' Make no mistake about this: *Wise people under the guidance of God will make the most of their time in knowing and doing God's will, where you see absolute trust and obedience in all of His ways in their active lives! Oh, the immense power of God's Wisdom, because of His wondrous grace, is the spiritual tool we need to ensure that His working process is ongoing in our lives as His children.*

Follow Up

Trust + Obedience = Genuine Faith

There is no greater formula in the Scriptures than this: trust + obedience = genuine saving faith. As a final follow-up and to ensure that our checks and balances of these components are active in our lives, let's delve into the depths of our hearts, minds, and spirits to gauge our progress as we reach the end of this journey. Because what we're going to discover is if we're really progressing in our daily walk with the Lord as His Citizens of Heaven on earth.

Unquestionably, this powerful prescription of holiness is needed in every Christian's life to ensure that their walk with the Lord is genuine, and they are living out their salvation for the glory of God. Consider this: It highlights the depths and measures of how these concepts interconnect in profound ways. Here's what I am trying to say: Faith in our God, Lord, and His Spirit is not merely intellectual assent, but a living, active force demonstrated through trust in His Sovereign plan and power.

In addition, when our trust is functioning in the Father, Son, and Holy Spirit, we will be obedient to all His principles and commands. In other words, we will not compromise, give way, or waffle from His guidance one inkling. This means that true faith is not passive but is actively expressed through our actions with a willingness and commitment to follow His instructions and teachings.

This is imperative because if this most divine process is at work in our lives, we're honoring the Father, Son, and Holy Spirit, which involves recognizing their distinct roles and functions within the Godhead, as the Holy Trinity. The Father is the origin of creation, the Son is the mediator, and the Holy Spirit is the one who brings every work to completion. You see, the Father creates the plan, the Son implements the plan, and the Holy Spirit administers the plan. And think: When our faith is producing spiritual trust and obedience to its fullest, we're glorifying God at the highest level.

If you seriously consider this formula above, it encompasses the Greatest Commandment, which is to love the Lord your God with all your heart, mind, soul, and strength (Matthew 22:37). It embodies every element of the Fruit of the Spirit in our daily lives. It leads us to act upon our conviction, trust the Lord in more practical ways, to commit our all to Him wholeheartedly, and to be not only a Bible Reader, but a Bible Doer. Let's look at the breakdown of this most profound principle.

Example: When we trust the Lord as described in Proverbs 3:5-6, it not only leads us to believe in His guidance but also enables us to experience His faithfulness and goodness in our lives. As we've seen throughout this book, trust and faith go hand in hand. Trust is essential for faith, as it allows us to rely on God's promises, His wisdom, and guidance, especially during all our troublesome times. Throughout God's Word, there are a myriad of verses that emphasize the importance of trusting God, which should definitely encourage us to submit our lives to Him, such as Psalm 56:3, 37:5, Isaiah 26:3, John 14:27, and Philippians 4:6-7.

And when we submit to Him wholly, it enables us to grow closer to God, which in turn elevates our prayer, worship, and fellowship with our Lord and Savior. And as we mature and are set apart for His glorious purpose, when we hear the word of God, we don't only read it, but receive it, accept it, apply it, and obey it! This deepens our spiritual connection with our Lord, allowing us to enjoy God's presence.

In that closeness, there's always that open invitation to seek Him and experience more of His grace, love, and His leading in our life's journey. By embracing trust, we can navigate life's challenges with confidence and find peace, joy, and even patience in knowing that God is always with us. And when this is enforced in our Christian Walk, we are more apt to obey His word, yield to all His ways, and yearn for more of His workings in our lives.

By now, we should know that trust is a fundamental aspect of our genuine faith, which leads to obedience. And as believers in today's swirling ways of uncertainties, we need to rely on God's guidance and promises more than ever. Consider this: When we trust God with all our beings, trust and obedience are intertwined, interlocked, and ingrained in our spiritual DNA because of that gift of faith from our Holy Father!

Look at the great Patriarch Abraham as our example. His willingness to obey God's command to sacrifice his son, demonstrating profound trust because of the faith he inherently possessed in God! Trusting God means putting our complete faith in Him, which influences our actions and decisions, prompting us to follow His will and plan in our lives, all for His glory. And we all know that God was pleased with Abraham because he put his faith to work for His Lord!

Ultimately, trust in God is essential for a deeper relationship with Him, as it allows us to align our lives with His purposes. These elements are not just a belief but a heartfelt response that encourages obedience to His will. And when we're in the will of our Father and Lord, because of our trust and obedience in all His ways, we have a level of inner peace that is unexplainable.

Never forget: In order to have the peace of God, we must have peace with God! We must understand that the Peace of God is a spiritual state of appreciation and faith that comes from submitting to His plan and trusting and obeying the commandments of God and our Lord. Please read John 14:27, Romans 5:1, and Philippians 4:7. That supernatural peace is when we trust in the promises of His word, where we give all our burdens and wearisome ways to our Lord so that we can take rest in Him fully! Please read Psalm 55:22, Matthew 11:28-30, and 1 Peter 5:7.

Remember what John (the one that Jesus loved) tells us in 1 John 5:3, "Loving God means keeping his commandments, and his commandments are not burdensome." This means that God's holy word and commandments are a source of love and guidance *for those who follow them, which proves our genuine saving faith.*

And when our relationship with the Lord reaches this level, as stated in the passage above in 1 John, we will undoubtedly experience His peace and joy, and develop greater patience in His timing because we take His word and promises to heart and believe them. Why? Because they provide us with profound pleasure and comfort! And once again, the ultimate results will be seen in our trust and obedience to His commandments in our everyday lives.

On the contrary, there is a danger zone for those who distrust God. As discussed in the last chapter, and as our daily reminder, if we don't trust in God, it can lead to extreme fear, anxiety, stress, and a separation from His presence. This will cause people to act on their own fleshly desires, which will lead to defiance, just like that first generation of Israelites. And here's the risk:

Like God's chosen ones thousands of years ago, because of their lack of trust in God, they fell into idolatry. That one generation of Israelites failed to trust and believe God, His promises, and His goodness, causing them to act on their own wisdom and desires, which led to disobedience and death. If we fall short of this prescribed method mentioned at the outset of this chapter in our lives, there's one formula we all must stray from, and it's this: distrust+disobedience=destruction.

And just as God's nation was then, so today, if people don't trust God, they may create other things to trust in, such as money, their career, individuals, sports teams, or a hobby, and the list could be endless. We cannot forget that our Holy God is a jealous God (Exodus 34:14). In other words, if anything gets in the way of placing God first in our lives, it is a sin, and that will indeed separate anyone from the will of God.

Always remember this as we move forward: God should ultimately *own all our loyalty, praise, worship, and service; nothing or no one else.* And when they do this, it is a clear sign that they are entrusted and committed followers of the Almighty One and our Lord! We cannot forget what happened to that first generation of Israelites from the Exodus, for they sought other things to believe in other than the One True God, which culminated in their doom! Our trust and belief must be sound and grounded in the truths of the Scriptures, or we will be deceived.

The second part of the formula is that when we obey the Lord, it means we love Him so much that we're dedicated to His guiding principles as outlined in His Holy Word. This type of obedience, enrobed in His love and grace, leads us to be gentler, kinder, good, and self-controlled in all that we say and do. Look at it this way: Obedience to God's commands fosters each element of the Fruit of the Spirit in our lives (Galatians 5:22–23). By embracing and engaging obedience, we can reflect God's love and grace in our daily lives, which in turn can impact and influence those around us.

When you examine the depths of this spiritual and biblical formula, it reveals that faith is not only the root that yields trust and obedience, but it's also the final summation of who we truly are as Christians; it proves our salvation. We cannot forget what the author tells us in Hebrews 11:6, "And it is impossible to please God without faith. Anyone who wants to come to him must believe that God exists and that he rewards those who sincerely seek him."

Obedience is not just about following rules; it's about responding to God's love and living out His Word in our lives. This begins with us knowing God and His goodness, allowing His truth to shape our choices and relationships. And as we progress in our sanctified lives, obedience is a response to faith, leading to blessings and transformation in our lives. There are numerous examples of obedience in the Bible, which illustrate how surrendering to God's will can lead to personal growth, a deeper connection with Him, and fulfilling His plan in our lives.

This involves a deep and abiding trust in God's wisdom and a belief in all His truths and promises as found in His Holy Word. It's a reliance on His powerful guidance, even when circumstances are challenging or uncertain. Obedience, in turn, is seen as a tangible expression of that trust.

Trust + Obedience = Genuine Faith

And when individuals trust in God, they are more likely to comply and follow His teachings and commands. This obedience is not born out of fear or compulsion, but from a place of love and devotion. It shows that we're living out our salvation with trembling and fear, as Paul notes in Philippians 2:12. This means that a person's faith is marked by a deep sense of reverence and seriousness toward God's command, which involves complete trust and obedience.

As one grows, they realize that salvation, by faith, is not a one-time event, but a continuous process that should lead to progress. It requires personal responsibility and a commitment to God and our Lord. When we do this, it highlights a respectful attitude towards God. Over time, the entrusted believer lives in a manner that reflects the worth and works of Christ in them, acknowledging the significance of their faith. What a privilege and honor to have a Christian Walk that is serious, with spiritual rewards and no eternal ramifications. However, it comes down to us choosing the right path!

This godly prescription emphasizes that trust and obedience are not separate entities, but rather two sides of the same coin. One cannot truly have faith without demonstrating both trust and obedience. Once again, obedience is seen as evidence of a genuine faith, and trust is the foundation upon which obedience is built. However, as we've seen throughout this book, just like that one generation of Israelites, there are severe consequences if we don't trust and obey God. Because without these two mastering components in our lives, there is no faith!

Jesus' half-brother James suggests in the second chapter of his epistle in verses 17–18 that faith without works (actions or obedience) is dead. We're not saying that works will get you to Heaven. Yes, we're saved by God's grace through faith in Christ alone (Eph 2:8–9), for this is the root of our salvation. But what James is saying is that there should be fruit from our salvation, which is the result of our true faith.

Similarly, John 14:15 states, "If you love me, keep my commandments". These verses emphasize the importance of obedience as a crucial component of faith. This understanding of faith moves beyond mere rituals or outward practices. True faith, as expressed through trust and obedience, is viewed as a transformative force that profoundly impacts one's life, character, and relationship with God and the Lord.

God's word reminds us profoundly in a set of passages in Deuteronomy 9:23–24 that when we do not trust and obey the Lord and all His ways, it leads to absolute rebellion against Yahweh. We must realize, with a discerning spirit, that in today's society and culture, we are living in a time when our homes, communities, states, country, and world are severely off course when it comes to complete trust and obedience to God's ways. And without complete trust and obedience in the Lord with all our hearts, minds, souls, and strength, it will only lead us to be disobedient. There is no foundation of His genuine saving faith in our lives if we don't live out every word that He's put forth before the eyes of our hearts, minds, and souls.

To expound: When this order and method of holiness and righteousness (not perfection) is alive and at work in us, it will produce unfathomable results in our homes, workplaces, streets, churches, and abroad. It elevates and strengthens our relationships as parents, spouses, employees, friends, servants, and brothers and sisters in Christ. Yes, it's that solid!

As we come to the end of this journey, we should now know whether we're truly *trusting and complying with God's working process in our lives*. As discussed frequently, trusting and obeying God is a spiritual approach that involves completely surrendering and submitting ourselves to His will, and believing that our Heavenly Father will work all things out for our good (Rom 8:28). In other words, we don't have any seeds of doubt in our mind, we believe in His workings supernaturally, like its second nature engrained in every fiber of our hearts and minds.

You see, it encompasses our absolute faith in the Lord, which leads to righteous actions and a fruitful life (Read the Parable of the Four Soils in Matthew 13). It is grounded in the absolute belief that God's plan is greater than ours, and regardless of the varying degrees of life's challenges, a trusting follower of the Lord believes in the truths of God's promises in the Bible.

Through it all, they hold themselves accountable to His Word and Spirit! Regardless of the trials and tribulations, they remain hopeful and faithful because they trust and wait for God's perfect timing. Is it hard at times? Yes! But when we yearn for more of His guidance in our lives and yield to His Sovereign Power, we will find it easier to deal with the difficulties and storms of everyday life. Refer back to the passage earlier in 1 John 5:3. Apply the power of that passage to your life so you can live it out with absolute trust and faith!

Just think: Even in all of our shortcomings and ignoring the guidance of a faithful God, isn't it wonderful that, regardless of our faithlessness, Yahweh is always faithful to us and is looking out for our best interests, which always aligns with His future plan (2 Tim 2:13)? God's faithfulness that He graciously showers upon us should be reciprocated from us to Him with wholehearted trust and obedience, like a constant cycle of sweet aroma flowing before His throne. This is all because we firmly believe in Him and all His ways, regardless of the hurdles and obstacles that are thrown before us.

This is paramount because when we allow those barriers to prevent us from trusting and obeying God with all our hearts, souls, and minds, we then try to take our lives into our own hands. As stated earlier, we then start making bad decisions, end up hurting ourselves and others, and find ourselves in a state of damage control. We must all realize that there are dire consequences if we don't trust and obey God, because when we don't, we will experience moments of weakness that test our faith and commitment to our Heavenly Father.

Ever since the fall of man (Genesis 3), we have fallen into the realm of imperfection, and chances are, if we're not relying wholeheartedly on God, we will give in to our weaknesses. When that happens, our flesh will decide to take the path of least resistance, and the world and man's ways become our daily guide. Then, the enemy has us snared in his own little devious plan, which is the opposite of God's desired plan for you and me (sound familiar?). Don't we realize that the enemy wants to confuse and deter us from trusting in God's most divine ways?

Look at it this way: If we are more focused on the things and directions of man's ways versus God, then we lack trust in His Sovereignty. If our emotions are driven more by our investments, the waves of the economy, leaders, and our careers, then we are not trusting in God's spiritual provisions. When we lean more towards the ways of man and this world, it will only lead us to become discontent, dissatisfied, and disgruntled, ultimately culminating in our not trusting all of God's promises and staying obedient to His working process in our lives.

Always remember this: *There's a wrong focus on the ways of this world and man that can lead us astray, and there's a right focus on the ways, truths, and life of Christ, which can keep us grounded on His righteous path.* As followers of Jesus, our Lord, we must be careful what we give our attention to. What do I mean? It seems that many of us pay more attention to the ways of man and this world in today's society and culture, which influence us more and more each passing day in unspiritual ways.

Over time, we become swayed and discipled by this dominant pull of unrighteousness, which distances us from our complete focus on God's ways. And here's the danger zone: If not corrected immediately (biblically and spiritually), it will eventually consume us and take over our lives. Here's another way to put it: Whatever fills our minds *the most* will ultimately fill our hearts and start to control us, which could lead to unspiritual pursuits if it's not of God.

You see, if we're truly transformed and born again, there should be a constant change of His empowering grace in our daily lives, which moves us from the unholy things of this world to His means of Holiness. Please keep this in mind: We cannot partner with the ways of this world and God at the same time (one is controlling us more than the other). But if we're on board with God's plan, here's an encouraging and motivational takeaway as we partner with Him in the future, and it's this:

When we engage and enforce God's working formula in our daily lives, it helps us overcome all the worrisome ways of this world while keeping us focused on the steps needed to develop mental and spiritual strength. Then, we can persevere through those tough times because adhering to Yahweh's plan promotes patience and confidence, which in turn elevate our participation in His plan.

And in God's timing, it will produce a powerfully positive outcome. Really, who is a follower of Christ who would not want to aspire to this godly action plan? Through the power of His Word and Spirit, He's provided us with the key sources to help us progress on this Side of Heaven (Please Read 2 Peter 1). What an invaluable lesson and teaching that the first generation of Israelites needed, particularly in terms of patience, confidence, and trusting in God's promises for the future, which could have led them to a greater purpose and outcome.

Undoubtedly, God's Word and His Spirit are our guiding compass and firm foundation, providing insight into God's nature and the scope of His work in our future lives. It emphasizes His sovereignty, wisdom, and love for us as we move forward with Him. If the power of His Word and Spirit is at work in us, it will illustrate our complete transparency as His committed partners (or not). It will expose and be the determining factor if we are willing participants in His long-term plan. Once again, I cannot stress this enough: There is a danger zone if the Lord is not part of our daily process; otherwise, we will fail in our future endeavors (Prov 16:9).

Surely, at this point, we realize that when we stick to and trust in God's faithful process, we can be resilient in the face of insurmountable setbacks and be empowered through His Word and Spirit to stay committed to our godly goals. Just as the second generation of Israelites, we must learn to rely on and depend on the guidance of God and His appointed Leader to reach our destined home. For you and me, that person is Jesus Christ. The first generation has already failed, but a new generation was given the chance to fulfill God's plan. And that same opportunity is there for us today!

Sadly, today, just like that generation of Israelites in the wilderness, millions lack trust in God. It can stem from a variety of reasons, including personal experiences with trauma or disappointment, a distorted image of God, fear of the unknown, past negative religious experiences, struggles with understanding the concept of a Higher Power, or simply not feeling a strong connection to a spiritual practice. Essentially, it can result from life experiences that make it very difficult to reconcile the concept of a Loving, Just, All-Powerful God with the realities of suffering and hardship in a world marked by so many pains, struggles, and unhealthy spiritual behaviors.

If someone has experienced significant affliction or mishaps in their life, mainly when they felt abandoned or unsupported, it can be challenging to trust an Almighty God to be there for them (Please read Nahum 1:7, Psalm 46:1, 62:8, John 14:1, and Romans 15:13). Unfortunately, past encounters with hurtful, judgmental, or hypocritical religious communities, people, or leaders can create distrust in an Almighty and Loving God. And this will only lead to that person never placing their trust and obedience in the ways of the Lord, all because of being misled by someone who did not set the example as an entrusted and genuine follower of Christ!

Undoubtedly, *it can lead a person not to have faith, love, and hope in our Heavenly Father and His Son.* And here's the root cause: When humans' fleshly actions, manmade philosophies, unspiritual behaviors, and unbiblical theories don't align with the Truths of the Bible and all its teachings, it gives a distorted image of our Holy Creator. It portrays our Heavenly Father as a punishing or vengeful entity that can make it difficult for anyone to trust Him. *And this is so far from the truth!* So, our job as believers and followers of the 'Real Truth' is to live a life of godliness and holiness that reflects our supernatural faith and trust in the One who will save us from all our pits of despair, discouragement, and disheartenment in this life.

Today, there are even reasons why Christians may lack complete trust in God. One is when we are not actively praying, meditating, or applying His word in our lives, which can lead to a decline in our genuine worship, fellowship, and service for our Lord. Other reasons include when we're more controlled by fear than faith, worrying too much about life circumstances versus entrusting them to God, and dwelling more on our past mistakes than on God's promising future. We must never forget that daily prayer, time with God, and the real-life application of His word in our lives are the cultivating tools toward a trusting relationship with Him. If we lack in any of these areas, they can and will hinder the development of our trust in His plan.

This is vital because if we're in that deficient state of not trusting God, it only opens the door to the enemy. When that happens, it can separate and distance us from the existence of a loving, merciful, and gracious God. Then, our anxiety around the uncertainties of life and death can make it hard to surrender and submit control to the One who has more authority and power than anyone else. Do you genuinely believe and have 100% trust in our Big God, who can transform even the most difficult situations for the spiritual good in our lives?

As we progress on this side of eternity, you and I will be put to the test, like that second generation of Israelites. We will realize 'Who' should be our leader daily if we are genuine followers of Christ. We will discover if we're His dedicated, good, and faithful servants living under the Freedom of Christ. If so, we're His bondservants, meaning we serve our Lord and others willingly and selflessly. When we do this, we're not only progressing toward our Promised Land but leading others down the same path, which is pleasing to God.

One thing should have surfaced as we come to the end of this journey, and it's this: we are either in the camp of that one generation of Israelites who failed and could not proceed to their Promised Land. Or we are like that succeeding generation who finally made it. Even in all their shortcomings, they came to believe, trust, and obey God's guidance as they navigated their new home. God chose them for such a time to fulfill His plan that would end their ill-fated journey, once and for all.

This should prompt us to examine our genuine faith and trust in the Lord. Have we passed the test and lived up to the standards of trusting God in every phase of our lives? In other words, we actively choose to believe and rely on God, even when faced with uncertainty or challenging circumstances. We've made the conscious decision to trust God's character, His love, and His plan for our lives, even when things don't make sense. This trust is not a passive feeling but an active choice to rely on God's strength and guidance. And trust me, as I mentioned earlier, we will not be disappointed. Go all in with your trusting and obeying Him and all His ways each and every day of your life! Just do it!

Please remember this daily: To live a life worthy of God's glory, honor, and praise, once we accept Jesus Christ as Lord of our life by faith, it will be evident in our trust and obedience to all His ways. We know that we will never be perfect on the side of eternity, but there must be a steady progression of spiritual and biblical maturity. That's the prescription of holiness that the Lord expects and desires in our lives daily!

In Closing

"Just Trust and Obey!"

Remember the old hymn, "Trust and Obey"? This song, written in 1887 by John H. Sammis and composed by Daniel B. Towner, encompasses two essential components that we've seen mentioned so often throughout this book and are necessary for every Christian's life today: Trust and Obedience. This hymn reminds us that obedience is the outflow of our absolute trust and faith in God. However, it also emphasizes a desire to live a life pleasing to God in response to His grace, mercy, and love, as demonstrated through His Son, Jesus Christ.

The profound theological words in this powerful song should encourage all genuine believers to cultivate a strong and trusting relationship with our Lord by faithfully obeying Him in every aspect of their lives. Many can sing this song without needing to look at the hymnal. Why? The lyrics of this song strike the internal chord of those two words that are instrumental in our lives as faithful followers of our Lord: 'Trust' and 'Obey.' If only God's chosen ones from thousands of years ago had complied with these words, their lives would have been blessed. This same guiding principle applies to you and me today!

If we pay close attention to these moving lyrics from this most memorable Christian song, we will see that God only sheds His glory on *those who walk in the Light of His word*. And for *those who desire His goodwill, He will abide with them still*. There is no doubt, fear, burden, sorrow, grief, loss, or even a sigh or tear that God cannot remove or wipe away. Woven in this hymn, we see that when we're in the Joy of our Lord, we discover His peace, favor, and endless love. And it's when we are in the sweetness of His fellowship that we'll walk by His side all the way. And no matter what He says, we will do it; wherever He sends us, we will go. And here's the summation of this great hymn: Trust and obey, for there's no other way. *To be happy in Jesus, but to trust and obey.*

As we've seen repeatedly throughout this book, trusting God with every fiber of our being depicts our faithful obedience to Him alone. Also, it reflects a believer's commitment to follow God's commands, trust Him in every part of their lives, and live according to His will and plan. It's not just a concept, but a statement, a command, and a desire of biblical reality from our Holy God. Why? Because it is deeply rooted in Scripture as our teaching and guide, which remains relevant to our application today. Our living example is exemplified by numerous biblical figures who demonstrated unwavering devotion to God by trusting Him through absolute faith and obedience in all His ways. A classic example is the life of Joshua.

Is it hard at times? Yes! Why? Once again, those who do not completely trust and obey God have not surrendered themselves to His loving grace. Plus, they must surround themselves with a strong community of believers who can help them stay the course when times are unbearable. It's not as complicated as you think when we're guided by the power of God's word and His Spirit (2 Pet 1:3-11)!

And consider this valid point: As noted in the last chapter, His word is not burdensome in our lives (1 John 5:3). This is crucial for Christians today because obedience to God proves our love for Him (John 14:15, 1 John 5:2-3). But it also demonstrates our faithfulness to His guiding principles (1 John 2:3-6). It proves that we trust Him in every area of our lives, which glorifies Him (1 Peter 2:12). Furthermore, in this growing phase of our lives, it opens up avenues of spiritual blessings (John 13:17).

When it comes to trusting God, as noted so often throughout this journey, many refer to Proverbs 3:5-6, a well-known passage that millions have memorized over the years, encouraging individuals to trust in the Lord rather than relying on their own understanding. These powerful verses emphasize the importance of acknowledging God in all aspects of our daily lives, and if we do, He'll guide and direct our paths. This passage also reminds us to relinquish control and believe in God's plan. It reminds us that God is in control, and if we follow Him, He will lead us through our troublesome times. I don't know about you, but that's a reminder that I need each and every day on this Side of Heaven—until I reach my eternal home.

Do we possess that burning desire to reach the future land where we can see our Lord face-to-face and hear those seven words we've waited for so many years? For us to hear those words, there is a godly process that must be incorporated and implemented in our lives, and it needs to be our daily reminder, and here it is: "You can't trust in God if you don't know Him, and you can't know Him if you never spend time with Him." Without

"Just Trust and Obey!"

trust in God, there can be no obedience. And this is because there's an issue with our genuine saving faith. It's time to return to the drawing board and reexamine our faith in Christ, as Paul notes in 2 Corinthians 13:5–6.

So, here's our challenge on this side of Heaven: Do you dedicate time to God's word where you observe, interpret, and apply His message to your daily life? Do you spend time in daily prayer and talks with the Lord? As stated so many times in this book, do you constantly meditate on His scriptures? Are you utilizing your gifts to their fullest for the sake of His Kingdom? Are you surrounding yourself with brothers and sisters in Christ who are there as your support group? What is the accurate measure of your times of praise, fellowship, and worship with God? How can you prioritize this in your life to ensure you're on His righteous path of Glory? We must ask ourselves: Are we genuine representatives of Jesus Christ for others to follow?

In today's challenging culture, the steps above are vital because if we're not using our time in biblical and spiritual ways, our efforts at productivity will be futile. If we place more trust in the guidance of man and this world in today's time, we're not setting the Christlike precedent. What do I mean? The truth is that Christianity plays a vital role in modern society, and that role is more critical now than ever before. You see, as followers of Christ, we have a responsibility to spread the truths and teachings of Jesus Christ so that they can know that trust and faith in Him are the key components to their future possession.

Today, where technology and social media dominate our lives, it can be challenging to connect with people on a spiritual level. However, it's more important than ever to find ways to reach those who are searching for meaning and purpose in their lives, as their trust is misplaced in the wrong things in life. When people place more trust in human ways versus God, you and I should be His example for others to follow. As dedicated servants of the Lord, the world must see a level of godly trust and obedience in our lives so they know that we have a faith, love, and hope that will lead to a greater outcome. This is more important than you realize because look at this study below:

A few years ago, the Pew Research Center conducted a survey to gauge people's trust in one another. Tragically, the results show that almost 80% of people in the United States cannot be trusted. In other words, there is very little confidence among millions when it comes to trusting people. You may ask, why is there such a problem with trusting others in this country? Here it is: Their study revealed that the levels of personal trust tend to be *more closely linked with people's broader views on institutions and civic life.* Do you see the underlying issue? When people tie their trust and beliefs around anything other than the sound words of God's truth, there will always be a level of mistrust and distortion. [1]

Fellow Christians, it's crucial to understand this fact in today's society, where disingenuous behaviors and false-hearted ways are prevalent. The reality is that humans, institutions, politicians, and, regrettably, even church leaders cannot be trusted 100%. We will all face this common encounter on this side of Heaven.

However, there is a reassuring Holy Presence that can help us navigate these challenges together in this shared battle because He is the Only One we can trust today, tomorrow, and in our future. Once again, this journey is a powerful reminder that we are not alone in this ongoing struggle of building our trust in our Heavenly Father and Lord, for He reminds us:

Isa 41:10, "Don't be afraid, for I am with you. Don't be discouraged, for I am your God. I will strengthen you and help you. I will hold you up with my victorious right hand."

Ps 46:1, "God is our refuge and strength, always ready to help in times of trouble."

Phil 4:6-7, "Don't worry about anything; instead, pray about everything. Tell God what you need and thank him for all he has done. Then, you will experience God's peace, which surpasses all understanding. His peace will guard your hearts and minds as you live in Christ Jesus."

Matt 11:28-30, "Then Jesus said, 'Come to me, all of you who are weary and carry heavy burdens, and I will give you rest. Take my yoke upon you. Let me teach you because I am humble and gentle at heart, and you will find rest for your souls. For my yoke is easy to bear, and the burden I give you is light."

Prov 3:1-6, "My child, never forget the things I have taught you. Store my commands in your heart. If you do this, you will live many years, and your life will be satisfying. Never let loyalty and kindness leave you! Tie them around your neck as a reminder. Write them deep within your heart. Then you will find favor with both God and people, and you will earn a good reputation. Trust in the Lord with all your heart; do not depend on your own understanding. Seek His will in all you do, and He will show you which path to take."

These scriptures lead me to ask: Are you trusting God with your future to His Promised Land? Is it evident in your life as a Christian? Are others looking to you as a Christlike example? Do they aspire to follow you because of your exemplary commitment, dedication, trust, faith, and obedience in all of God's ways?

---

1. Pew Research. Americans Trust in One Another.

"Just Trust and Obey!"

In other words, the world sees that you are fully clothed by the ways of God's Word and Spirit. And this is what we want as genuine followers of Christ: "For unbelievers and the weaker in faith to see someone like you and me, who are not shaken by the ways of this world and man because of our unwavering faith, because it's all due to our solid trust and obedience in God's sovereign plan."

Throughout this book, we've obtained some significant nuggets that can help us trust our God and Lord more than ever. As we conclude this incredible journey, never forget that you can demonstrate trust in God through consistent prayer, study, application of His Word to your lives, seeking His guidance in everyday decisions, and living a life that reflects His divine characteristics, even in the most difficult times.

Always remember: During our most difficult struggles in life, if we express more joy than sadness, our trust in God is rock solid. If we're guided by more of His convictions, counsel, and comfort than the ways of man and this world, then our trust in God is steadfast. If we rely more on His wisdom and knowledge rather than our own desires and feelings, then our understanding of complete trust and faith in God remains intact and will continue to deepen.

Just think: If we're patiently waiting on God's timing to bring a plan to fruition, then our trust in God is more loyal than disloyal. If we've reached a state of complete contentment with the things God has provided in our lives, then our relationship with the Lord has genuinely grown beyond all measures. If we're experiencing more of His peace than the turbulent times of life's uncertainty, our trust in God is apparent, internally and externally. When we trust God in these areas, our love for Him grows because we know He's our Source for all things.

You see, trusting that God can handle all the unfortunate conditions of our lives for our spiritual good will help us to realize that He cares for us and is loving and just in all He does, which will elevate our adherence to His ultimate plan. This will lead us to be more obedient to the scriptures because we trust His Promises, Provision, Providence, and Protection. And when we wholeheartedly rely on God's Word and His Promises, we know He is faithful and will keep His word, just as He did for the new generation of Israelites as they journeyed to their Promised Land.

As noted earlier and as a reminder, we should know why trusting God is so important. It gives us that peace that surpasses all our understanding (Phil 4:7). Trusting God can bring a sense of calmness, especially during our most difficult stages of life. It gives us strength and enables us to find the courage to face our fears, make good choices, and endure life's trials and tribulations. It helps us mature and develop our character of Christlikeness while giving us a sense of security and assurance, where we can find contentment in God alone.

And think: It helps us to let go of unimportant things that don't matter to God so that we can focus more on Him and the realities of our future Heaven (read Colossians 3). Trusting God keeps us centered in His presence and His will for our lives, knowing that our Heavenly Father has our back, will help us, care for us, and carry us through all of life's good, bad, and ugly situations with His loving hands. Don't we realize that He knows what is best for us and always has a better plan for us on the other side? When we trust God, we know He will never leave or forsake us, for victory is undoubtedly on the horizon (Joshua 1:5, Deuteronomy 31:8, Hebrews 13:5).

Just as thousands of years ago, today's times can reveal challenges or crises that expose undeveloped trust in our lives, but these are also opportunities to strengthen our faith and grow in our reliance on God. Recognize and pay close attention to God's Work in your life as He fulfills His Promises and uses you for His purposes.

In these times of faithlessness, God's children must spend time in His Word, in prayer, fellowship, and worship, seeking to draw closer to God and cultivate a relationship built on trust in Him for all things. It's imperative that we seek His presence and dwell in it, for it's our place of refuge that will sustain you and me until our Day of Glory. But while we're here on this side, please never forget this:

Our God is a Big God! What does this mean? Our Heavenly Father is All-Knowing, All-Powerful, and Ever-Present. He possesses immense and sovereign power, wisdom, and knowledge, which should remind believers that God can handle any situation. He can help us to deal with any problem or trial we will face on this Side of Heaven. When we firmly believe and trust that our God is a BIG God, it can offer comfort and hope, reminding believers that even in the face of overwhelming challenges, God is greater and capable of providing us with all the solutions.

When we reach that place of complete reverence, respect, awe, and wonder for our Holy Creator and BIG God, for all He has done, is doing, and will do, we will come to have trust and hope in what is to come. No matter what, never forget that God is more significant than any trial we will face on this side of Heaven. He's preparing you and me right now, in this very moment, for a Plan beyond our wildest dreams.

Today, as we witness the truths of God's promises and plans come to fruition in our own lives, do they bring us to our knees in absolute respect to the One Who will see us to the other Side of Eternity? We should all know that *not one word of God's truths has failed,* *(then and now)* as He pledged through His servants Moses and Joshua. Never forget this: Our response to His faithful promises and all His truths will be evident in our complete trust and obedience to Him.

You see, when we stand upon the truths of God's word, it will surely help us when we encounter warfare with our enemy in the coming days on this Side of Heaven. Because when we stand firmly on the Truths of God's word and believe in them with all our hearts, minds, and souls with all our might, we will trust Him and obey His guiding principles. Please read these passages below, for they are our daily lessons that can aid us in our ongoing fights against Satan: Heb 6:1-3, 2 Cor 5:16-21, Psalm 133, 1 Peter 4, 2 Pet 1:3-11, 2 Tim 3:16-17, Heb 4:12-13, and Acts 2:42-47.

We can never forget how Jesus Christ countered Satan when he tempted our Lord in the wilderness. Our Lord thwarted the enemy with the truths of the Word of God, as recorded in Matthew 4:1-11. You see, with the power of God's Word and His Spirit before us, we now have that opportunity, right now, not to waste God's most precious truths in our lives that will help us in the areas of trust and obedience; especially when the enemy is trying to prevent us from trusting and obeying the Lord in our daily lives. And just like Joshua, we cannot trust our Lord and serve Him wholeheartedly if we do not apply all His truths to our lives.

Once again, are we trusting Him each step in this life journey to that Spectacular Place where we will be with Him forever? Please never forget this: Heaven is not a default option simply because we claim to believe in Christ, perform good deeds, and serve Him in various capacities. Our true measurement is seen through our genuine saving faith (Heb 11:6), which will produce 100% trust and obedience to all of God's ways in our lives, which will be Christlikeness.

As His entrusted followers, we must put ourselves to the test of biblical and spiritual truth each day while there's still time! The Lord is waiting for you and me to respond with complete trust and obedience so the world will see where our true faith lies. And our reward is to hear those most precious words we have longed to hear for so many years. *"Well done, my good and faithful servant."*

When the world and people all around us seem to be falling apart (day by day), our true faith stands secure on God's rock-solid and trustworthy promises in His Word. It's a humbling affirmation that God is faithful to the very end of our lives. He is Who He says He is—and will do what He has promised in our lives. Once again, please read Jeremiah 29:11-13.

This is imperative because faith, in its purest form, is more than just belief; it's an unshakeable trust in something greater than ourselves. In the Christian journey, this faith is not just a feeling or a fleeting hope, but a firm conviction rooted in God's promises. Hebrews 10:23 encapsulates this powerful guarantee. The author reminds us, "Let us hold tightly without wavering to the hope we affirm, for God can be trusted to keep his promise." Remember, "Walking closely with the Lord involves a life of genuine saving faith where we cling to all of God's promises." Applying this becomes our spiritual staying power, and we will know that our obedience and trust in His word will have rich rewards—where all of His promises will be fulfilled one day soon, just like that second generation of Israelites!

When we embrace God's promises, they anchor us in the unwavering power of faith! In a world of uncertainty, untruths, and unbelief, we need to trust in the sound truths of God's promises, which will provide us with hope, assurance, and reliance, knowing that His words are not just words; they are the very foundation upon which we build our lives of faith, confident that His promises will be fulfilled, soon. We need this belief in our hearts, minds, souls, and spirits like never before! Why?

Regrettably, today, we cannot escape humankind's unholy traits and acts of carelessness and neglect to the truths of the Holy Scriptures because we live in a society and culture that is scarred by sin. But once again, there is one guarantee in life: "God Can Be Counted on No Matter What!" With all the brokenness we're seeing in people's lives, homes, schools, churches, communities, politics, workplaces, streets, states, countries, and globally, there is one assurance that we all can rest upon, and it's all the "Unbroken Promises that God has laid out in the Bible!" These promises are words of validity and a testament to God's reliability and trustworthiness, which we can always count on.

In a world where hopes, dreams, and visions are too often shattered, we can find trust and security in the enduring nature of God's promises. His truths are a constant reassurance in the face of all our life's broken promises. Our Loving and Caring God's 'Word of Honor' should be our mainstay and foundation in all the storms of dismay, leading us to our spiritual restoration. This constant expectation, rooted in our faith in God's promises, is our source of comfort, stability, and dependability as we navigate life's challenges.

When we firmly believe that the Lord is our refuge and strength, we can trust in the promises of His word and know beyond a shadow of a doubt that He is always there. This faith is not just a shield but a powerful weapon against all the negative emotions that disappointment can bring. Almighty God is our sustaining strength and protection, and His presence should be a yearning in our daily journey because He's a beacon of light in the darkness of all our dissatisfactions. This genuine faith equips and enables us to rise above all our displeasures in life and find hope in God's promises. It fills us with a sense of enduring empowerment through the Holy Spirit.

Surely, by now, we realize that when we firmly believe and accept God's most sovereign plan, it will reveal to us that trust is our bridge from yesterday to tomorrow and into our future. We should ponder an old idiom: "Faith is the bridge over the gap you and I have chosen to get us from this side to God's Side." You see, our bridge of faith connects our belief with action. Even when our future path seems uncertain, this bridge guides us to trust in God's promises, no matter what.

Those are profound words, but if we're going to trust God and obey His guiding ways as we move toward our future Promise Land, we must ensure that we're building on the paths of righteousness and holiness. Paul reminds us powerfully in 1 Corinthians 3 that we should be building our lives and others on the foundation of Jesus Christ, for He is the only way to the Father (John 14:6). Never forget this: "We can't build our godly bridge of faith and trust with scaffoldings of mistruths, lies, and deceptions."

Let there be no doubt: Despite all our heartaches on this side of Heaven, our Lord, Jesus Christ, has set things right. We are now reconciled with our Heavenly Father and restored, renewed, and prepared for extraordinary things. Jesus has rescued us from a land of deficiencies and shortcomings to His land of fulfillment and perfect abundance. There is now a paved crossing for anyone who willingly surrenders and submits their all to the Lord. He desires to guide as many as He can to His Promised Land, where there is no more brokenness and death.

This promise of a life free from brokenness and death should fill us with hope and inspiration every day. This can happen all because of the life we've chosen in our Redeemer and Savior. Imagine what awaits us because of God's promises. We have the opportunity to dwell in a realm where we will no longer be violated because, under God's long-term care, we're untouched and undefiled. This is beyond my comprehension, but once again, I put my trust in the promises of God's word, and you can too.

If you want to be saved from the perils of this destructive world, give your life faithfully to the Lord Jesus Christ, trust Him in every aspect of your life, and obey His guiding principles with all your heart, mind, soul, and spirit. Then, you will be on God's path to the Promised Land that He has destined for those who are His entrusted followers and believers to the very end of this journey!

Ps 116:3-6, "Death wrapped its ropes around me; the terrors of the grave overtook me. I saw only trouble and sorrow. Then I called on the name of the Lord: "Please, Lord, save me!" How kind the Lord is! How good he is! So merciful, this God of ours! The Lord protects those of childlike faith; I was facing death, and he saved me."

A final note: I am not sure about you, but as we progress in this life journey as His entrusted Christians on this Side of Heaven, we need to ensure we're living the type of life that will one day hear those words, Well done, my good and faithful servant versus those words from the lips of Christ below, which are the scariest words known to man, found in Matt 7:21–23: Jesus says, "Not everyone who calls out to me, 'Lord! Lord!' will enter the Kingdom of Heaven. Only those who actually do the will of my Father in heaven will enter. On judgment day, many will say to me, 'Lord! Lord! We prophesied in your name and cast out demons in your name and performed many miracles in your name.' But I will reply, 'I never knew you. Get away from me, you who break God's laws.'

Please ensure that you're on God's faithful path today more than ever, by living out your trust and obedience to all His ways with all you have! Be steadfast in your daily commitment to sticking to God's working plans in your life, which will lead to a future outcome that is beyond our comprehension. Make that ultimate decision right now to live by the ways of our Father, Son, and Holy Spirit with unwavering and undeniable faith, like never before. It will be worth it all in the end!

Bibliography

Anderson. Michael. "The Spiritual Significance of Brokenness in the Bible." John Baptist Church, Org Site. https://johnbaptistchurch.org/biblical-meaning-concepts/brokenness

Anxious Faith Blog. "Six People Who Struggled with Their Mental Health." https://www.anxiousfaith.org/blog/6-people-in-the-bible-who-struggled-with-theirmental-health

Barna Group. "Most Americans Do Not Believe that Satan or the Holy Spirit Exist." April 13, 2009. https://www.barna.com/research/most-american-christians-do-not-believe-that-satan-or-the-holy-spirit-exist/

———. "Two-thirds of Christians Face Doubt:" July 25, 2017. https://www.barna.com/research/two-thirds-christians-face-doubt/

———. "Doubt & Faith: Top Reasons Why People Question Christianity." March 1, 2023. https://www.barna.com/research/doubt-faith/

———. "Annual Study Reveals America Is Spiritually Stagnant." March 5, 2001. https://www.barna.com/research/annual-study-reveals-america-is-spiritually-stagnant/

Bible Study Tools Site. "Baker's Evangelical Dictionary of Biblical Theology Know, Knowledge" https://www.biblestudytools.com/dictionary/know-knowledge/

Bloom, Jon. Desiring God Site. "The Greatest Thing You Can Do with Your Life." August 10, 2018. https://www.desiringgod.org/articles/the-greatest-thing-you-can-do-with-your-life

———. Desiring God Site. "You Don't Need to Understand Now." March 21, 2021. https://www.desiringgod.org/articles/you-dont-need-to-understand-now

Brainy Quote Site. "Rush Limbaugh Quotes." https://www.brainyquote.com/quotes/rush_limbaugh_153259Brown. Gregory.

Christian Quotes Site. "Twenty Powerful Quotes About Boldness," https://www.christianquotes.info/top-quotes/20-powerful-quotes-about-boldness/

Connaughton. Aidan, Moncus. J.J. Pew Research Center Site: "Around the world, people who trust others are more supportive of international cooperation." December 15, 2020. https://www.pewresearch.org/short-reads/2020/12/15/around-the-world-people-who-trust-others-are-more-supportive-of-international-cooperation/

Eller. Jack David. Boston Review Site. "Why Do We Pledge Allegiance." September 6, 2018. https://www.bostonreview.net/articles/jack-david-eller-pledge-allegiance/

Enduring Word. "Joshua 15, 16 and 16. The Inheritance of Judah, Ephraim, and Western Manasseh." https://enduringword.com/bible-commentary/joshua-15-16-17/

———. Joshua 5. "Circumcision and Passover at Gilgal." https://enduringword.com/bible-commentary/joshua-5/

Bibliography

———. Joshua 9. "The Gibeon Deception." https://enduringword.com/bible-commentary/joshua-9/

———. Joshua 11. "The Northern Canaanite Armies Defeated." https://enduringword.com/bible-commentary/joshua-11/

———. Joshua 18, 19. "Inheritance of the Remaining Tribes." https://enduringword.com/bible-commentary/joshua-18-19/

———. "Joshua 20. The Cities of Refuge." https://enduringword.com/bible-commentary/joshua-20/

———. "Joshua 21. Cities Appointed for the Levites." https://enduringword.com/bible-commentary/joshua-21/

———. "Joshua 23. Joshua's Farewell Address." https://enduringword.com/bible-commentary/joshua-23/

Freedom in Christ Site. Neil Anderson. The Origin, Theology, and Rationale of The Steps to Freedom in Christ. "The Results of Brokenness." https://www.ficm.org/steps-to-freedom-in-christ/neil-andersons-the-origin-theology-rationale-of-the-steps-to-freedom-in-christ/

Goodreads Site. Quote by Eric Metaxas on German Pastor Bonhoeffer. https://www.goodreads.com/quotes/325420-when-someone-asked-bonhoeffer-whether-he-shouldn-t-join-the-german

Got Questions. "What is Regeneration According to the Bible?" https://www.gotquestions.org/regeneration-Bible.html

———. "Does God Cause Suffering?" https://www.gotquestions.org/does-God-cause-suffering.html

———. "Why Does God Allow the Innocent to Suffer?" https://www.gotquestions.org/innocent-suffer.html

———. "What is the Latter and Former Rain in Hosea 6:3?" https://www.gotquestions.org/latter-and-former-rain.html

———. "Why was Abraham Promised Land that Belonged to Others?" https://www.gotquestions.org/Abraham-promised-land.html

———. "What are some examples of metaphor in the Bible?' https://www.gotquestions.org/metaphor-in-the-Bible.html

———. "How Can I Learn to Trust in the Faithfulness of God?" https://www.gotquestions.org/faithfulness-of-God.html

———. "Why Did God Choose Abraham?" https://www.gotquestions.org/why-did-God-choose-Abraham.html

———. What does "If God is for us, who can be against us" mean? Romans 8:31. https://www.gotquestions.org/if-God-is-for-us-who-can-be-against-us.html

———. "What Should We Learn from the Story of the Rich Man and Lazarus in Luke 16?" https://www.gotquestions.org/rich-man-and-Lazarus.html

———. "What Does the Bible Say About Boldness." https://www.gotquestions.org/Bible-boldness.html

———. "What Value is There in Christian Journaling." https://www.gotquestions.org/Christian-journaling.html

———. "What Were the Cities of Refuge in the Old Testament?" https://www.gotquestions.org/cities-of-refuge.html

———. "Why Did Reuben, Gad, and the Half-Tribe of Manasseh want to live on the East of the Jordan?" https://www.gotquestions.org/east-of-Jordan.html

Bibliography

———. "How Can We Enter into God's Rest?" https://www.gotquestions.org/enter-Gods-rest.html

———. "What Does the Bible Say About Fighting?" https://www.gotquestions.org/Bible-fighting.html

———. "What Did Paul Mean When He Said He Fought the Good Fight?" https://www.gotquestions.org/fought-the-good-fight.html

Haynes Jr. Clarence L. Bible Study Tool Site. "How Can We Grow in the Knowledge and Understanding of God?" April 14, 2023. https://www.biblestudytools.com/bible-study/topical-studies/how-we-can-grow-in-theknowledge-and-understanding-of-god.html

Hilpert, Tom. Clear Bible Blog. "1 Samuel #15, Trusting Obedience." January 27, 2024. https://clearbible.blog/2024/01/27/1-samuel-15-trusting-obedience/

Lifeway Research. "A Third of Americans Trust the Church." July 24, 2024. https://research.lifeway.com

Lucado, Max. Words of Hope and Help Site. "Fully Trusting in God's Word." https://maxlucado.com/listen/fully-trusting-gods-word/

MacArthur, John. "Grace to You Site. "What is Truth?" August 4, 2009. https://www.gty.org/library/Articles/A379/What-Is-Truth

Macinnis. Adam. "26 million Americans Stopped Reading the Bible Regularly During COVID 19." Christianity Today Site. April 20, 2022. https://www.christianitytoday.com/news/2022/april/state-of-bible-reading-decline-report-26-million.html

McKim. Daniel P. Washington Post. "Fruit of a Godless Society." Washington Post Site Column. September 23, 2023. https://www.washingtonpost.com/archive/opinions/1989/05/25/fruit-of-a-godless-society/d1c96a32-ee1a-42b0-9fe8-2b8bb758e46c/

Newport. Frank. Gallup Poll Site. "Fewer in U.S. Now See Bible as Literal Word of God." July 6, 2022. https://news.gallup.com/poll/394262/fewer-bible-literal-word-god.aspx

Oswald, Dwight. Live Ready, Southview Bible Church Site." April 15, 2020, Devotional. God Breaks Us To Make Us | Southview Bible Church.

Pew Research Center. "In U.S., Decline of Christianity Continues at Rapid Pace." October 17, 2019. https://www.pewresearch.org/religion/2019/10/17/in-u-s-decline-of-christianity-continues-at-rapid-pace/

———. "Americans Trust in One Another." May 8, 2025. https://www.pewresearch.org/2025/05/08/americans-trust-in-one-another/

Piper. John. Desiring God Site. "What Does It Mean to Seek the Lord?" August 19, 2009. https://www.desiringgod.org/articles/what-does-it-mean-to-seek-the-lord

Pringle. Phil. Bible Study. "The Broken Spirit." https://philpringle.wordpress.com/2015/07/16/the-broken-spirit/

Roundy. Antone. The Art of Ethical Persuasion• White Hat Crew Site. "A Mere One-Degree Difference." https://whitehatcrew.com/blog/a-mere-one-degree-difference/

The Bible. Org Site. "Conquering Temptation (James 1:13-15). https://bible.org/seriespage/4-conquering-temptation-james-113-15#:~:text=Trials%20and%20temptations%20always%20go%20together.%20We%20can,away%20from%20God%20%28and%20others%29%20because%20of%20them.

Ziglar Site. "Character, Commitment and Discipline." https://www.ziglar.com/quotes/character commitment-and-discipline/.